A TREATISE ON THE THEORY OF INVARIANTS

OLIVER E. GLENN, PH.D.
PROFESSOR OF MATHEMATICS
IN THE UNIVERSITY OF PENNSYLVANIA

Published by

Hawk Press
4836/24, Ansari Road, Daryaganj
New Delhi – 110 002
Phones : 9643330713, + 91-11-23278618, + 91-11-35676207
E-mail : thehawkpress@gmail.com
www.thehawkpress.com

Copyright © 2022, Editor
ISBN : 978-93-93971-47-0
All rights reserved.

No part of this book may be reproduced, stored in a retrieval
system, transmitted or utilised in any form or by any means,
electronic, mechanical, photocopying, recording or otherwise,
without the prior permission of the copyright owner.
Application for such permission should be addressed to the
publisher.

PREFACE

The object of this book is, first, to present in a volume of medium size the fundamental principles and processes and a few of the multitudinous applications of invariant theory, with emphasis upon both the nonsymbolical and the symbolical method. Secondly, opportunity has been taken to emphasize a logical development of this theory as a whole, and to amalgamate methods of English mathematicians of the latter part of the nineteenth century–Boole, Cayley, Sylvester, and their contemporaries–and methods of the continental school, associated with the names of Aronhold, Clebsch, Gordan, and Hermite.

The original memoirs on the subject, comprising an exceedingly large and classical division of pure mathematics, have been consulted extensively. I have deemed it expedient, however, to give only a few references in the text. The student in the subject is fortunate in having at his command two large and meritorious bibliographical reports which give historical references with much greater completeness than would be possible in footnotes in a book. These are the article "Invariantentheorie" in the "Enzyklopädie der mathematischen Wissenschaften" (I B 2), and W. Fr. Meyer's "Bericht über den gegenwärtigen Stand der Invarianten-theorie" in the "Jahresbericht der deutschen Mathematiker-Vereinigung" for 1890-1891.

The first draft of the manuscript of the book was in the form of notes for a course of lectures on the theory of invariants, which I have given for several years in the Graduate School of the University of Pennsylvania.

The book contains several constructive simplifications of standard proofs and, in connection with invariants of finite groups of transformations and the algebraical theory of ternariants, formulations of fundamental algorithms which may, it is hoped, be of aid to investigators.

While writing I have had at hand and have frequently consulted the following texts:

- CLEBSCH, Theorie der binären Formen (1872).

- CLEBSCH, LINDEMANN, Vorlesungen uher Geometrie (1875).

- DICKSON, Algebraic Invariants (1914).

- DICKSON, Madison Colloquium Lectures on Mathematics (1913). I. Invariants and the Theory of lumbers.

- ELLIOTT, Algebra of Quantics (1895).

- FAÀ DI BRUNO, Theorie des formes binaires (1876).

- GORDAN, Vorlesungen über Invariantentheorie (1887).

- GRACE and YOUNG, Algebra of Invariants (1903).

- W. FR. MEYER, Allgemeine Formen und Invariantentheorie (1909).

- W. FR. MEYER, Apolarität und rationale Curven (1883).

- SALMON, Lessons Introductory to Modern Higher Algebra (1859; 4th ed., 1885).

- STUDY, Methoden zur Theorie der temaren Formen (1889).

O. E. GLENN
PHILADELPHIA, PA.

Contents

Chapter 1

THE PRINCIPLES OF INVARIANT THEORY

1.1 The nature of an invariant. Illustrations

We consider a definite entity or system of elements, as the totality of points in a plane, and suppose that the system is subjected to a definite kind of a transformation, like the transformation of the points in a plane by a linear transformation of their coördinates. Invariant theory treats of the properties of the system which persist, or its elements which remain unaltered, during the changes which are imposed upon the system by the transformation.

By means of particular illustrations we can bring into clear relief several defining properties of an invariant.

1.1.1 An invariant area.

Given a triangle ABC drawn in the Cartesian plane with a vertex at the origin. Suppose that the coordinates of A are (x_1, y_1); those of B (x_2, y_2). Then the area Δ is

$$\Delta = \frac{1}{2}(x_1 y_2 - x_2 y_1),$$

or, in a convenient notation,

$$\Delta = \frac{1}{2}(xy).$$

Let us transform the system, consisting of all points in the plane, by the substitutions

$$x = \lambda_1 x' + \mu_1 y', y = \lambda_2 x' + \mu_2 y'.$$

The area of the triangle into which Δ is then carried will be

$$\Delta' = \frac{1}{2}(x_1'y_1' - x_2'y_1') = \frac{1}{2}(x'y'),$$

and by applying the transformations directly to Δ,

$$\Delta = (\lambda_1\mu_2 - \lambda_2\mu_1)\Delta'. \qquad (1)$$

If we assume that the determinant of the transformation is unity,

$$D = (\lambda\mu) = 1,$$

then

$$\Delta' = \Delta.$$

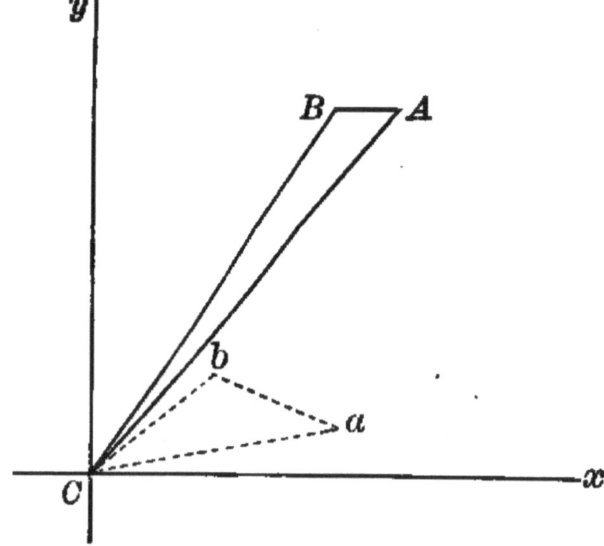

Thus the area Δ of the triangle ABC remains unchanged under a transformation of determinant unity and is an invariant of the transformation. The triangle itself is not an invariant, but is carried into abC. The area Δ is called an *absolute* invariant if $D = 1$. If $D \neq 1$, all triangles having a vertex at the origin will have their areas multiplied by the same number D^{-1} under the transformation. In such a case Δ is said to be a *relative* invariant. The adjoining figure illustrates the transformation of $A(5, 6)$, $B(4, 6)$, $C(0, 0)$ by means of

$$x = x' + y', y = x' + 2y'.$$

1.1.2 An invariant ratio.

In I the points (elements) of the transformed system are located by means of
two lines of reference, and consist of the totality of points in a plane. For a
second illustration we consider the system of all points on a line EF.

We locate a point C on this line by referring it to two fixed points of reference
P, Q. Thus C will divide the segment PQ in a definite ratio. This ratio,

$$PC/CQ,$$

is unique, being positive for points C of internal division and negative for points
of external division. The point C is said to have for coordinates any pair of
numbers (x_1, x_2) such that

$$\lambda \frac{x_1}{x_2} = \frac{PC}{CQ}, \tag{2}$$

where λ is a multiplier which is constant for a given pair of reference points
P, Q. Let the segment PC be positive and equal to μ. Suppose that the point
C is represented by the particular pair (p_1, p_2), and let $D(q_1, q_2)$ be any other
point. Then we can find a formula for the length of CD. For,

$$\frac{CQ}{p_2} = \frac{PC}{\lambda p_1} = \frac{PQ}{\lambda p_1 + p_2} = \frac{\mu}{\lambda p_1 + p_2},$$

and

$$\frac{DQ}{q_2} = \frac{\mu}{\lambda q_1 + q_2}.$$

Consequently

$$CD = CQ = DQ = \frac{\lambda \mu (qp)}{(\lambda q_1 + q_2)(\lambda p_1 + p_2)}. \tag{3}$$

Theorem. *The anharmonic ratio $\{CDEF\}$ of four points $C(p_2, p_2)$, $D(q_1, q_2)$,
$E(r_1, r_2)$, $F(\delta_1, \delta_2)$, defined by*

$$\{CDEF\} = \frac{CD \cdot EF}{CF \cdot ED}.$$

is an invariant under the general linear transformation

$$T : x_1 = \lambda_1 x_1' + \mu_1 x_2', \ x_2 = \lambda_2 x_1' + \mu_2 x_2', \ (\lambda \mu) \neq 0. \tag{3_1}$$

3

In proof we have from (3)

$$\{CDEF\} = \frac{(qp)(\delta r)}{(\delta p)(qr)}.$$

But under the transformation (cf. (1)),

$$(qp) = (\lambda\mu)(q'p'), \qquad\qquad (4)$$

and so on. Also, C, D, E, F are transformed into the points

$$C'(p_1', p_2'), D'(q_1', q_2'), E'(r_1', r_2'), F'(s_1', s_2'),$$

respectively. Hence

$$\{CDEF\} = \frac{(qp)(sr)}{(sp)(qr)} = \frac{(q'p')(s'r')}{(s'p')(q'r')} = \{C'D'E'F'\},$$

and therefore the anharmonic ratio is an absolute invariant.

1.1.3   An invariant discriminant.

A homogeneous quadratic polynomial,

$$f = a_0 x_1^2 + 2a_1 x_1 x_2 + a_2 x_2^2,$$

when equated to zero, is an equation having two roots which are values of the ratio x_1/x_2. According to II we may represent these two ratios by two points $C(p_1, p_2), D(q_1, q_2)$ on the line EF. Thus we may speak of the roots $(p_1, p_2), (q_1, q_2)$ of f.

These two points coincide if the discriminant of f vanishes, and conversely; that is if

$$D = 4(a_0 a_2 - a_1^2) = 0$$

If f be transformed by T, the result is a quadratic polynomial in x_1', x_2', or

$$f' = a_0' x_1'^2 + 2a_1' x_1' x_2' + a_2' x_2'^2,$$

Now if the points C, D coincide, then the two transformed points C', D' also coincide. For if $CD = 0$, (3) gives $(qp) = 0$. Then (4) gives $(q'p') = 0$, since by hypothesis $(\lambda\mu) \neq 0$. Hence, as stated, $C'D' = 0$.

It follows that the discriminant D' of f' must vanish as a consequence of the vanishing of D. Hence

$$D' = KD.$$

The constant K may be determined by selecting in place of f the particular quadratic $f_1 = 2x_1 x_2$ for which $D = -4$. Transforming f_1 by T we have

$$f_1' = 2\lambda_1\lambda_2 x_1^2 + 2(\lambda_1\mu_2 + \lambda_2\mu_1)x_1 x_2 + 2\mu_1\mu_2 x_2^2;$$

and the discriminant of f_1' is $D' = -4(\lambda\mu)^2$. Then the substitution of these particular discriminants gives

$$-4(\lambda\mu)^2 = -4K,$$
$$K = (\lambda\mu)^2.$$

We may also determine K by applying the transformation T to f and computing the explicit form of f'. We obtain

$$\begin{aligned}
a_0' &= a_0\lambda_1^2 + 2a_1\lambda_1\lambda_2 + a_2\lambda_2^2, \\
a_1' &= a_0\lambda_1\mu_1 + a_1(\lambda_1\mu_2 + \lambda_2\mu_1) + a_2\lambda_2\mu_2, \\
a_2' &= a_0\mu_1^2 + 2a_1\mu_1\mu_2 + a_2\mu_2^2,
\end{aligned} \tag{5}$$

and hence by actual computation,

$$4(a_0'a_2' - a_1'^2) = 4(\lambda\mu)^2(a_0a_2 - a_1^2),$$

or, as above,

$$D' = (\lambda\mu)^2 D.$$

Therefore the discriminant of f is a relative invariant of T (Lagrange 1773); and, in fact, the discriminant of f' is always equal to the discriminant of f multiplied by the square of the determinant of the transformation..

Preliminary Geometrical Definition.

If there is associated with a geometric figure a quantity which is left unchanged by a set of transformations of the figure, then this quantity is called an absolute invariant of the set (Halphen). In I the set of transformations consists of all linear transformations for which $(\lambda\mu) = 1$. In II and III the set consists of all for which $(\lambda\mu) \neq 0$.

1.1.4   An Invariant Geometrical Relation.

Let the roots of the quadratic polynomial f be represented by the points $(p_1, p_2), (r_1, r_2)$, and let ϕ be a second polynomial,

$$\phi = b_0x_1^2 + 2b_1x_1x_2 + b_2x_2^2,$$

whose roots are represented by (q_1, q_2), (s_1, s_2), or, in a briefer notation, by (q), (s). Assume that the anharmonic ratio of the four points (p), (q), (r), (s), equals minus one,

$$\frac{(qp)(sr)}{(sp)(qr)} = -1 \tag{6}$$

The point pairs $f = 0, \phi = 0$ are then said to be harmonic conjugates. We have from (6)

$$2h \equiv 2p_2 r_2 s_1 q_1 + 2p_1 r_1 s_2 q_2 - (p_1 r_2 + p_2 r_1)(q_1 s_2 + q_2 s_1) = 0.$$

But

$$f = (x_1 p_2 - x_2 p_1)(x_1 r_2 - x_2 r_1),$$
$$\phi = (x_1 q_2 - x_2 q_1)(x_1 s_2 - x_2 s_1).$$

Hence

$$a_0 = p_2, \quad 2a_1 = -(p_2 r_1 + p_1 r_2), \quad a_2 = p_1 r_1,$$
$$b_0 = q_2 s_2, \quad 2b_1 = -(q_2 s_1 + q_1 s_2), \quad b_2 = q_1 s_1,$$

and by substitution in $(2h)$ we obtain

$$h \equiv a_0 b_2 - 2a_1 b_1 + a_2 b_0 = 0. \tag{7}$$

That h is a relative invariant under T is evident from (6): for under the transformation f, ϕ become, respectively,

$$f' = (x_1' p_2' - x_2' p_1')(x_1' r_2' - x_2' r_1'),$$
$$\phi' = (x_1' q_2' - x_2' q_1')(x_1' s_2' - x_2' s_1'),$$

where

$$p_1' = \mu_2 p_1 - \mu_1 p_2, \quad p_2' = -\lambda_2 p_1 + \lambda_1 p_2,$$
$$r_1' = \mu_2 r_1 - \mu_1 r_2, \quad r_2' = -\lambda_2 r_1 + \lambda_1 r_2,$$

Hence

$$(q'p')(s'r') + (s'p')(q'r') = (\lambda\mu)^2[(qp)(sr) + (sp)(qr)].$$

That is,

$$h' = (\lambda\mu)^2 h.$$

Therefore the bilinear function h of the coefficients of two quadratic polynomials, representing the condition that their root pairs be harmonic conjugates, is a relative invariant of the transformation T. It is sometimes called a joint invariant, or simultaneous invariant of the two polynomials under the transformation.

1.1.5 An invariant polynomial.

To the pair of polynomials f, ϕ, let a third quadratic polynomial be adjoined,

$$\psi = c_0 x_1^2 + 2c_1 x_2 x_2 + c_2 x_2^2$$
$$= (x_1 u_2 - x_2 u_1)(x_1 v_2 - x_2 v_1).$$

Let the points (u_1, u_2) (v_1, v_2), be harmonic conjugate to the pair (p), (r); and also to the pair (q), (s). Then

$$c_0 a_2 - 2c_1 a_1 - c_2 a_0 = 0,$$
$$c_0 b_2 - 2c_1 b_1 - c_2 b_0 = 0,$$
$$c_0 x_1^2 + 2c_1 x_1 x_2 + c2 x_2^2 = 0.$$

Elimination of the c coefficients gives

$$C = \begin{vmatrix} a_0 & a_1 & a_2 \\ b_0 & b_1 & b_2 \\ x_2^2 & -x_1 x_2 & x_1^2 \end{vmatrix} = 0 \tag{8}$$

This polynomial,

$$C = (a_0 b_1 - a_1 b_0)x_1^2 + (a_0 b_2 - a_2 b_0)x_1 x_2 + (a_1 b_2 - a_2 b_1)x_2^2,$$

is the one existent quadratic polynomial whose roots form a common harmonic conjugate pair, to each of the pairs f, ϕ.

We can prove readily that C is an invariant of the transformation T. For we have in addition to the equations (5),

$$b_0' = b_0 \lambda_1^2 + 2b_1 \lambda_1 \lambda_2 + b_2 \lambda_2^2,$$
$$b_1' = b_0 \lambda_1 \mu_1 + b_1(\lambda_1 \mu_2 + \lambda_2 \mu_1) + b_2 \lambda_2 \mu_2, \tag{9}$$
$$b_2' = b_0 \mu_1^2 + 2b_1 \mu_1 \mu_2 + b_2 \mu_2^2.$$

Also if we solve the transformation equations T for x_1', x_2' in terms of x_1, x_2 we obtain

$$x_1' = (\lambda\mu)^{-1}(\mu_2 x_1 - \mu_1 x_2),$$
$$x_2' = (\lambda\mu)^{-1}(-\lambda_2 x_1 + \lambda_1 x_2), \tag{10}$$

Hence when f, ϕ are transformed by T, C becomes

$$C' = \tag{11}$$
$$\{(a_0\lambda_1^2 + 2a_1\lambda_1\lambda_2 + a_2\lambda_2^2)[b_0\lambda_1\mu_1 + b_1(\lambda_1\mu_2 + \lambda_2\mu_1) + b_2\lambda_2\mu_2]$$
$$-(b_0\lambda_1^2 + 2b_1\lambda_1\lambda_2 + b_2\lambda_2^2[a_0\lambda_1\mu_1 + a_1(\lambda_1\mu_2 + \lambda_2\mu_1) + a_2\lambda_2\mu_2]\}$$
$$\times(\lambda\mu)^{-2}(\mu_2 x_1 - \mu_1 x_2)^2 + \cdots .$$

When this expression is multiplied out and rearranged as a polynomial in x_1, x_2, it is found to be $(\lambda\mu)C$. That is,

$$C' = (\lambda\mu)C$$

and therefore C is an invariant.

It is customary to employ the term invariant to signify a function of the coefficients of a polynomial, which is left unchanged, save possibly for a numerical multiple, when the polynomial is transformed by T. If the invariant function involves the variables also, it is ordinarily called a *covariant*. Thus D in III is a relative invariant, whereas C is a relative covariant.

The Inverse of a Linear Transformation.

The process (11) of proving by direct computation the invariancy of a function we shall call *verifying* the invariant or covariant. The set of transformations (10) used in such a verification is called the *inverse* of T and is denoted by T^{-1}.

1.1.6   An invariant of three lines.

Instead of the Cartesian coördinates employed in I we may introduce homogeneous variables (x_1, x_2, x_3) to represent a point P in a plane. These variables may be regarded as the respective distances of N from the three sides of a triangle of reference. Then the equations of three lines in the plane may be written

$$a_{11}x_1 + a_{12}x_2 + a_{13}x_3 = 0,$$
$$a_{21}x_1 + a_{22}x_2 + a_{23}x_3 = 0,$$
$$a_{31}x_1 + a_{32}x_2 + a_{33}x_3 = 0.$$

The eliminant of these,

$$D = \begin{vmatrix} a_{11} & a_{12} & a_{13} \\ a_{21} & a_{22} & a_{23} \\ a_{31} & a_{32} & a_{33} \end{vmatrix},$$

evidently represents the condition that the lines be concurrent. For the lines are concurrent if $D = 0$. Hence we infer from the geometry that D is an invariant, inasmuch as the transformed lines of three concurrent lines by the following transformations, S, are concurrent:

$$S: \begin{aligned} x_1 &= \lambda_1 x_1' + \mu_1 x_2' + \nu_1 x_3', \\ x_2 &= \lambda_2 x_1' + \mu_2 x_2' + \nu_2 x_3', \\ x_1 &= \lambda_3 x_1' + \mu_3 x_2' + \nu_3 x_3'. \end{aligned} \qquad (\lambda\mu\nu) \neq 0. \qquad (12)$$

To verify algebraically that D is an invariant we note that the transformed of

$$a_{i1}x_1 + a_{i2}x_2 + a_{i3}x_3 \quad (i = 1, 2, 3),$$

by S is

$$(a_{i1}\lambda_1 + a_{i2}\lambda_2 + a_{i3}\lambda_3)x_1' + (a_{i1}\mu_1 + a_{i2}\mu_2 + a_{i3}\mu_3)x_2' + (a_{i1}\nu_1$$
$$+a_{i2}\nu_2 + a_{i3}\nu_3)x_3' \quad (i = 1, 2, 3). \tag{13}$$

Thus the transformed of D is

$$D' = \begin{vmatrix} a_{11}\lambda_1 + a_{12}\lambda_2 + a_{13}\lambda_3 & a_{11}\mu_1 + a_{12}\mu_2 + a_{13}\mu_3 & a_{11}\nu_1 + a_{12}\nu_2 + a_{13}\nu_3 \\ a_{21}\lambda_1 + a_{22}\lambda_2 + a_{23}\lambda_3 & a_{21}\mu_1 + a_{22}\mu_2 + a_{23}\mu_3 & a_{21}\nu_1 + a_{22}\nu_2 + a_{23}\nu_3 \\ a_{31}\lambda_1 + a_{32}\lambda_2 + a_{33}\lambda_3 & a_{31}\mu_1 + a_{32}\mu_2 + a_{33}\mu_3 & a_{31}\nu_1 + a_{32}\nu_2 + a_{33}\nu_3 \end{vmatrix}$$
$$= (\lambda\mu\nu)D. \tag{14}$$

The latter equality holds by virtue of the ordinary law of the product of two determinants of the third order. Hence D is an invariant.

1.1.7 A Differential Invariant.

In previous illustrations the transformations introduced have been of the linear homogeneous type. Let us next consider a type of transformation which is not linear, and an invariant which represents the differential of the arc of a plane curve or simply the distance between two consecutive points (x, y) and $(x + dx, y + dy)$ in the (x, y) plane.

We assume the transformation to be given by

$$x' = X(x, y, a), \quad y' = Y(x, y, a),$$

where the functions X, Y are two independent continuous functions of x, y and the parameter a. We assume (a) that the partial derivatives of these functions exist, and (b) that these are continuous. Also (c) we define X, Y to be such that when $a = a_0$

$$X(x, y, a_0) = x, \ Y(x.y, a_0) = y.$$

Then let an increment δa be added to a_0 and expand each function as a power series in δa by Taylor's theorem. This gives

$$x' = X(x, y, a_0) + \frac{\partial X(x, y, a_0)}{\partial a_0}\delta a + \ldots,$$
$$y' = Y(x, y, a_0) + \frac{\partial Y(x, y, a_0)}{\partial a_0}\delta a + \ldots. \tag{15}$$

Since it may happen that some of the partial derivatives of X, Y may vanish for $a = a_0$, assume that the lowest power of δa in (15) which has a non-vanishing coefficient is $(\delta a)^k$, and write $(\delta a)^k = \delta t$. Then the transformation, which is infinitesimal, becomes

$$I: \begin{aligned} x' &= x + \xi\delta t, \\ y' &= y + \eta\delta t. \end{aligned}$$

where ξ, η are continuous functions of x, y. The effect of operating I upon the coördinates of a point P is to add infinitesimal increments to those coördinates, viz.

$$\begin{aligned} \delta x &= \xi\delta t, \\ \delta y &= \eta\delta t. \end{aligned} \tag{16}$$

Repeated operations with I produce a continuous motion of the point P along a definite path in the plane. Such a motion may be called a stationary streaming in the plane (Lie).

Let us now determine the functions ξ, η, so that

$$\sigma = dx^2 + dy^2$$

shall be an invariant under I.

By means of I, σ receives an infinitesimal increment $\delta\sigma$. In order that σ may be an absolute invariant, we must have

$$\frac{1}{2}\delta\sigma = dx\delta dx + dy\delta dy = 0,$$

or, since differential and variation symbols are permutable,

$$dx d\delta x + dy d\delta y = dx d\xi + dy d\eta = 0.$$

Hence

$$(\xi_x dx + \xi_y dy)dx + (\eta_x dx + \eta_y dy)dy = 0.$$

Thus since dx and dy are independent differentials

$$\xi_x = \eta_y = 0, \quad \xi_y + \eta_x = 0.$$

That is, ξ is free from x and η from y. Moreover

$$\xi_{xy} = \eta_{xx} = \xi_{yy} = 0.$$

Hence ξ is linear in y, and η is linear in x; and also from

$$\begin{aligned} \xi_y &= -\eta_x, \\ \xi &= \alpha y + \beta, \quad \eta = -\alpha x + \gamma. \end{aligned} \tag{17}$$

Thus the most general infinitesimal transformation leaving σ invariant is

$$I: x' = x + (\alpha y + \beta)\delta t, \quad y' = y + (-\alpha x + \gamma)\delta t. \tag{18}$$

Now there is one point in the plane which is left invariant, viz.

$$x = \gamma/\alpha, \quad y = -\beta/\alpha.$$

The only exception to this is when $\alpha = 0$. But the transformation is then completely defined by

$$x' = x + \beta\delta t, \quad y' = y + \gamma\delta t,$$

and is an infinitesimal translation parallel to the coördinate axes. Assuming then that $\alpha \neq 0$, we transform coördinate axes so that the origin is moved to the invariant point. This transformation,

$$x = x + \gamma/\alpha, \quad y = y - \beta/\alpha,$$

leaves σ unaltered, and I becomes

$$x' = x + \alpha y\delta t, \quad y' = y - \alpha x\delta t. \tag{19}$$

But (19) is simply an infinitesimal rotation around the origin. We may add that the case $\alpha = 0$ does not require to be treated as an exception since an infinitesimal translation may be regarded as a rotation around the point at infinity. Thus,

Theorem. *The most general infinitesimal transformation which leaves $\sigma = dx^2 + dy^2$ invariant is an infinitesimal rotation around a definite invariant point in the plane.*

We may readily interpret this theorem geometrically by noting that if σ is invariant the motion is that of a rigid figure. As is well known, any infinitesimal motion of a plane rigid figure in a plane is equivalent to a rotation around a unique point in the plane, called the instantaneous center. The invariant point of I is therefore the instantaneous center of the infinitesimal rotation.

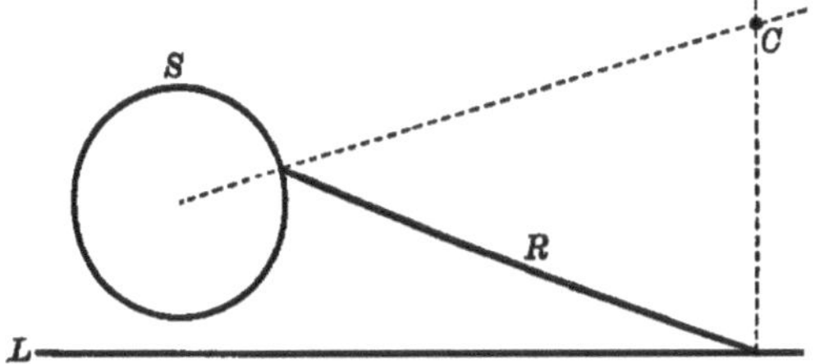

The adjoining figure shows the invariant point (C) when the moving figure is a rigid rod R one end of which slides on a circle S, and the other along a straight line L. This point is the intersection of the radius produced through one end of the rod with the perpendicular to L at the other end.

1.1.8 An Arithmetical Invariant.

Finally let us introduce a transformation of the linear type like

$$T : x_l = \lambda_1 x_1' + \mu_1 x_2', \quad x_2 = \lambda_2 x_1' + \mu_2 x_2',$$

but one in which the coefficients λ, μ are positive integral residues of a prime number p. Call this transformation T_p. We note first that T_p may be generated by combining the following three particular transformations:

$$(a)\ x_1 = x_1' + t x_2', \quad x_2 = x_2',$$
$$(b)\ x_1 = x_1', \quad x_2 = \lambda x_2', \tag{20}$$
$$(c)\ x_1 = x_2', \quad x_2 = -x_1',$$

where t, λ are any integers reduced modulo p. For (a) repeated gives

$$x_1 = (x_1'' + t x_2'') + t x_2'' = x_1'' + 2t x_2'', \quad x_2 = x_2''.$$

Repeated r times (a) gives, when $rt \equiv u \pmod{p}$,

$$(d)\ x_1 = x_1' + u x_2', \quad x_2 = x_2'.$$

Then (c) combined with (d) becomes

$$(e)\ x_1 = -u x_1' + x_2', \quad x_2 = -x_1'.$$

Proceeding in this way T_p may be built up.

Let

$$f = a_0 x_1^2 + 2 a_1 x_1 x_2 + a_2 x_2^2,$$

where the coefficients are arbitrary variables; and

$$g = a_0 x_1^4 + a_1 (x_1^3 x_2 + x_1 x_2^3) + a_2 x_2^4, \tag{21}$$

and assume $p = 3$. Then we can prove that g is an arithmetical covariant; in other words a covariant modulo 3. This is accomplished by showing that if f be transformed by T_3 then g' will be identically congruent to g modulo 3. When f is transformed by (c) we have

$$f' = a_2 x_1'^2 - 2 a_1 x_1' x_2' + a_0 x_2'^2.$$

That is,

$$a_0' = a_2, \quad a_1' = -a_1, \quad a_2' = a_0.$$

The inverse of (c) is $x_2' = x_1$, $x_1' = -x_2$. Hence

$$g' = a_2 x_2^4 + a_1 (x_1 x_2^3 + x_1^3 x_2) + a_0 x_1^4 = g,$$

and g is invariant, under (c).

Next we may transform f by (a); and we obtain

$$a_0' = a_0, \quad a_1' = a_0 t + a_1, \quad a_2' = a_0 t^2 + 2 a_1 t + a_2.$$

The inverse of (a) is

$$x_2' = x_2, \ x_1' = x_1 - tx_2.$$

Therefore we must have

$$\begin{aligned}
g' &= a_0(x_1 - tx_2)^4 + (a_0t + a_1)\left[(x_1 - tx_2)^3 x_2 + (x_1 - tx_2)x_2^3\right] \\
&\quad + (a_0t^2 + 2a_1t + a_2)x_2^4 \\
&\equiv a_0x_1^4 + a_1(x_1^3x_2 + x_1x_2^3) + a_2x_2^4 \ (\mathrm{mod} \ 3)
\end{aligned} \tag{22}$$

But this congruence follows immediately from the following case of Fermat's theorem:

$$t^3 \equiv t(\mathrm{mod} \ 3).$$

Likewise g is invariant with reference to *(b)*. Hence g is a formal modular covariant of f under T_3.

1.2 Terminology and Definitions. Transformations

We proceed to formulate some definitions upon which immediate developments depend.

1.2.1 An invariant.

Suppose that a function of n variables, f, is subjected to a definite set of transformations upon those variables. Let there be associated with f some definite quantity ϕ such that when the corresponding quantity ϕ' is constructed for the transformed function f' the equality

$$\phi' = M\phi$$

holds. Suppose that M depends only upon the transformations, that is, is free from any relationship with f. Then ϕ is called an invariant of f under the transformations of the set.

The most extensive subdivision of the theory of invariants in its present state of development is the theory of invariants of algebraical polynomials under linear transformations. Other important fields are differential invariants and number-theoretic invariant theories. In this book we treat, for the most part, the algebraical invariants.

1.2.2 Quantics or forms.

A homogeneous polynomial in n variables $x_1, x_2, \ldots, x_n$ of order m in those variables is called a *quantic*, or *form*, of order m. Illustrations are

$$f(x_1, x_2) = a_0x_1^3 + 3a_1x_1^2x_2 + 3a_2x_1x_2^2 + a_3x_2^3,$$

$$f(x_1, x_2, x_3) = a_{200}x_1^2 + 2a_{110}x_1x_2 + a_{020}x_2^2 + 2a_{101}x_1x_3 + 2a_{011}x_2x_3 + a_{002}x_3^2$$

With reference to the number of variables in a quantic it is called binary, ternary; and if there are n variables, n-ary. Thus $f(x_1, x_2)$ is a binary cubic form; $f(x_1, x_2, x_3)$ a ternary quadratic form. In algebraic invariant theories of binary forms it is usually most convenient to introduce with each coefficient a_i the binomial multiplier $\binom{m}{i}$ as in $f(x_1, x_2)$. When these multipliers are present, a common notation for a binary form of order m is (Cayley)

$$f(x_1, x_2) = (a_0, a_1, \cdots, a_m \ ) \ x_1, x_2)^m = a_0 x_1^m + m a_1 x_1^{m-1} x_2 + \cdots .$$

If the coefficients are written without the binomial numbers, we abbreviate

$$f(x_1, x_2) = (a_0, a_1, \cdots, a_m \ ) \ x_1, x_2)^m = a_a x_1^m + a_1 x_1^{m-1} x_2 + \cdots .$$

The most common notation for a ternary form of order m is the generalized form of $f(x_1, x_2, x_3)$ above. This is

$$f(x_1, x_2, x_3) = \sum_{p,q,r=0}^{m} \frac{m!}{p!q!r!} a_{pqr} x_1^p x_2^q x_3^r,$$

where p, q, r take all positive integral values for which $p + q + r = m$. It will be observed that the multipliers associated with the coefficients are in this case multinomial numbers. Unless the contrary is stated, we shall in all cases consider the coefficients a of a form to be arbitrary variables. As to coordinate representations we may assume (x_1, x_2, x_3), in a ternary form for instance, to be homogenous coördinates of a point in a plane, and its coefficients a_{pqr} to be homogenous coordinates of planes in M-space, where $M + 1$ is the number of the a's. Thus the ternary form is represented by a point in M dimensional space and by a curve in a plane.

1.2.3 Linear Transformations.

The transformations to which the variables in an n-ary form will ordinarily be subjected are the following linear transformations called collineations:

$$\begin{aligned}
x_1 &= \lambda_1 x_1' + \mu_1 x_2' + \ldots + \sigma_1 x_n' \\
x_2 &= \lambda_2 x_1' + \mu_2 x_2' + \ldots + \sigma_2 x_n' \\
&\cdots \\
x_n &= \lambda_n x_1' + \mu_n x_2' + \ldots + \sigma_n x_n' .
\end{aligned} \tag{23}$$

In algebraical theories the only restriction to which these transformations will be subjected is that the inverse transformation shall exist. That is, that it be possible to solve for the primed variables in terms of the un-primed variables (cf. (10)). We have seen in Section 1, V (11), and VIII (22) that the verification of a covariant and indeed the very existence of a covariant depends upon the existence of this inverse transformation.

Theorem. *A necessary and sufficient condition in order that the inverse of (23) may exist is that the determinant or modulus of the transformation,*

$$M = (\lambda\mu\nu\ldots\sigma) = \begin{vmatrix} \lambda_1, & \mu_1, & \nu_1, & \cdots & \sigma_1 \\ \lambda_2, & \mu_2, & \nu_2, & \cdots & \sigma_2 \\ \vdots & \vdots & \vdots & \ddots & \vdots \\ \lambda_n, & \mu_n, & \nu_n, & \cdots & \sigma_n \end{vmatrix},$$

shall be different from zero.

In proof of this theorem we observe that the minor of any element, as of μ_i, of M equals $\frac{\partial M}{\partial \mu_i}$. Hence, solving for a variable as x'_2, we obtain

$$x'_2 = M^{-1}\left(x_1\frac{\partial M}{\partial \mu_1} + x_2\frac{\partial M}{\partial \mu_2} + \ldots + x_n\frac{\partial M}{\partial \mu_n}\right),$$

and this is a defined result in all instances except when $M = 0$, when it is undefined. Hence we must have $M \neq 0$.

1.2.4   A theorem on the transformed polynomial.

Let f be a polynomial in x_1, x_2 of order m,

$$f(x_1, x_2) = a_0 x_1^m + m a_1 x_1^{m-1} x_2 + \binom{m}{2} a_2 x_1^{m-2} x_2^2 + \ldots + a_m x_2^m.$$

Let f be transformed into f' by T (cf. 3_1)

$$f' = a'_0 x_1'^m + m a'_1 x_1'^{m-1} x'_2 + \cdots + \binom{m}{r} a'_r x_1'^{m-r} x_2'^r + \cdots + a'_m x_2'^m.$$

We now prove a theorem which gives a short method of constructing the coefficients a'_r in terms of the coefficients $a_0, \ldots, a_m$.

Theorem. *The coefficients a'_r of the transformed form f' are given by the formulas*

$$a'_r = \frac{(m-r)!}{m!}\left(\mu_1\frac{\partial}{\partial \lambda_1} + \mu_2\frac{\partial}{\partial \lambda_2}\right)^r f(\lambda_1, \lambda_2) \quad (r = 0, \ldots, m). \tag{23_1}$$

In proof of this theorem we note that one form of f' is $f(\lambda_1 x'_1 + \mu_1 x'_2, \lambda_2 x'_1 + \mu_2 x'_2)$. But since f' is homogeneous this may be written

$$f' = x_1'^m f(\lambda_1 + \mu_1 x'_2/x'_1, \lambda_2 + \mu_2 x'_2/x'_1).$$

We now expand the right-hand member of this equality by Taylor's theorem, regarding x'_2/x'_1 as a parameter,

$$f' = x_1'^m \left[f(\lambda_1, \lambda_2) + \frac{x_2'}{x_1'} \left(\mu \frac{\partial}{\partial \lambda} \right) f(\lambda_1, \lambda_2) \right.$$

$$+ \frac{1}{2!} \left(\frac{x_2'}{x_1'} \right)^2 \left(\mu \frac{\partial}{\partial \lambda} \right)^2 f(\lambda_1, \lambda_2) + \cdots$$

$$\left. + \frac{1}{r!} \left(\frac{x_2'}{x_1'} \right)^r \left(\mu \frac{\partial}{\partial \lambda} \right)^r f(\lambda_1, \lambda_2) + \cdots \right],$$

where

$$\left(\mu \frac{\partial}{\partial \lambda} \right) = \left(\mu_1 \frac{\partial}{\partial \lambda_1} + \mu_2 \frac{\partial}{\partial \lambda_2} \right),$$

$$f' = f(\lambda_1, \lambda_2) x_1'^m + \cdots + \frac{1}{r!} \left(\mu \frac{\partial}{\partial \lambda} \right)^r f(\lambda_1, \lambda_2) x_1'^{m-r} x_2'^r + \cdots$$

$$+ \frac{1}{m!} \left(\mu \frac{\partial}{\partial \lambda} \right)^m f(\lambda_1, \lambda_2) x_2'^m.$$

Comparison of this result with the above form of f' involving the coefficients a_r' gives (23_1).

An illustration of this result may be obtained from (5). Here $m = 2$, and

$$a_0' = a_0 \lambda_1^2 + 2a_1 \lambda_1 \lambda_2 + a_2 \lambda_2^2 = f(\lambda_1, \lambda_2) = f_0,$$

$$a_1' = a_0 \lambda_1 \mu_1 + a_1(\lambda_1 \mu_2 + \lambda_2 \mu_1) + a_2 \lambda_2 \mu_2 = \frac{1}{2} \left(\mu \frac{\partial}{\partial \lambda} \right) f(\lambda_1, \lambda_2), \qquad (24)$$

$$a_2' = a_0 \mu_1^2 + 2a_1 \nu_1 \mu_2 + a_2 \mu_2^2 = \frac{1}{2} \left(\mu \frac{\partial}{\partial \lambda} \right)^2 f(\lambda_1, \lambda_2).$$

1.2.5   A group of transformations.

If we combine two transformations, as T and

$$T' : \begin{array}{l} x_1' = \xi_1 x_1'' + \eta_1 x_2'', \\ x_2' = \xi_2 x_2'' + \eta_2 x_2'', \end{array}$$

there results

$$TT' : \begin{array}{l} x_1 = (\lambda_1 \xi_1 + \mu_1 \xi_2) x_1'' + (\lambda_1 \eta_1 + \mu_1 \eta_2) x_2'', \\ x_2 = (\lambda_2 \xi_1 + \mu_2 \xi_2) x_1'' + (\lambda_2 \eta_1 + \mu_2 \eta_2) x_2'', \end{array}$$

This is again a linear transformation and is called the product of T and T'. If now we consider $\lambda_1, \lambda_2, \mu_1, \mu_2$ in T to be independent continuous variables assuming, say, all real values, then the number of linear transformations is infinite, $i.e.$ they form an infinite set, but such that the product of any two transformations of the set is a third transformation of the set. Such a set of transformations is said to form a *group*. The complete abstract definition of a group is the following:

Given any set of distinct operations $T, T'', T''', \cdots$, finite or infinite in number and such that:

(α) The result of performing successively any two operations of the set is another definite operation of the set which depends only upon the component operations and the sequence in which they are carried out:

(β) The inverse of every operation T exists in the set; that is, another operation T^{-l} such that TT^{-l} is the identity or an operation which produces no effect.

This set of operations then forms a group.

The set described above therefore forms an infinite group. If the transformations of this set have only integral coefficients consisting of the positive residues of a prime number p, it will consist of only a finite number of operations and so will form a finite group.

1.2.6   The induced group.

The equalities (24) constitute a set of linear transformations on the variables a_0, a_1, a_2. Likewise in the case of formulas (23_1). These transformations are said to be *induced* by the transformations T. If T carries f into f' and T'' carries f' into f'', then

$$a_r'' = \frac{(m-r)!}{m!} \left(\eta \frac{\partial}{\partial \xi} \right)^r f'(\xi_1, \xi_2)$$

$$= \frac{(m-r)!}{m!} \left(\eta \frac{\partial}{\partial \xi} \right) \sum_{s=0}^{m} \frac{1}{s!} \left(\mu \frac{\partial}{\partial \lambda} \right)^s f(\lambda_1, \lambda_2) \xi_1^{m-2} \xi_2^s. \quad (24_1)$$

$$(r = 0, 1, \cdots, m).$$

This is a set of linear transformations connecting the a_r'' directly with $a_0, \cdots, a_m$. The transformations are induced by applying T, T'' *in succession* to f. Now *the induced transformations (23_1) form a group*; for the transformations induced by applying T and T' in succession is identical with the transformation induced by the product TT'. This is capable of formal proof. For by (28_1) the result of transforming f by TT' is

$$a_r'' = \frac{(m-r)!}{m!} \Delta^r f(\lambda_1 \xi_1 + \mu_1 \xi 2, \lambda_2 \xi_1 + \mu_2 \xi_2),$$

where

$$\Delta = (\lambda_1 \eta_1 + \mu_1 \eta_2) \frac{\partial}{\partial(\lambda_1 \xi_1 + \mu_1 \xi_2)} + (\lambda_2 \eta_1 + \mu_2 \eta_2) \frac{\partial}{\partial(\lambda_2 \xi_1 + \mu_2 \xi_2)}$$

But

$$(\lambda_1\eta_1 + \mu_1\eta_2)\frac{\partial}{\partial(\lambda_1\xi_1 + \mu_1\xi_2)}$$

$$= \eta_1\frac{\partial}{(\lambda_1\xi_1 + \mu_1\xi_2)}\frac{\partial(\lambda_1\xi_1 + \mu_1\xi_2)}{\partial\xi_1}$$

$$+ \eta_2\frac{\partial}{(\lambda_1\xi_1 + \mu_1\xi_2)}\frac{\partial(\lambda_1\xi_1 + \mu_1\xi_2)}{\partial\xi_2}$$

$$= \eta_1\frac{\partial}{\partial\xi_1} + \eta_2\frac{\partial}{\partial\xi_2}.$$

Hence

$$\Delta = \left(\eta\frac{\partial}{\partial\xi}\right) + \left(\eta\frac{\partial}{\partial\xi}\right)$$

and by the method of (IV) combined with this value of Δ

$$a_r'' = \frac{(m-r)!}{m!}\left(\eta\frac{\partial}{\partial\xi}\right)^r \sum_0^m \frac{1}{s!}\left(\mu\frac{\partial}{\partial\lambda}\right)^s f(\lambda_1, \lambda_2)\xi_1^{m-s}\xi_2^s.$$

But this is identical with (24_1). Hence the induced transformations form a group, as stated. This group will be called the *induced group*.

Definition.

A quantic or form, as for instance a binary cubic f, is a function of two distinct sets of variables, *e.g.* the variables x_1, x_2, and the coefficients $a_0, \ldots, a_3$. It is thus quaternary in the coefficients and binary in the variables x_1, x_2. We call it a quaternary-binary function. In general, if a function F is homogeneous and of degree i in one set of variables and of order ω in a second set, and if the first set contains m variables and the second set n, then F is said to be an m-ary-n-ary function of *degree-order* (i, ω). If the first set of variables is $a_0, \ldots, a_m$, and the second and the second $x_1, \ldots, x_n$, we frequently employ the notation

$$F = (a_0, \ldots, a_m)^i(x_1, \ldots, x_n)^\omega.$$

1.2.7   Cogrediency.

In many invariant theory problems two sets of variables are brought under consideration simultaneously. If these sets $(x_1, x_2, \cdots, x_n)$, $(y_1, y_2, \cdots, y_n)$ are subject to the same scheme of transformations, as (23), they are said to be cogredient sets of variables.

As an illustration of cogredient sets we first take the modular binary transformations,

$$T_p : x_1 = \lambda_1 x_1' + \mu_1 x_2', x_2 = \lambda_2 x_1' + \mu_2 x_2',$$

where the coefficients λ, μ are integers reduced modulo p as in Section 1, VIII. We can prove that with reference to T_p the quantities x_1^p, x_2^p, are cogredient to

x_1, x_2. For all binomial numbers $\binom{p}{i}$, where p is a prime, are divisible by p except $\binom{p}{0}$ and $\binom{p}{p}$. Hence, raising the equations of T_p to the pth power, we have

$$x_1^p \equiv \lambda_1^p x_1'^p + \mu_1^p x_2'^p,\ x_2^p \equiv \lambda_2^p x_1'^p + \mu_2^p x_2'^p \ (\mathrm{mod}\ p).$$

But by Fermat's theorem,

$$\lambda_i^p \equiv \lambda_i,\ \mu_i^p \equiv \mu_i \ (\mathrm{mod}\ p)\ (i = 1, 2).$$

Therefore

$$x_1^p = \lambda_1 x_1'^p + \mu_1 x_2'^p,\ x_2^p = \lambda_2 x_1'^p + \mu_2 x_2'^p,$$

and the cogrediency of x_1^p, x_2^p with x_1, x_2 under T_p is proved.

1.2.8   Theorem on the roots of a polynomial.

Theorem. *The roots* $(r_1^{(1)}, r_2^{(1)}), (r_1^{(2)}, r_2^{(2)}), \cdots, ((r_1^{(m)}, r_2^{(m)})$ *of a binary form*

$$f = a_0 x_1^m + m a_1 x_1^{m-1} x_2 + \dots + a_m x_2^m,$$

are cogredient to the variables.

To prove this we write

$$f = (r_2^{(1)} x_1 - r_1^{(1)} x_2)(r_2^{(2)} x_1 - r_1^{(2)} x_2) \cdots (r_2^{(m)} x_1 - r_1^{(m)} x_2),$$

and transform f by T. There results

$$f' = \prod_{i=1}^{m} \left[(r_2^{(i)} \lambda_1 - r_1^{(i)} \lambda_2) x_1' + (r_2^{(i)} \mu_1 - r_1^{(i)} \mu_2) x_2' \right].$$

Therefore

$$r_2'^{(i)} = r_2^{(i)} \lambda_1 - r_1^{(i)} \lambda_2;\ r_1'^{(i)} = -(r_2^{(i)} \mu_1 - r_1^{(i)} \mu_2).$$

Solving these we have

$$(\lambda \mu) r_1^{(i)} = \lambda_1 r_1'^{(i)} + \mu_1 r_2'^{(i)},$$
$$(\lambda \mu) r_2^{(i)} = \lambda_2 r_1'^{(i)} + \mu_2 r_2'^{(i)}.$$

Thus the r's undergo the same transformation as the x's (save for a common multiplier $(\lambda \mu)$), and hence are cogredient to x_1, x_2 as stated.

1.2.9   Fundamental postulate.

We may state as a fundamental postulate of the invariant theory of quantics subject to linear transformations the following: Any covariant of a quantic or system of quantics, *i.e.* any invariant formation containing the variables $x_1, x_2, \ldots$ will keep its invariant property unaffected when the set of elements $x_1, x_2, \ldots$ is replaced by any cogredient set.

This postulate asserts, in effect, that the notation for the variables may be changed in an invariant formation provided the elements introduced in place of the old variables are subject to the same transformation as the old variables.

Since invariants may often be regarded as special cases of covariants, it is desirable to have a term which includes both types of invariant formations. We shall employ the word *concomitant* in this connection.

BINARY CONCOMITANTS

Since many chapters of this book treat mainly the concomitants of binary forms, we now introduce several definitions which appertain in the first instance to the binary case.

1.2.10 Empirical definition.

Let

$$f = a_0 x_1^m + m a_1 x_1^{m-1} x_2 + \frac{1}{2} m(m-1) a_2 x_1^{m-2} x_2^2 + \cdots + a_m x_2^m,$$

be a binary form of order m. Suppose f is transformed by T into

$$f' = a_0' x_1'^m + m a_1' x_1'^{m-1} x_2' + \cdots + a_m' x_2'^m.$$

We construct a polynomial ϕ in the variables and coefficients of f. If this function ϕ is such that it needs at most to be multiplied by a power of the determinant or modulus of the transformation $(\lambda\mu)$, to be made equal to the same function of the variables and coefficients of f', then ϕ is a concomitant of f under T. If the order of ϕ in the variables x_1, x_2 is zero, ϕ is an invariant. Otherwise it is a covariant. An example is the discriminant of the binary quadratic, in Paragraph III of Section 1.

If ϕ is a similar invariant formation of the coefficients of two or more binary forms and of the variables x_1, x_2, it is called a simultaneous concomitant. Illustrations are h in Paragraph IV of Section 1, and the simultaneous covariant C in Paragraph V of Section 1.

We may express the fact of the invariancy of ϕ in all these cases by an equation

$$\phi' = (\lambda\mu)^k \phi,$$

in which ϕ' is understood to mean the same function of the coefficients a_0', a_1', ..., and of x_1', x_2' that ϕ is of a_0, a_1, ..., and x_1, x_2. Or we may write more explicitly

$$\phi(a_0', a_1', \ldots; x_1', x_2') = (\lambda\mu)^k \phi(a_0, a_1, \ldots; x_1, x_2). \tag{25}$$

We need only to replace T by (23) and $(\lambda\mu)$ by $M = (\lambda\mu\cdots\sigma)$ in the above to obtain an empirical definition of a concomitant of an n-ary form f under (23). The corresponding equation showing the concomitant relation is

$$\phi(a'; x_1', x_2', \ldots, x_n') = M^k \phi(a; x_1, x_2, \ldots, x_n). \tag{26}$$

An equation such as (25) will be called *the invariant relation* corresponding to the invariant ϕ.

1.2.11 Analytical definition.

[1] We shall give a proof in Chapter II that no essential particularization of the above definition of an invariant ϕ of a binary form f is imposed by assuming that ϕ is homogeneous both in the a's and in the x's. Assuming this, we define a concomitant ϕ of f as follows:

(1) Let ϕ be a function of the coefficients and variables of f, and ϕ' the same function of the coefficients and variables of f'. Assume that it is a function such that

$$\mu_1 \frac{\partial \phi'}{\partial \lambda_1} + \mu_2 \frac{\partial \phi'}{\partial \lambda_2} = 0, \quad \lambda_1 \frac{\partial \phi'}{\partial \mu_1} + \lambda_2 \frac{\partial \phi'}{\partial \mu_2} = 0. \tag{27}$$

(2) Assume that ϕ' is homogeneous in the sets λ_1, λ_2; μ_1, μ_2 and of order k in each.

Then ϕ is called a concomitant of f.

We proceed to prove that this definition is equivalent to the empirical definition above.

Since ϕ' is homogeneous in the way stated, we have by Euler's theorem and (1) above

$$\lambda_1 \frac{\partial \phi'}{\partial \lambda_1} + \lambda_2 \frac{\partial \phi'}{\partial \lambda_2} = k\phi', \quad \left(\mu \frac{\partial}{\partial \lambda} \right) \phi' = 0, \tag{28}$$

where k is the order of ϕ' in λ_1, λ_2. Solving these,

$$\frac{\partial \phi'}{\partial \lambda_1} = k\mu_2 \phi'(\lambda\mu)^{-1}, \quad \frac{\partial \phi'}{\partial \lambda_2} = -k\mu_1 \phi'(\lambda\mu)^{-1}.$$

Hence

$$d\phi' = \frac{\partial \phi'}{\partial \lambda_1} d\lambda_1 + \frac{\partial \phi'}{\partial \lambda_2} d\lambda_2 = (\lambda\mu)^{-1} k\phi'(\mu_2 d\lambda_1 - \mu_1 d\lambda_2).$$

Separating the variables and integrating we have

$$\frac{d\phi'}{\phi'} = k\frac{d(\lambda\mu)}{(\lambda\mu)}, \quad \phi' = C(\lambda\mu)^k,$$

where C is the constant of integration. To determine C, let T be particularized to

$$x_1 = x_1', \quad x_2 = x_2'.$$

Then $a_i' = a_i (i = 0, 1, 2, \cdots, m)$, and $\phi' \equiv \phi$. Also $(\lambda\mu) = 1$. Hence by substitution

$$\phi' = (\lambda\mu)^k \phi,$$

---

[1]The idea of an analytical definition of invariants is due to Cayley. Introductory Memoir upon Quantics. Works, Vol. II.

and this is the same as (25). If we proceed from

$$\left(\lambda\frac{\partial}{\partial\mu}\right)\phi' = 0, \quad \left(\mu\frac{\partial}{\partial\mu}\right)\phi' = k\phi',$$

we arrive at the same result. Hence the two definitions are equivalent.

1.2.12 Annihilators.

We shall now need to refer back to Paragraph IV (23_1) and Section 1 (10) and observe that

$$\left(\mu\frac{\partial}{\partial\lambda}\right)a'_r = (m-r)a'_{r+1}, \quad \left(\mu\frac{\partial}{\partial\lambda}\right)x'_1 = 0, \quad \left(\mu\frac{\partial}{\partial\lambda}\right)x'_2 = -x'_1. \qquad (29)$$

Hence the operator $\left(\mu\frac{\partial}{\partial\lambda}\right)$ applied to ϕ', regarded as a function of $\lambda_1, \lambda_2, \mu_1, \mu_2$, has precisely the same effect as some other linear differential operator involving only $a'_i (i = 0, \cdots, m)$ and x'_1, x'_2, which would have the effect (29) when applied to ϕ' regarded as a function of a'_i, x'_1, x'_2 alone. Such an operator exists. In fact we can see by empirical considerations that

$$O' - x'_1\frac{\partial}{\partial x'_2} \equiv ma'_1\frac{\partial}{\partial a'_0} + (m-1)a'_2\frac{\partial}{\partial a'_1} + \cdots + a'_m\frac{\partial}{\partial a'_{m-1}} - x'_1\frac{\partial}{\partial x'_2} \qquad (29_1)$$

is such an operator. We can also derive this operator by an easy analytical procedure. For,

$$\left(\mu\frac{\partial}{\partial\lambda}\right)\phi' = \frac{\partial\phi'}{\partial a'_0}\left(\mu\frac{\partial a'_0}{\partial\lambda}\right) + \frac{\partial\phi'}{\partial a'_1}\left(\mu\frac{\partial a'_1}{\partial\lambda}\right) + \cdots + \frac{\partial\phi'}{\partial a'_m}\left(\mu\frac{\partial a'_m}{\partial\lambda}\right) + \frac{\partial\phi'}{\partial x'_2}\left(\mu\frac{\partial x'_2}{\partial\lambda}\right) = 0,$$

or, by (29)

$$\left(O' - x'_1\frac{\partial}{\partial x'_2}\right)\phi' = 0.$$

In the same manner we can derive from $(\lambda\frac{\partial}{\partial\mu})\phi' = 0$,

$$\left(\Omega' - x'_2\frac{\partial}{\partial x'_1}\right)\phi' \equiv \left(a'_0\frac{\partial}{\partial a'_1} + 2a'_1\frac{\partial}{\partial a'_2} + \cdots + ma'_{m-1}\frac{\partial}{\partial a'_m} - x'_2\frac{\partial}{\partial x'_1}\right)\phi' = 0.$$

$$(29_2)$$

The operators (29_1), (29_2) are called *annihilators* (Sylvester). Since ϕ is the same function of $a_i, x_1 x_2$, that ϕ' is of $a'_i, x'_1 \, x'_2$ we have, by dropping primes, the result:

Theorem. *A set of necessary and sufficient conditions that a homogeneous function, ϕ, of the coefficients and variables of a binary form f should be a concomitant is*

$$\left(O - x_1\frac{\partial}{\partial x_2}\right)\phi = 0, \quad \left(\Omega - x_2\frac{\partial}{\partial x_1}\right)\phi = 0.$$

In the case of invariants these conditions reduce to $O\phi = 0$, $\Omega\phi = 0$. These operators are here written again, for reference, and in the un-primed variables:

$$O = ma_1\frac{\partial}{\partial a_0} + (m-1)a_2\frac{\partial}{\partial a_1} + \cdots + a_m\frac{\partial}{\partial a_{m-1}},$$

$$\Omega = a_0\frac{\partial}{\partial a_1} + 2a_1\frac{\partial}{\partial a_2} + \cdots + ma_{m-1}\frac{\partial}{\partial a_m}.$$

A simple illustration is obtainable in connection with the invariant

$$D_1 = a_0 a_2 - a_1^2 \ \text{(Section 1, III)}.$$

Here $m = 2$:

$$\Omega = a_0\frac{\partial}{\partial a_1} + 2a_1\frac{\partial}{\partial a_2}, \ O = 2a_1\frac{\partial}{\partial a_0} + a_2\frac{\partial}{\partial a_1}.$$

$$\Omega D_1 = -2a_0 a_1 + 2a_0 a_1 \equiv 0, \ O D_1 = 2a_1 a_2 - 2a_1 a_2 \equiv 0.$$

It will be noted that this method furnishes a convenient means of checking the work of computing any invariant.

1.3 Special Invariant Formations

We now prove the invariancy of certain types of functions of frequent occurrence in the algebraic theory of quantics.

1.3.1 Jacobians.

Let $f_1, f_2, \cdots, f_n$ be n homogeneous forms in n variables $x_1, x_2, \cdots, x_n$. The determinant,

$$J = \begin{vmatrix} f_{1x_1}, & f_{1x_2}, & \cdots, & f_{1x_n} \\ f_{2x_1}, & f_{2x_2}, & \cdots, & f_{2x_n} \\ \multicolumn{4}{c}{\cdots\cdots} \\ f_{nx_1}, & f_{nx_2}, & \cdots, & f_{nx_n} \end{vmatrix} \tag{30}$$

in which $f_{1x_1} = \frac{\partial f_1}{\partial x_1}$, etc., is the functional determinant, or Jacobian of the n forms. We prove that J is invariant when the forms f_i are transformed by (23), *i.e.* by

$$x_i = \lambda_i x_1' + \mu_i x_2' + \cdots + \sigma_i x_n' (i = 1, 2, \cdots, n). \tag{31}$$

To do this we construct the Jacobian J' of the transformed quantic f_j'. We have from (31),

$$\frac{\partial f_j'}{\partial x_2'} = \frac{\partial f_j'}{\partial x_1}\frac{\partial x_1}{\partial x_2'} + \frac{\partial f_j'}{\partial x_2}\frac{\partial x_2}{\partial x_2'} + \cdots + \frac{\partial f_j'}{\partial x_n}\frac{\partial x_n}{\partial x_2'}.$$

But by virtue of the transformations (31) we have in all cases, identically,

$$f_j' = f_j(j = 1, 2, \cdots, n). \tag{32}$$

Hence

$$\frac{\partial f'_j}{\partial x'_2} = \mu_1 \frac{\partial f_j}{\partial x_1} + \mu_2 \frac{\partial f_j}{\partial x_2} + \cdots + \mu_n \frac{\partial f_j}{\partial x_n}, \tag{33}$$

and we obtain similar formulas for the derivatives of f'_j with respect to the other variables. Therefore

$$J' = \begin{vmatrix} \lambda_1 f_{1x_1} + \lambda_2 f_{1x_2} + \cdots + \lambda_n f_{1x_n}, & \mu_1 f_{1x_1} + \mu_2 f_{1x_2} + \cdots + \mu_n f_{1x_n}, & \cdots \\ \cdots\cdots\cdots\cdots\cdots \\ \lambda_1 f_{nx_1} + \lambda_2 f_{nx_2} + \cdots + \lambda_n f_{nx_n}, & \mu_1 f_{nx_1} + \mu_2 f_{nx_2} + \cdots + \mu_n f_{nx_n}, & \cdots \end{vmatrix}. \tag{1.1}$$

But this form of J' corresponds exactly with the formula for the product of two nth order determinants, one of which is J and the other the modulus M. Hence

$$J' = (\lambda\mu\cdots\sigma)J,$$

and J is a concomitant. It will be observed that the covariant C in Paragraph V of Section 1 is the Jacobian of f and ϕ.

1.3.2 Hessians.

If f is an n-ary form, the determinant

$$H = \begin{vmatrix} f_{x_1x_1}, & f_{x_1x_2}, & \cdots, & f_{x_1x_n} \\ f_{x_2x_1}, & f_{x_2x_2}, & \cdots, & f_{x_2x_n} \\ \vdots & \vdots & \ddots & \vdots \\ f_{x_nx_1}, & f_{x_nx_2}, & \cdots, & f_{x_nx_n} \end{vmatrix} \tag{34}$$

is called the Hessian of f. That H possesses the invariant property we may prove as follows: Multiply H by $M = (\lambda\mu\upsilon\cdots\sigma)$, and make use of (33). This gives

$$MH \equiv \begin{vmatrix} \lambda_1 & \mu_1 & \cdots & \sigma_1 \\ \lambda_2 & \mu_2 & \cdots & \sigma_2 \\ \vdots & \vdots & \ddots & \vdots \\ \lambda_n & \mu_n & \cdots & \sigma_n \end{vmatrix} H = \begin{vmatrix} \frac{\partial}{\partial x'_1}\frac{\partial f}{\partial x_1}, & \frac{\partial}{\partial x'_2}\frac{\partial f}{\partial x_1}, & \cdots, & \frac{\partial}{\partial x'_n}\frac{\partial f}{\partial x_1} \\ \frac{\partial}{\partial x'_1}\frac{\partial f}{\partial x_2}, & \frac{\partial}{\partial x'_2}\frac{\partial f}{\partial x_2}, & \cdots, & \frac{\partial}{\partial x'_n}\frac{\partial f}{\partial x_2} \\ \vdots & \vdots & \ddots & \vdots \\ \frac{\partial}{\partial x'_1}\frac{\partial f}{\partial x_n}, & \frac{\partial}{\partial x'_2}\frac{\partial f}{\partial x_n}, & \cdots, & \frac{\partial}{\partial x'_n}\frac{\partial f}{\partial x_n} \end{vmatrix}.$$

Replacing f by f' as in (32) and writing

$$\frac{\partial}{\partial x'_1}\frac{\partial f}{\partial x_1} = \frac{\partial}{\partial x_1}\frac{\partial f'}{\partial x'_1}, etc.,$$

we have, after multiplying again by M,

$$M^2 H = \begin{vmatrix} f'_{x'_1x'_1}, & f'_{x'_2x'_1}, & \cdots, & f'_{x'_nx'_1} \\ f'_{x'_1x'_2}, & f'_{x'_2x'_1}, & \cdots, & f'_{x'_nx'_2} \\ \vdots & \vdots & \ddots & \vdots \\ f'_{x'_1x'_n}, & f'_{x'_2x'_n}, & \cdots, & f'_{x'_nx'_n} \end{vmatrix},$$

that is to say,
$$H' = (\lambda\mu\nu\cdots\sigma)^2 H,$$

and H is a concomitant of f.

It is customary, and avoids extraneous numerical factors, to define the Hessian as the above determinant divided by $\frac{1}{2}m^n \times (m-1)^n$. Thus the Hessian covariant of the binary cubic form

$$f = a_0 x_1^3 + 3a_1 x_1^2 x_2 + 3a_2 x_1 x_2^2 + a_3 x_2^3,$$

is[2]

$$\Delta = 2\begin{vmatrix} a_0 x_1 + a_1 x + 2, a_1 x_1 + a_2 x_2 \\ a_1 x_1 + a_2 x_2, a_2 x_1 + a_3 x_2 \end{vmatrix},$$
$$= 2(a_0 a_2 - a_1^2)x_1^2 + 2(a_0 a_3 - a_1 a_2)x_1 x_2 + 2(a_1 a_3 - a_2^2)x_2^2. \tag{35}$$

1.3.3 Binary resultants.

Let f, ϕ be two binary forms of respective orders, m, n;

$$f = a_0 x_1^m + m a_1 x_1^{m-1} x_2 + \cdots + a_m x_2^m = \prod_{i=1}^{m}(r_2^{(i)} x_1 - r_1^{(i)} x_2),$$

$$\phi = b_0 x_1^n + n b_1 x_1^{n-1} x_2 + \cdots + b_n x_2^n = \prod_{j=1}^{n}(s_2^{(j)} x_1 - s_1^{(j)} x_2).$$

It will be well known to students of the higher algebra that the following symmetric function of the roots $(r_1^{(i)}, r_2^{(i)})$, $(s_1^{(j)}, s_2^{(j)})$, $R(f, \phi)$ is called the resultant of f and ϕ. Its vanishing is a necessary and sufficient condition in order that f and ϕ should have a common root.

$$R(f, \phi) = \prod_{j=1}^{n}\prod_{i=1}^{m}(r_1^{(i)} s_2^{(j)} - r_2^{(i)} s_1^{(j)}). \tag{36}$$

To prove that R is a simultaneous invariant of f and ϕ it will be sufficient to recall that the roots (r_1, r_2), (s_1, s_2) are cogredient to x_1, x_2. Hence when f, ϕ are each transformed by T, R undergoes the transformation

$$(\lambda\mu)r_1^{(i)} = \lambda_1 r_1'^{(i)} + \mu_1 r_2'^{(i)}, \; (\lambda\mu)r_2^{(i)} = \lambda_2 r_1'^{(i)} + \mu_2 r_2'^{(i)},$$
$$(\lambda\mu)s_1^{(j)} = \lambda_1 s_1'^{(j)} + \mu_1 s_2'^{(j)}, \; (\lambda\mu)s_2^{(j)} = \lambda_2 s_1'^{(j)} + \mu_2 s_2'^{(j)},$$

in which, owing to homogeneity the factors $(\lambda\mu)$ on the left may be disregarded. But under these substitutions,

$$r_1^{(i)} s_2^{(j)} - r_2^{(i)} s_1^{(j)} = (\lambda\mu)^{-1}(r_1'^{(i)} s_1'^{(j)} - r_2'^{(t)} s_1'^{(j)}).$$

---

[2] Throughout this book the notation for particular algebraical concomitants is that of Clebsch.

Hence
$$R'(f', \phi') = (\lambda\mu)^{mn} R(f, \phi),$$
which proves the invariancy of the resultant.

The most familiar and elegant method of expressing the resultant of two forms f, ϕ in terms of the coefficients of the forms is by Sylvester's dialytic method of elimination. We multiply f by the n quantities $x_1^{n-1}, x_1^{n-2}x_2, ..., x_2^{n-1}$ in succession, and obtain

$$a_0 x_1^{m+n-1} + ma_1 x_1^{m+n-2} x_2 + ... + a_m x_1^{n-1} x_2^m,$$
$$a_0 x_1^{m+n-2} x_2 + ... + ma_{m-1} x_1^{n-2} x_2^{m+1} + a_m x_1^{n-1} x_2^m, \tag{37}$$
$$\cdots\cdots\cdots$$
$$a_0 x_1^m x_2^{n-1} + ... + ma_{m-1} x_1 x_2^{m+n-2} + a_m x_2^{m+n-1}.$$

Likewise if we multiply ϕ by the succession $x_1^{m-1}, x_1^{m-2}x_2, ..., x_2^{m-1}$, we have the array

$$b_0 x_1^{m+n-1} + nb_1 x_1^{m+n-2} x_2 + ... + b_n x_1^{m-1} x_2^n,$$
$$\cdots\cdots\cdots$$
$$b_0 x_1^n x_2^{m-1} + ... + nb_{n-1} x_1 x_2^{m+n-2} + b_n x_2^{m+n-1}. \tag{38}$$

The eliminant of these two arrays is the resultant of f and ϕ, viz.

$$R(f, \phi) = \begin{vmatrix} \begin{array}{l} n \text{ rows} \begin{cases} \\ \\ \\ \end{cases} \\ m \text{ rows} \begin{cases} \\ \\ \\ \end{cases} \end{array} & \begin{array}{cccccccc} a_0 & ma_1 & \cdots & \cdots & a_m & 0 & 0\cdots & 0 \\ 0 & a_0 & ma_1 & \cdots & ma_{m-1} & a_m & 0\cdots & 0 \\ \cdots\cdots & & & & & & & \\ 0 & 0 & 0 & \cdots & \cdots & \cdots & \cdots & a_m \\ b_0 & nb_1 & \cdots & \cdots & \cdots & \cdots & \cdots & \cdots \\ 0 & b_0 & nb_1 & \cdots & \cdots & \cdots & \cdots & \cdots \\ \cdots\cdots & & & & & & & \\ 0 & 0 & 0 & \cdots & \cdots & \cdots & \cdots & b_n \end{array} \end{vmatrix}.$$

A particular case of a resultant is shown in the next paragraph. The degree of $R(f, \phi)$ in the coefficients of the two forms is evidently $m + n$.

1.3.4 Discriminant of a binary form.

The discriminant D of a binary form f is that function of its coefficients which when equated to zero furnishes a necessary and sufficient condition in order that $f = 0$ may have a double root. Let

$$f = f(x_1, x_2) = a_0 x_1^m + ma_1 x_1^{m-1} x_2 + \cdots + a_m x_2^m,$$

and let $f_{x_1}(x_1, x_2) = \frac{\partial f}{\partial x_1}$, $f_{x_2}(x_1, x_2) = \frac{\partial f}{\partial x_2}$. Then, as is well known, a common root of $f = 0$, $\frac{\partial f}{\partial x_1} = 0$ is a double root of $f = 0$ and conversely. Also

$$x_2^{-1}\left(mf - x_1\frac{\partial f}{\partial x_1}\right) = \frac{\partial f}{\partial x_2};$$

hence a double root of $f = 0$ is a common root of $f = 0$, $\frac{\partial f}{\partial x_1} = 0$, $\frac{\partial f}{\partial x_2} = 0$, and conversely; or D is equal either to the eliminant of f and $\frac{\partial f}{\partial x_1}$, or to that of f and $\frac{\partial f}{\partial x_2}$. Let the roots of $f_{x_1}(x_1, x_2) = 0$ be $(s_1^{(i)}, s_2^{(i)})(i = 1, \cdots, m-1)$, those of $f_x(x_1, x_2) = 0$, $(t_1^{(i)}, t_2^{(i)})(i = 1, \cdots, m-1)$, and those of $f = 0$ be $(r_1^{(j)}, r_2^{(j)})(j = 1, 2, \cdots, m)$. Then

$$a_0 D = f(s_1^{(1)}, s_2^{(1)}) f(s_1^{(2)}, s_2^{(2)}) \cdots f(s_1^{(m-1)}, s_2^{(m-1)}),$$
$$a_m D = f(t_1^{(1)}, t_2^{(1)}) f(t_1^{(2)}, t_2^{(2)}) \cdots f(t_1^{(m-1)}, t_2^{(m-1)}).$$

Now $Of(x_1, x_2) = x_1 \frac{\partial f}{\partial x_2}$, $\Omega f(x_1, x_2) = x_2 \frac{\partial f}{\partial x_1}$, where O and Ω are the annihilators of Section 2, XII. Hence

$$OD = \sum t_1^{(1)} f_{x_2}(t_1^{(1)}, t_2^{(1)}) f(t_1^{(2)}, t_2^{(2)}) \cdots f(t_1^{(m-1)}, t_2^{(m-1)}) \equiv 0,$$
$$\Omega D = \sum s_2^{(1)} f_{x_1}(s_1^{(1)}, s_2^{(1)}) f(s_1^{(2)}, s_2^{(2)}) \cdots f(s_1^{(m-1)}, s_2^{(m-1)}) \equiv 0,$$

Thus the discriminant satisfies the two differential equations $OD = O$, $\Omega D = 0$ and is an invariant. Its degree is $2(m-1)$.

An example of a discriminant is the following for the binary cubic f, taken as the resultant of $\frac{\partial f}{\partial x_1}$, $\frac{\partial f}{\partial x_2}$:

$$-\frac{1}{2}R = \begin{vmatrix} a_0 & 2a_1 & a_2 & 0 \\ 0 & a_0 & 2a_1 & a_2 \\ a_1 & 2a_2 & a_3 & 0 \\ 0 & a_1 & 2a_2 & a_3 \end{vmatrix} \tag{39}$$
$$= (a_0 a_3 - a_1 a_2)^2 - 4(a_0 a_2 - a_1^2)(a_1 a_3 - a_2^2).$$

1.3.5 Universal covariants.

Corresponding to a given group of linear transformations there is a class of invariant formations which involve the variables only. These are called universal covariants of the group. If the group is the infinite group generated by the transformations T in the binary case, a universal covariant is

$$d = (xy) = x_1 y_2 - x_2 y_1,$$

where (y) is cogredient to (x). This follows from

$$d = \begin{vmatrix} \lambda_1 x_1' + \mu_1 x_2', & \lambda_2 x_1' + \mu_2 x_2' \\ \lambda_1 y_1' + \mu_1 y_2', & \lambda_2 y_1' + \mu_2 y_2' \end{vmatrix} = (\lambda\mu)(x'y'). \tag{40}$$

If the group is the finite group modulo p, given by the transformations T_p, then since x_1^p, x_2^p are cogredient to x_1, x_2, we have immediately, from the above result for d, the fact that

$$L = x_1^p x_2 - x_1 x_2^p \tag{41}$$

is a universal covariant of this modular group.[3]

Another group of linear transformations, which is of consequence in geometry, is given by the well-known transformations of coördinate axes from a pair inclined at an angle ω to a pair inclined at an angle $\omega' = \beta - \alpha$, viz.

$$x_1 = \frac{sin(\omega - \alpha)}{sin\omega} x_1' + \frac{sin(\omega - \beta)}{sin\omega} x_2',$$

$$x_2 = \frac{sin\alpha}{sin\omega} x_1' + \frac{sin\beta}{sin\omega} x_2'. \tag{42}$$

Under this group the quadratic,

$$x_1^2 + 2x_1 x_2 cos\omega + x_2^2 \tag{43}$$

is a universal covariant.[4]

---

[3] Dickson, Transactions Amer. Math. Society, vol. 12 (1911)

[4] Study, Leipz. Ber. vol. 40 (1897).

Chapter 2

PROPERTIES OF INVARIANTS

2.1 Homogeneity of a Binary Concomitant

2.1.1 Homogeneity.

A binary form of order m

$$f = a_0 x_1^m + m a_1 x_1^{m-1} x_2 + \cdots + a_m x_2^m,$$

is an $(m+1)$-ary-binary function, of degree-order $(1, m)$. A concomitant of f is an $(m+1)$-ary-binary function of degree-order (i, ω). Thus the Hessian of the binary cubic (Chap. I, §3, II),

$$\Delta \equiv 2(a_0 a_2 - a_1^2)x_1^2 + 2(a_0 a_3 - a_1 a_2)x_1 x_2 + 2(a_1 a_3 - a_2^2)x_2^2, \qquad (44)$$

is a quaternary-binary function of degree-order $(2,\ 2)$. Likewise $f + \Delta$ is quaternary-binary of degree-order $(2,\ 3)$, but non-homogeneous.

An invariant function of degree-order $(i, 0)$ is an *invariant* of f. If the degree-order is $(0, \omega)$, the function is a universal covariant (Chap. I, §3, V). Thus $a_2 a_2 - a_1^2$ of degree-order $(2,\ 0)$ is an invariant of the binary quadratic under T, whereas $x_1^p x_2 - x_1 x_2^p$ of degree-order $(0, p+1)$ is a universal modular covariant of T_p.

Theorem. *If* $C \equiv (a_0, a_1, \cdots, a_m)^i (x_1, x_2)^\omega$ *is a concomitant of* $f = (a_0, \cdots, a_m)(x_1, x_2)^m$, *its theory as an invariant function loses no generality if we assume that it is homogeneous both as regards the variables* x_1, x_2 *and the variables* $a_0, \cdots, a_m$.

Assume for instance that it is non-homogeneous as to x_1, x_2. Then it must equal a sum of functions which are separately homogeneous in x_1, x_2. Suppose

$$C = C_1 + C_2 + \cdots + C_s,$$

where $C_j = (a_0, a_1, \cdots, a_m)i'(x_1, x_2)\omega_j$ $(j = 1, 2, \cdots, s)$ $i' \leq i$. Suppose now that we wish to verify the covariancy of C, directly. We will have

$$C' = (a_0', a_1', \cdots, a_m')^i (x_1', x_2')^\omega = (\lambda\mu)^k C, \tag{45}$$

in which relation we have an identity if a_i' is expressed as the appropriate linear expression in $a_0, \cdots, a_m$ and the x_i' as the linear expression in x_1, x_2, of Chapter I, Section 1 (10). But we can have

$$\sum_{j=1}^{s} C_j' = (\lambda\mu)^k \sum_{j=1}^{s} C_j,$$

identically in x_1, x_2 only provided

$$C_j' = (\lambda\mu)^k C_j \ (j = 1, \cdots, s).$$

Hence C_j is itself a concomitant, and since it is homogeneous as to x_1, x_2, no generality will be lost by assuming all invariant functions C homogeneous in x_1, x_2.

Next assume C to be homogeneous in x_1, x_2 but not in the variables $a_0, a_1, \cdots, a_m$. Then

$$C = \Gamma_1 + \Gamma_2 + \cdots + \Gamma_\sigma,$$

where Γ_i is homogeneous both in the a's and in the x's. Then the above process of verification leads to the fact that

$$\Gamma_j' = (\lambda\mu)^k \Gamma_j,$$

and hence C may be assumed homogeneous both as to the a's and the x's; which was to be proved. The proof applies equally well to the cases of invariants, covariants, and universal covariants.

2.2 Index, Order, Degree, Weight

In a covariant relation such as (45) above, k, the power of the modulus in the relation, shall be called the *index* of the concomitant. The numbers i, ω are respectively the *degree* and the *order* of C.

2.2.1 Definition.

Let $\tau = a_0^p a_1^q a_2^r \cdots a_m^v x_1^\mu x_2^{\omega-\mu}$ be any monomial expression in the coefficients and variables of a binary m-ic f. The degree of τ is of course $i = p + q + r + \cdots + v$. The number

$$w = q + 2r + 3s + \cdots + mv + \mu \tag{46}$$

is called the *weight* of τ. It equals the sum of all of the subscripts of the letters forming factors of τ *excluding the factors* x_2. Thus a_3 is of weight 3; $a_0 a_1^2 a_4$ of weight 6; $a_1^3 a_4 x_1^2 x_2^3$ of weight 9. Any polynomial whose terms are of the type

τ and all of the same weight is said to be an *isobaric* polynomial. We can, by a method now to be described, prove a series of facts concerning the numbers ω, i, k, w.

Consider the form f and a corresponding concomitant relation

$$C' = (a_0', a_1', \cdots, a_m')^i (x_1', x_2')^\omega = (\lambda\mu)^k (a_0, a_1, \cdots, a_m)^i (x_1, x_2)^\omega. \qquad (47)$$

This relation holds true when f is transformed by any linear transformation

$$T : \begin{matrix} x_1 = \lambda_1 x_1' + \mu_1 x_2', \\ x_2 = \lambda_2 x_1' + \mu_2 x_2'. \end{matrix}$$

It will, therefore, certainly hold true when f is transformed by any particular case of T. It is by means of such particular transformations that a number of facts will now be proved.

2.2.2 Theorem on the index.

Theorem. *The index k, order ω, and degree i of C satisfy the relation*

$$k = \frac{1}{2}(im - \omega). \qquad (48)$$

And this relation is true of invariants, i.e. (48) holds true when $\omega = 0$.

To prove this we transform

$$f = a_0 x_1^m + m a_1 x_1^{m-1} x_2 + \cdots + a_m x_2^m,$$

by the following special case of T:

$$x_1 = \lambda x_1', x_2 = \lambda x_2'$$

The modulus is now λ^2, and $a_j' = \lambda^m a_j (j = 0, \cdots, m)$. Hence from (47),

$$(\lambda^m a_0, \lambda^m a_1, \cdots, \lambda^m a_m)^i (\lambda^{-1} x_1, \lambda^{-1} x_2)^\omega = \lambda^{2k} (a_0, a_1, \cdots, a_m)^i (x_1, x_2)^\omega. \qquad (49)$$

But the concomitant C is homogeneous. Hence, since the degree-order is (i, ω),

$$\lambda^{im-\omega} (a_0, \cdots, a_m)^i (x_1, x_2)^\omega = \lambda^{2k} (a_0, \cdots, a_m)^i (x_1, x_2)^\omega$$

Hence

$$2K = im - \omega.$$

2.2.3 Theorem on weight.

Theorem. *Every concomitant C of f is isobaric and the weight is given by*

$$w = \frac{1}{2}(im + \omega), \qquad (50)$$

where (i, ω) is the degree-order of C, and m the order of f. The relation is true for invariants, i.e. if $\omega = 0$.

In proof we transform f by the special transformation

$$x_1 = x_1', x_2 = \lambda x_2'. \tag{51}$$

Then the modulus is λ, and $a_j' = \lambda^i a_i (j = 0, 2, \cdots, m)$. Let

$$\tau = a_0^p a_1^q a_2^r \cdots x_1^\mu x_2^{\omega - \mu}$$

be any term of C and τ' the corresponding term of C', the transformed of C by (51). Then by (47),

$$\tau' = \lambda^{q + 2r + \cdots + \mu - \omega} a_0^p a_1^q a_2^r \cdots x_1^\mu x_2^{\omega - \mu} = \lambda^k \tau.$$

Thus

$$w - \omega = k = \frac{1}{2}(im - \omega),$$

or

$$w = \frac{1}{2}(im + \omega).$$

COROLLARY 1. The weight of an invariant equals its index,

$$w = k = \frac{1}{2}im.$$

COROLLARY 2. The degree-order (i, ω) of a concomitant C cannot consist of an even number and an odd number except when m is even. Then i may be odd and ω even. But if m is even ω cannot be odd.

These corollaries follow directly from (48), (50).

As an illustration, if C is the Hessian of a cubic, (44), we have

$$i = 2, \omega = 2, m = 3,$$

$$w = \frac{1}{2}(2 \cdot 3 + 2) = 4,$$

$$k = \frac{1}{2}(2 \cdot 3 - 2) = 2.$$

These facts are otherwise evident (cf. (44), and Chap. I, Section 3, II).

COROLLARY 3. The index k of any concomitant of f is a positive integer. For we have

$$w - \omega = k,$$

and evidently the integer w is positive and $\omega \leqq w$.

2.3   Simultaneous Concomitants

We have verified the invariancy of two simultaneous concomitants. These are the bilinear invariants of two quadratics (Chap. I, Section 1, IV),

$$\psi = a_0 x^2{}_1 + 2a_1 x_1 x_2 + a_2 x^2{}_2,$$

$$\phi = b_0 x^2{}_1 + 2b_1 x_1 x_2 + b_2 x^2{}_2,$$

$$\text{viz. } h = a_0 b_2 - 2a_1 b_1 + a_2 b_0,$$

and the Jacobian C of ψ and ϕ (cf. (8)). For another illustration we may introduce the Jacobian of ϕ and the Hessian, Δ, of a binary cubic f. This is (cf. (44))

$$
\begin{aligned}
J_{\phi,\Delta} \;=\; & [b_0(a_0a_3 - a_1a_2) - 2b_1(a_0a_2 - a^2{}_1)]x^2{}_1 \\
+\; & 2[b_0(a_1a_3 - a^2{}_2) - b_2(a_0a_2 - a^2{}_1)]x_1x_2 \\
+\; & [2b_1(a_1a_3 - a^2{}_2) - b_2(a_0a_3 - a_1a_2)]x^2{}_2,
\end{aligned}
$$

and it may be verified as a concomitant of ϕ and

$$
f = a_0 x^3{}_1 + \ldots .
$$

The degree-order of J is $(3, 2)$. This might be written $(1 + 2, 2)$, where by the sum $1 + 2$ we indicate that J is of partial degree 1 in the coefficients of the first form ϕ and of partial degree 2 in the coefficients of the second form f.

2.3.1 Theorem on index and weight.

Theorem. *Let $f, \phi, \psi, \cdots$ be a set of binary forms of respective orders $m_1, m_2, m_3, \cdots$. Let C be a simultaneous concomitant of these forms of degree-order*

$$
(i_1 + i_2 + i_3 + \cdots, \omega)
$$

Then the index and the weight of C are connected with the numbers m, i, ω by the relations

$$
k = \frac{1}{2}\left(\sum i_1 m_1 - \omega\right), \; w = \frac{1}{2}\left(\sum i_1 m_1 + \omega\right), \tag{52}
$$

and these relations hold true for invariants (i.e. when $\omega = 0$).

The method of proof is similar to that employed in the proofs of the theorems in Section 2. We shall prove in detail the second formula only. Let

$$
f = a_0 x_1^{m_1} + \cdots, \quad \phi = b_0 x_1^{m_2} + \cdots, \quad \psi = c_0 x_1^{m_3} + \cdots, \cdots .
$$

Then a term of C will be of the form

$$
\tau = a_0^{q_1} a_1^{r_1} a_2^{s_1} \cdots b_0^{q_2} b_1^{r_2} b_2^{s_2} \cdots x_1^{\mu} x_2^{\omega - \mu}.
$$

Let the forms be transformed by $x_1 = x'_1, x_2 = \lambda x'_2$. Then $a'_j = \lambda^j a_j, b'_j = \lambda^j b_j, \cdots (j = 0, \cdots, m_i)$, and if τ' is the term corresponding to τ in the transformed of C by this particular transformation, we have

$$
\tau' = \lambda^{r_1 + 2s_1 + \cdots + r_2 + 2s_2 + \cdots + \mu - \omega}\tau = \lambda^k \tau.
$$

Hence

$$
w - \omega = k = \frac{1}{2}\left(\sum i_1 m_1 - \omega\right),
$$

which proves the theorem.

We have for the three simultaneous concomitants mentioned above; from formulas (52)

$$
\begin{array}{ccc}
h & C & J \\
k = 2 & k = l & k = 3 \\
w = 2 & w = 3 & w = 5
\end{array}
$$

2.4 Symmetry. Fundamental Existence Theorem

We have shown that the binary cubic form has an invariant, its discriminant, of degree 4, and weight 6. This is (cf. (39))

$$
\frac{1}{2} R = -(a_0 a_3 - a_1 a_2)^2 + 4(a_0 a_2 - a_1^2)(a_1 a_3 - a_2^2).
$$

2.4.1 Symmetry.

We may note concerning it that it is unaltered by the substitution $(a_0 a_1)(a_1 a_2)$. This fact is a case of a general property of concomitants of a binary form of order m. Let $f = a_0 x_1^m + \cdots$; and let C be a concomitant, the invariant relation being

$$
C' = (a_0', a_1', \ldots, a_m')^i (x_1', x_2')^\omega = (\lambda \mu)^k (a_0, \ldots, a_m)^i (x_1, x_2)^\omega.
$$

Let the transformation T of f be particularized to

$$
x_1 = x_2', \quad x_2 = x_1'.
$$

The modulus is -1. Then $a_j' = a_{m-j}$, and

$$
C' = (a_m, a_{m-1}, \ldots, a_0)^i (x_2, x_1)^\omega = (-1)^k (a_0, \ldots, a_m)^i (x_1, x_2)^\omega. \tag{53}
$$

That is; any concomitant of even index is unchanged when the interchanges $(a_0 a_m)(a_1 a_{m-1}) \cdots (x_1 x_2)$ are made, and if the index be odd, the concomitant changes only in sign. On account of this property a concomitant of odd index is called a skew concomitant. There exist no skew invariants for forms of the first four orders 1, 2, 3, 4. Indeed the simplest skew invariant of the quintic is quite complicated, it being of degree 18 and weight 45 [1] (Hermite). The simplest skew covariant of a lower form is the covariant T of a quartic of (125) (Chap. IV, §1).

We shall now close this chapter by proving a theorem that shows that the number of concomitants of a form is infinite. We state this fundamental existence theorem of the subject as follows:

Theorem. *Every concomitant K of a covariant C of a binary form f is a concomitant of f.*

---

[1] Faà di Bruno, Walter. Theorie der Binären Formen, p. 320.

That this theorem establishes the existence of an infinite number of concomitants of f is clear. In fact if f is a binary quartic, its Hessian covariant H (Chap. I, §3) is also a quartic. The Hessian of H is again a quartic, and is a concomitant of f by the present theorem. Thus, simply by taking successive Hessians we can obtain an infinite number of covariants of f, all of the fourth order. Similar considerations hold true for other forms.

In proof of the theorem we have

$$f = a_0 x_1^m + \cdots,$$
$$C = (a_0, \cdots, a_m)^i (x_1, x_2)^\omega = c_0 x_1^\omega + \omega c_1 x_1^{\omega-1} x_2 + \cdots,$$

where c_i is of degree i in $a_0, \cdots, a_m$.

Now let f be transformed by T. Then we can show that this operation *induces* a linear transformation of C, and precisely T. In other words when f is transformed, then C is transformed by the same transformation. For when f is transformed into f', C goes into

$$C' \equiv (\lambda\mu)^k (c_0 x_1^\omega + \omega c_1 x_1^{\omega-1} x_2 + \cdots).$$

But when C is transformed directly by T, it goes into a form which equals C itself by virtue of the equations of transformation. Hence the form C, induced by transforming f, is identical with that obtained by transforming C by T directly, save for the factor $(\lambda\mu)^k$. Thus by transformation of either f or C,

$$c_0' x_1'^\omega + \omega c_1' x_1'^{\omega-1} x_2' + \cdots = (\lambda\mu)^k c_0 x_1^\omega + \omega(\lambda\mu)^k c_1 x_1^{\omega-1} x_2 + \cdots \tag{54}$$

is an equality holding true by virtue of the equations of transformation. Now an invariant relation for K is formed by forming an invariant function from the coefficients and variables of the left-hand side of (54) and placing it equal to $(\lambda\mu)^k$ times the same function of the coefficients and the variables of the right-hand side,

$$K' = (c_0', \ldots, c_\omega')^\iota (x_1', x_2')^\epsilon$$
$$= (\lambda\mu)^\kappa ((\lambda\mu)^k c_0, \ldots, (\lambda\mu)^k c_\omega)^\iota (x_1, x_2)^\epsilon.$$

But K' is homogeneous and of degree-order (ι, ϵ). Hence

$$K' = (c_0', \ldots, c_\omega')^\iota (x_1', x_2')^\epsilon = (\lambda\mu)^{\iota k + \kappa} (c_0, \ldots, c_\omega)^\iota (x_1, x_2)^\epsilon \tag{55}$$
$$= (\lambda\mu)^{\iota k + \kappa} K.$$

Now c_j' is the same function of the $a_0', \ldots, a_m'$ that c_j is of $a_0, \ldots, a_m$. When the c''s and c's in (55) are replaced by their values in terms of the a's, we have

$$K' = [a_0', \ldots, a_m']^{\iota i} (x_1', x_2')^\epsilon = (\lambda\mu)^{\iota k + \kappa} [a_0, \ldots, a_m]^{\iota i} (x_1, x_2)^\epsilon \tag{56}$$
$$= (\lambda\mu)^{\iota k + \kappa} K.$$

where, of course, $[a_0, \ldots, a_m]^{\iota i} (x_1, x_2)^\epsilon$ considered as a function, is different from $(a_0, \ldots, a_m)^{\iota i} (x_1, x_2)^\epsilon$. But (56) is a covariant relation for a covariant of f. This proves the theorem.

The proof holds true *mutatis mutandis* for concomitants of an n-ary form and for simultaneous concomitants.

The *index* of K is

$$\rho = \iota \cdot \frac{1}{2}(im - \omega) + \frac{1}{2}(\iota\omega - \epsilon)$$
$$= \frac{1}{2}(\iota\iota m - \epsilon),$$

and its weight,

$$w = \frac{1}{2}(\iota\iota m + \epsilon).$$

Illustration. If f is a binary cubic,

$$f = a_0 x_1^3 + 3a_1 x_1^2 x_2 + 3a_2 x_1 x_2^2 + a_2 x_2^3,$$

then its Hessian,

$$\Delta = 2[(a_0 a_2 - a_1^2)x_1^2 + (a_0 a_3 - a_1 a_2)x_1 x_2 + (a_1 a_3 - a_2^2)x_2^2],$$

is a covariant of f. The Hessian $2R$ of Δ is the discriminant of Δ, and it is also twice the discriminant of f,

$$2R = 4[-(a_0 a_3 - a_1 a_2)^2 + 4(a_0 a_2 - a_1^2)(a_1 a_2 - a_2^2)].$$

Chapter 3

THE PROCESSES OF INVARIANT THEORY

3.1 Invariant Operators

We have proved in Chapter II that the system of invariants and covariants of a form or set of forms is infinite. But up to the present we have demonstrated no methods whereby the members of such a system may be found. The only methods of this nature which we have established are those given in Section 3 of Chapter I on special invariant formations, and these are of very limited application. We shall treat in this chapter the standard known processes for finding the most important concomitants of a system of quantics.

3.1.1 Polars.

In Section 2 of Chapter I some use was made of the operations $\lambda_1 \frac{\partial}{\partial \mu_1} + \lambda_2 \frac{\partial}{\partial \mu_2}, \mu_1 \frac{\partial}{\partial \lambda_1} + \mu_2 \frac{\partial}{\partial \lambda_2}$. Such operators may be extensively employed in the construction of invariant formations. They are called *polar* operators.

Theorem. *Let* $f = a_0 x_1^m + \cdots$ *be an n-ary quantic in the variables* $x_1, \cdots, x_n$ *and* ϕ *a concomitant of* f*, the corresponding invariant relation being*

$$\phi' = (a_0', \cdots)^i (x_1', \cdots, x_n')^\omega$$
$$= (\lambda \mu \cdots \sigma)^k (a_0, \cdots)^i (x_1, \cdots, x_n)^\omega = M^k \phi. \tag{57}$$

Then if $y_1, y_2, \cdots, y_n$ *are cogredient to* $x_1, x_2, \cdots, x_n$*, the function*

$$\left(y \frac{\partial}{\partial x} \right) \phi \equiv \left(y_1 \frac{\partial}{\partial x_1} + y_2 \frac{\partial}{\partial x_2} + \cdots + y_n \frac{\partial}{\partial x_n} \right) \phi$$

is a concomitant of f*.*

It will be sufficient to prove that

$$\left(y' \frac{\partial}{\partial x'} \right) \phi' = M^{\kappa} \left(y \frac{\partial}{\partial x} \right) \phi; \tag{58}$$

the theorem will then follow directly by the definition of a covariant. On account of cogrediency we have

$$\begin{aligned}
x_i &= \lambda_i x'_1 + \mu_i x'_2 + \cdots + \sigma_i x'_n, \\
y_i &= \lambda_i y'_1 + \mu_i y'_2 + \cdots + \sigma_i y'_n \, (i = 1, \cdots, n).
\end{aligned} \tag{59}$$

Hence

$$\frac{\partial}{\partial x'_1} = \frac{\partial}{\partial x_1} \frac{\partial x_1}{\partial x'_1} + \frac{\partial}{\partial x_2} \frac{\partial x_2}{\partial x'_1} + \cdots + \frac{\partial}{\partial x_n} \frac{\partial x_n}{\partial x'_1},$$

$$\frac{\partial}{\partial x'_1} = \lambda_1 \frac{\partial}{\partial x_1} + \lambda_2 \frac{\partial}{\partial x_2} + \cdots + \lambda_n \frac{\partial}{\partial x_n},$$

$$\frac{\partial}{\partial x'_2} = \mu_1 \frac{\partial}{\partial x_1} + \mu_2 \frac{\partial}{\partial x_2} + \cdots + \mu_n \frac{\partial}{\partial x_n},$$

$$\cdots\cdots\cdots\cdots\cdots$$

$$\frac{\partial}{\partial x'_n} = \sigma_1 \frac{\partial}{\partial x_1} + \sigma_2 \frac{\partial}{\partial x_2} + \cdots + \sigma_n \frac{\partial}{\partial x_n}.$$

Therefore

$$\begin{aligned}
y'_1 \frac{\partial}{\partial x'_1} + \cdots + y'_n \frac{\partial}{\partial x'_n} &= (\lambda_1 y'_1 + \mu_1 y'_2 + \cdots + \sigma_1 y'_n) \frac{\partial}{\partial x_n} \\
&\quad + \cdots + (\lambda_n y'_1 + \mu_n y'_2 + \cdots + \sigma_n y'_n) \frac{\partial}{\partial x_n} \\
&= y_1 \frac{\partial}{\partial x_1} + \cdots + y_n \frac{\partial}{\partial x_n}.
\end{aligned}$$

Hence (58) follows immediately when we operate upon (57) by

$$\left(y' \frac{\partial}{\partial x'} \right) = \left(y \frac{\partial}{\partial x} \right). \tag{60}$$

The function $(y \frac{\partial}{\partial x}) \phi$ is called the first *polar covariant* of ϕ, or simply the first polar of ϕ. It is convenient, however, and avoids adventitious numerical factors, to define as *the* polar of ϕ the expression $(y \frac{\partial}{\partial x}) \phi$ times a numerical factor. We give this more explicit definition in connection with polars of f itself without loss of generality. Let f be of order m. Then

$$\frac{\underline{|m-r}}{\underline{|m}} \left(y_1 \frac{\partial}{\partial x_1} + \cdots + y_n \frac{\partial}{\partial x_n} \right)^r f \equiv f_{y^r}, \tag{61}$$

the right-hand side being merely an abbreviation of the left-hand side, is called the rth y-polar of f. It is an absolute covariant of f by (60).

For illustration, the first polars of

$$f = a_0 x_1^3 + 3a_1 x_1^2 x_2 + 3a_2 x_1 x_2^2 + a_3 x_2^3,$$
$$g = a_{200} x_1^2 + 2a_{110} x_1 x_2 + a_{020} x_2^2 + 2a_{101} x_1 x_3 + 2a_{011} x_2 x_3 + a_{002} x_3^2,$$

are, respectively,

$$f_y = (a_0 x_1^2 + 2a_1 x_1 x_2 + a_2 x_2^2)y_1 + (a_1 x_1^2 + 2a_2 x_1 x_2 + a_3 x_2^2)y_2,$$
$$g_y = (a_{200} x_1 + a_{110} x_2 + a_{101} x_3)y_1 + (a_{110} x_1 + a_{020} x_2 + a_{011} x_3)y_2$$
$$+ (a_{101} x_1 + a_{011} x_2 + a_{002} x_3)y_3.$$

Also,

$$f_{y^2} = (a_0 y_1^2 + 2a_1 y_1 y_2 + a_2 y_2^2)x_1 + (a_1 y_1^2 + 2a_2 y_1 y_2 + a_3 y_2^2)x_2.$$

If $g = 0$ is the conic C of the adjoining figure, and $(y) = (y_1, y_2, y_3)$ is the point P, then $g_y = 0$ is the chord of contact AB, and is called the polar line of P and the conic. If P is within the conic, $g_y = 0$ joins the imaginary points of contact of the tangents to C from P.

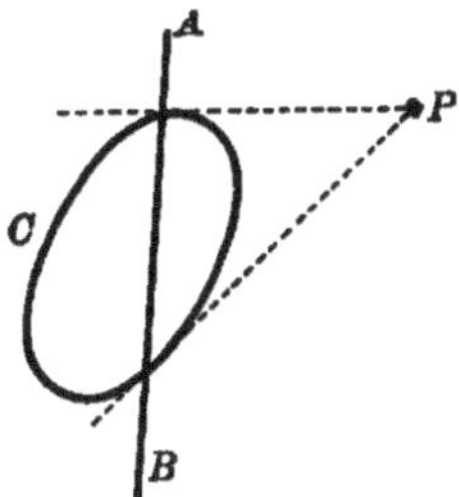

We now restrict the discussion in the remainder of this chapter to binary forms.

We note that *if the variables (y) be replaced by the variables (x) in any polar of a form f the result is f itself,* i.e. the original polarized form. This follows by Euler's theorem on homogeneous functions, since

$$\left(y\frac{\partial}{\partial x}\right) f\big]_{y=x} = \left(x_1\frac{\partial}{\partial x_1} + x_2\frac{\partial}{\partial x_2}\right) f = mf. \tag{62}$$

In connection with the theorem on the transformed form of Chapter I, Section 2, we may observe that *the coefficients of the transformed form are given by the polar formulas*

$$a_0' = f(\lambda_1, \lambda_2) = f_0 . a_1' = f_{0\mu}, a_2' = f_{0\mu^2}, ..., a_m' = f_{0\mu^m}. \tag{63}$$

The rth y-polar of f is a *doubly binary* form in the sets $(y_1, y_2), (x_1, x_2)$ of degree-order $(r, m - r)$. We may however *polarize a number of times as to* (y) *and then a number of times as to another cogredient set* (z);

$$f_{y^r}]_{z^2} = \frac{(m - r)!(m - r - s)!}{m!(m - r)!} \left(y \frac{\partial}{\partial x} \right)^r \left(z \frac{\partial}{\partial x} \right)^s f. \tag{64}$$

This result is a function of three cogredient sets $(x), (y), (z)$.

Since the polar operator is a linear differential operator, it is evident that the polar of a sum of a number of forms equals the sum of the polars of these forms,

$$(f + \phi + \cdots)_{y^r} = f_{y^r} + \phi_{y^r} + \cdots.$$

3.1.2 The polar of a product.

We now develop a very important formula giving the polar of the product of two binary forms in terms of polars of the two forms.

If $F(x_1, x_2)$ is any binary form in x_1, x_2 of order M and (y) is cogredient to (x), we have by Taylor's theorem, k being any parameter,

$$F(x_1 + ky_1, x_2 + ky_2)$$

$$= F(x_1, x_2) + k \left(y \frac{\partial}{\partial x} \right) F + k^2 \left(y \frac{\partial}{\partial x} \right)^2 \frac{F}{2!} + \cdots + k^r \left(y \frac{\partial}{\partial x} \right)^r \frac{F}{r!} + \cdots$$

$$= F + \binom{M}{1} F_y k + \binom{M}{2} F_{y^2} k^2 + \cdots + \binom{M}{r} F_{y^r} k^r + \cdots. \tag{65}$$

Let $F = f(x_1, x_2)\phi(x_1, x_2)$, the product of two binary forms of respective orders m, n. Then the rth polar of this product will be the coefficient of k^r in the expansion of

$$f(x_1 + ky_1, x_2 + ky_2) \times \phi(x_1 + ky_1, x_2 + ky_2),$$

divided by $\binom{m+n}{r}$, by (65). But this expansion equals

$$\left[f + \binom{m}{1} f_y k + \binom{m}{2} f_{y^2} k^2 + \cdots + \binom{m}{r} f_{y^r} k^r + \cdots \right] \left[\phi + \binom{n}{1} \phi_y k \right.$$

$$\left. + \binom{n}{2} \phi_{y^2} k^2 + \cdots + \binom{n}{r} \phi_{y^r} k^r + \cdots \right].$$

Hence by direct multiplication,

$$f\phi \Big]_{y^r} = \frac{1}{\binom{m+n}{r}} \left[\binom{m}{0}\binom{n}{r} f\phi_{y^r} + \binom{m}{1}\binom{n}{r-1} f_y \phi_{y^{r-1}} + \cdots + \binom{m}{r}\binom{n}{0} f_{y^r}\phi \right],$$

or

$$f\phi \Big]_{y^r} = \frac{1}{\binom{m+n}{r}} \sum_{s=0}^{r} \binom{m}{s}\binom{n}{r-s} f_{y^s}\phi_{y^{r-s}} \tag{66}$$

This is the required formula.

The sum of the coefficients in the polar of a product is unity. This follows from the fact (cf. (62)) that if (y) goes into (x) in the polar of a product it becomes the original polarized form.

An illustration of formula (66) is the following:

Let $f = a_0 x_1^4 + \ldots$, $\phi = b_0 x_1^2 + \ldots$. Then

$$f\phi\bigg]_{y^3} = \frac{1}{20}\left[\binom{4}{3}\binom{2}{0} f_{y^3}\phi + \binom{4}{2}\binom{2}{1} f_{y^2}\phi_y + \binom{4}{1}\binom{2}{2} f_y\phi_{y^2}\right]$$

$$= \frac{1}{5} f_{y^3}\phi + \frac{3}{5} f_{y^2}\phi_y + \frac{1}{5} f_y\phi_{y^3}.$$

3.1.3 Aronhold's polars.

The coefficients of the transformed binary form are given by

$$a_r' = f_{\mu^r}(\lambda_1, \lambda_2)\ (r = 0, \ldots, m).$$

These are the linear transformations of the induced group (Chap. I, §2). Let ϕ be a second binary form of the same order as f,

$$\phi = b_0 x_1^m + m b_1 x_1^{m-1} x_2 + \ldots.$$

Let ϕ be transformed by T into ϕ'. Then

$$b_r' = \phi_{u^r}(\lambda_1, \lambda_2).$$

Hence the set $b_0, b_1, \cdots, b_m$ is cogredient to the set $a_0, a_1, \cdots, a_m$, under the induced group. It follows immediately by the theory of Paragraph I that

$$\left(b'\frac{\partial}{\partial a'}\right) \equiv b_o'\frac{\partial}{\partial a_0'} + \cdots + b_m'\frac{\partial}{\partial a_m'}$$

$$= b_0\frac{\partial}{\partial a_0} + \cdots + b_m\frac{\partial}{\partial a_m} \equiv \left(b\frac{\partial}{\partial a}\right). \qquad (67)$$

That is, $\left(b\frac{\partial}{\partial a}\right)$ is an invariant operation. It is called the Aronhold operator but was first discovered by Boole in 1841. Operated upon any concomitant of f it gives a simultaneous concomitant of f and ϕ. If $m = 2$, let

$$I = a_0 a_2 - a_1^2.$$

Then

$$\left(b\frac{\partial}{\partial a}\right) I = \left(b_0\frac{\partial}{\partial a_0} + b_1\frac{\partial}{\partial a_1} + b_2\frac{\partial}{\partial a_2}\right) I = a_0 b_2 - 2a_1 b_1 + a_2 b_0.$$

This is h (Chap. I, §1). Also

$$2\left(b\frac{\partial}{\partial a}\right)^2 I = 4(b_0 b_2 - b_1^2),$$

the discriminant of ϕ. In general, if ψ is any concomitant of f,

$$\psi' = (a'_0, \cdots, a'_m)^i (x'_1, x'_2)^\omega = (\lambda\mu)^\kappa (a_0, \cdots, a_m)^i (x_1, x_2)^\omega,$$

then

$$\left(b'\frac{\partial}{\partial a'}\right)^r \psi' = (\lambda\mu)^\kappa \left(b\frac{\partial}{\partial a}\right)^r \psi \quad (r = 0, 1, \cdots, i) \tag{68}$$

are concomitants of f and ϕ. When $r = i$, the concomitant is

$$x = (b_0, \cdots, b_m)^i (x_1, x_2)^\omega.$$

The other concomitants of the series, which we call a series of Aronhold's polars of ψ, are said to be *intermediate* to ψ and χ, and of the same *type* as ψ. The theory of *types* will be referred to in the sequel.

All concomitants of a series of Aronhold's polars have the same index k.

Thus the following series has the index $k = 2$, as may be verified by applying (52) of Section 3, Chapter II to each form ($f = a_0 x_1^3 + \cdots ; \phi = b_0 x_1^3 + \cdots$):

$$H = (a_0 a_2 - a_1^2) x_1^2 + (a_0 a_3 - a_1 a_2) x_1 x_2 + (a_1 a_3 - a_2^2) x_2^2,$$

$$\left(b\frac{\partial}{\partial a}\right) H = (a_0 b_2 - 2 a_1 b_1 + a_2 b_0) x_1^2 + (a_0 b_3 + a_3 b_0 - a_1 b_2 - a_2 b_1) x_1 x_2$$

$$+ (a_1 b_3 - 2 a_2 b_2 + a_3 b_1) x_2^2,$$

$$\frac{1}{2}\left(b\frac{\partial}{\partial a}\right)^2 H = (b_0 b_2 - b_1^2) x_1^2 + (b_0 b_3 - b_1 b_2) x_1 x_2 + (b_1 b_3 - b_2^2) x_2^2.$$

3.1.4   Modular polars.

Under the group T_p, we have shown, x_1^p, x_2^p are cogredient to x_1, x_2. Hence the polar operation

$$\delta_p = x_1^p \frac{\partial}{\partial x_1} + x_2^p \frac{\partial}{\partial x_2}, \tag{69}$$

applied to any algebraic form f, or covariant of f, gives a formal modular concomitant of f. Thus if

$$f = a_0 x_1^2 + 2 a_1 x_1 x_2 + a_2 x_2^2,$$

then,

$$\frac{1}{2}\delta_3 f = a_0 x_1^4 + a_1 (x_1^3 x_2 + x_1 x_2^3) + a_2 x_2^4.$$

This is a covariant of f modulo 3, as has been verified in Chapter I, Section 1. Under the induced modular group $a_0^p, x_1^p, \cdots, a_m^p$ will be cogredient to $a_0, a_1, \cdots, a_m$. Hence we have the modular Aronhold operator

$$d_p = a_0^p \frac{\partial}{\partial a_0} + \cdots + a_m^p \frac{\partial}{\partial a_m}.$$

If $m = 2$, and

$$D = a_0 a_2 - a_1^2,$$

then

$$d_p D \equiv a_0^p a_2 - 2a_1^{p+1} + a_0 a_2^p \quad (\text{mod } p).$$

This is a formal modular invariant modulo p. It is not an algebraic invariant; that is, not invariantive under the group generated by the transformations T.

We may note in addition that the line

$$l = a_0 x_1 + a_1 x_2 + a_2 x_3$$

has among its covariants modulo 2, the line and the conic

$$d_2 l = a_0^2 x_1 + a_1^2 x_2 + a_2^2 x_3,$$
$$\delta_2 l = a_0 x_1^2 + a_1 x_2^2 + a_2 x_3^2.$$

3.1.5 Operators derived from the fundamental postulate.

The fundamental postulate on cogrediency (Chap. I, §2) enables us to replace the variables in a concomitant by any set of elements cogredient to the variables, without disturbing the property of invariance.

Theorem. *Under the binary transformations T the differential operators $\frac{\partial}{\partial x_2}, -\frac{\partial}{\partial x_1}$ are cogredient to the variables.*

From T we have

$$\frac{\partial}{\partial x_1'} = \lambda_1 \frac{\partial}{\partial x_1} + \lambda_2 \frac{\partial}{\partial x_2},$$
$$\frac{\partial}{\partial x_2'} = \mu_1 \frac{\partial}{\partial x_1} + \mu_2 \frac{\partial}{\partial x_2}.$$

Hence

$$(\lambda\mu) \frac{\partial}{\partial x_2} = \lambda_1 \frac{\partial}{\partial x_2'} + \mu_1 \left(-\frac{\partial}{\partial x_1'} \right),$$
$$-(\lambda\mu) \frac{\partial}{\partial x_1} = \lambda_2 \frac{\partial}{\partial x_2'} + \mu_2 \left(-\frac{\partial}{\partial x_1'} \right).$$

This proves the theorem.

It follows that if $\phi = (a_0, \ldots, a_m)^i (x_1, x_2)^\omega$ is any invariant function, *i.e.* a concomitant of a binary form f, then

$$\partial\phi = (a_0, \ldots, a_m)^i \left(\frac{\partial}{\partial x_2}, -\frac{\partial}{\partial x_1} \right)^\omega \tag{70}$$

is an invariant operator (Boole). If this operator is operated upon any covariant of f, it gives a concomitant of f, and if operated upon a covariant of any set of forms g, h, $\ldots$, it gives a simultaneous concomitant of f and the set. This process is a remarkably prolific one and enables us to construct a great variety of invariants and covariants of a form or a set of forms. We shall illustrate it by means of several examples.

Let f be the binary quartic and let ϕ be the form f itself. Then

$$\partial\phi = \partial f = a_0\frac{\partial_4}{\partial x_2^4} - 4a_1\frac{\partial^4}{\partial x_2^3 \partial x_1} + 6a_2\frac{\partial^4}{\partial x_2^2 \partial x_1^2} - 4a_3\frac{\partial^4}{\partial x_2 \partial x_1^3} + a_4\frac{\partial^4}{\partial x_1^4},$$

and

$$\frac{1}{24}\delta f \cdot f = 2(a_0 a_4 - 4a_1 a_3 + 3a_2^2) = i.$$

This second degree invariant i represents the condition that the four roots of the quartic form a self-apolar range. If this process is applied in the case of a form of odd order, the result vanishes identically.

If H is the Hessian of the quartic, then

$$\partial H = (a_0 a_2 - a_1^2)\frac{\partial^4}{\partial x_2^4} - 2(a_0 a_3 - a_1 a_2)\frac{\partial^4}{\partial x_2^3 \partial x_1}$$

$$+ (a_0 a_4 + 2a_1 a_3 - 3a_2^2)\frac{\partial^4}{\partial x_2^2 \partial x_1^2} - 2(a_1 a_4 - a_2 a_3)\frac{\partial^4}{\partial x_2 \partial x_1^3}$$

$$+ (a_2 a_4 - a_3^2)\frac{\partial^4}{\partial x_1^4}.$$

And

$$\frac{1}{12}\partial H \cdot f = 6(a_0 a_2 a_4 + 2a_1 a_2 a_3 - a_0 a_3^2 - a_2^3) = J. \tag{70_1}$$

This third-degree invariant equated to zero gives the condition that the roots of the quartic form a harmonic range.

If H is the Hessian of the binary cubic f and

$$g = b_0 x_1^3 + \cdots,$$

then

$$\frac{1}{6}\partial H \cdot g = [b_0(a_1 a_3 - a_2^2) + b_1(a_1 a_2 - a_0 a_3) + b_2(a_0 a_2 - a_1^2)]x_1$$

$$+ [b_1(a_1 a_3 - a_2^2) + b_2(a_1 a_2 - a_0 a_3) + b_3(a_0 a_2 - a_1^2)]x_2;$$

a linear covariant of the two cubics.

Bilinear Invariants

If $f = a_0 x_1^m + \cdots$ is a binary form of order m and $g = b_0 x_1^m + \cdots$ another of the same order, then

$$\frac{1}{m!}\partial f \cdot g = a_0 b_m - \binom{m}{1}a_1 b_{m-1} + \cdots + (-1)^r \binom{m}{r}a_r b_{m-r} + \cdots + (-1)^m a_m b_0. \tag{71}$$

This, the *bilinear invariant* of f and g, is the simplest joint invariant of the two forms. If it is equated to zero, it gives the condition that the two forms be *apolar*. If $m = 2$, the apolarity condition is the same as the condition that the two quadratics be harmonic conjugates (Chap. I, §1, IV).

3.1.6   The fundamental operation called transvection.

The most fundamental process of binary invariant theory is a differential operation called transvection. In fact it will subsequently appear that all invariants and covariants of a form or a set of forms can be derived by this process. We proceed to explain the nature of the process. We first prove that the following operator Ω is an invariant:

$$\Omega = \begin{vmatrix} \frac{\partial}{\partial x_1}, & \frac{\partial}{\partial x_2} \\ \frac{\partial}{\partial y_1}, & \frac{\partial}{\partial y_2} \end{vmatrix} \tag{72}$$

where (y) is cogredient to (x). In fact by (70),

$$\Omega' = \begin{vmatrix} \lambda_1 \frac{\partial}{\partial x_1} + \lambda_2 \frac{\partial}{\partial x_2}, & \mu_1 \frac{\partial}{\partial x_1} + \mu_2 \frac{\partial}{\partial x_2} \\ \lambda_1 \frac{\partial}{\partial y_1} + \lambda_2 \frac{\partial}{\partial y_2}, & \mu_1 \frac{\partial}{\partial y_1} + \mu_2 \frac{\partial}{\partial y_2} \end{vmatrix} = (\lambda\mu)\Omega,$$

which proves the statement.

Evidently, to produce any result, Ω must be applied to a doubly binary function. One such type of function is a y-polar of a binary form. But

Theorem. *The result of operating Ω upon any y-polar of a binary form f is zero.*

For, if $f = a_0 x_1^m + \cdots$,

$$P = \frac{m!}{(m-r)!} f_y^r = \left(y \frac{\partial}{\partial x} \right)^r f$$
$$= \left(y_1^r \frac{\partial^r f}{\partial x_1^y} + \binom{r}{1} y_1^{r-1} y_2 \frac{\partial^r f}{\partial x_1^{r-1} \partial x_2} + \cdots + y_2^r \frac{\partial^r f}{\partial x_2^r} \right).$$

Hence

$$\Omega P = \binom{r}{1} y_1^{r-1} \frac{\partial^{r+1} f}{\partial x_1^r \partial x_2} + \cdots + r y_2^{r-1} \frac{\partial^{r+1} f}{\partial x_1 \partial x_2^r}$$
$$- r y_1^{r-1} \frac{\partial^{r+1} f}{\partial x_1^r \partial x_2} - \cdots - \binom{r}{1} y_2^{r-1} \frac{\partial^{r+1} f}{\partial x_1 \partial x_2^r},$$

and this vanishes by cancellation.

If Ω is operated upon another type of doubly binary form, not a polar, as for instance upon fg, where f is a binary form in x_1, x_2 and g a binary form in y_1, y_2, the result will generally be a doubly binary invariant formation, not zero.

DEFINITION.

If $f(x) = a_0 x_1^m + \cdots$ is a binary form in (x) of order m, and $g(y) = b_0 y_1^n + \cdots$ a binary form in (y) of order n, then if y_1, y_2 be changed to x_1, x_2 respectively in

$$\frac{(m-r)!(n-r)!}{m!n!} \Omega^r f(x) g(y), \tag{73}$$

after the differentiations have been performed, the result is called the rth transvectant (Cayley, 1846) of $f(x)$ and $g(x)$. This will be abbreviated $(f, g)^r$, following a well-established notation. We evidently have for a general formula

$$(f, g)^r = \frac{(m-r)!(n-r)!}{m!n!} \sum_{s=0}^{r} (-1)^s \binom{r}{s} \frac{\partial^r f(x)}{\partial x_1^{r-s} \partial x_2^s} \cdot \frac{\partial^r g(x)}{\partial x_1^s \partial x_2^{r-s}}. \tag{74}$$

We give at present only a few illustrations. We note that the Jacobian of two binary forms is their first transvectant. Also the Hessian of a form f is its second transvectant. For

$$H = \frac{2}{m^2(m-1)^2} (f_{x_1 x_1} f_{x_2 x_2} - f_{x_1 x_2}^2)$$

$$= \frac{(\lfloor m-2)^2}{(\lfloor m)^2} (f_{x_1 x_1} f_{x_2 x_2} - 2f_{x_1 x_1}^2 + f_{x_2 x_2} f_{x_1 x_1})$$

$$= (f, f)^2.$$

As an example of multiple transvection we may write the following covariant of the cubic f:

$$\begin{aligned} Q = (f, (f, f)^2)^1 &= (a_0^2 a_3 - 3a_0 a_1 a_2 + 2a_1^3) x^3 \\ &+ 3(a_0 a_1 a_3 - 2a_0 a_2^2 + a_1^2 a_2) x_1^2 x_2 \\ &- 3(a_0 a_2 a_3 - 2a_1^2 a_3 + a_1 a_2^2) x_1 x_2^2 \\ &- (a_0 a_3^2 - 3a_1 a_2 a_3 + 2a_2^3) x_2^3 \end{aligned} \tag{74_1}$$

If f and g are two forms of the same order m, then $(f, g)^m$ is their bilinear invariant. By forming multiple transvections, as was done to obtain Q, we can evidently obtain an unlimited number of concomitants of a single form or of a set.

3.2 The Aronhold Symbolism. Symbolical Invariant Processes

3.2.1 Symbolical Representation.

A binary form f, written in the notation of which

$$f = a_0 x_1^3 + 3a_1 x_1^2 x_2 + 3a_2 x_1 x_2^2 + a_3 x_2^3$$

is a particular case, bears a close formal resemblance to a power of linear form, here the third power. This resemblance becomes the more noteworthy when we observe that the derivative $\frac{\partial f}{\partial x_1}$ bears the same formal resemblance to the derivative of the third power of a linear form:

$$\frac{\partial f}{\partial x_1} = 3(a_0 x_1^2 + 2a_1 x_1 x_2 + a_2 x_2^2).$$

That is, it resembles three times the square of the linear form. When we study the question of how far this formal resemblance may be extended we are led to a completely new and strikingly concise formulation of the fundamental processes of binary invariant theory. Although $f = a_0 x^m + \cdots$ is not an exact power, we assume the privilege of placing it equal to the mth power of a purely symbolical linear form $\alpha_1 x_1 + \alpha_2 x_2$ which we abbreviate α_x.

$$f = (\alpha_1 x_1 + \alpha_2 x_2)^m = \alpha_x^m = a_0 x^m + \cdots .$$

This may be done provided we assume that the only defined combinations of the symbols α_1, α_2, that is, the only combinations which have any definite meaning, are the monomials of degree m in α_1, α_2;

$$\alpha_1^m = a_0,\, \alpha_1^{m-1}\alpha_2 = a_0, \cdots ,\alpha_2^m = a_m,$$

and linear combinations of these. Thus $\alpha_1^m + 2\alpha_1^{m-1}\alpha_2^2$ means $a_0 + 2a_2$. But of $\alpha_1^{m-2}\alpha_2$ is meaningless; an umbral expression (Sylvester). An expression of the second degree like $a_0 a_8$ cannot then be represented in terms of α's alone, since $\alpha_1^m \cdot \alpha_1^{m-3}\alpha_2^3 = \alpha_1^{2m-3}\alpha_2^3$ is undefined. To avoid this difficulty we give f a series of symbolical representations,

$$f = \alpha_x^m = \beta_x^m = \gamma_x^m \cdots ,$$

wherein the symbols $(\alpha_1,\ \alpha_2)$, $(\beta_1,\ \beta_2)$, $(\gamma_1,\ \gamma_2)$, ... are said to be equivalent symbols as appertaining to the same form f. Then

$$\alpha_1^m = \beta_1^m = \gamma_1^m \cdots = a_0,\, \alpha_1^{m-1}\alpha_2 = \beta_1^{m-1}\beta_2 = \gamma_1^{m-1}\gamma_2 \cdots = a_1, \cdots .$$

Now $a_0 a_3$ becomes $(\alpha_1^m \beta_1^{m-3}\beta_2^3)$ and this is a defined combination of symbols.

In general an expression of degree i in the a's will be represented by means of i equivalent symbol sets, the symbols of each set entering the symbolical expressions only to the mth degree; moreover there will be a series of (equivalent) symbolical representations of the same expression, as

$$a_0 a_3 = \alpha_1^m \beta_1^{m-3}\beta_2^3 = \alpha_1^m \gamma_1^{m-3}\gamma_2^3 = \beta_1^m \gamma_1^{m-3}\gamma_2^3 = \cdots .$$

Thus the discriminant of

$$f = \alpha_x^2 = \beta_x^2 = \ldots = a_0 x_1^2 + 2a_1 x_1 x_2 + a_2 x_2^2$$

is

$$D = 4(\alpha_0 a_2 - a_1^2) = 4(\alpha_1^2 \beta_2^2 - \alpha_1 \alpha_2 \beta_1 \beta_2)$$
$$= 2(\alpha_1^2 \beta_2^2 - 2\alpha_1 \alpha_2 \beta_1 \beta_2 + \alpha_2^2 \beta_1^2),$$

or

$$D = 2(\alpha\beta)^2,$$

a very concise representation of this invariant.

Conversely, if we wish to know what invariant a given symbolical expression represents, we proceed thus. Let f be the quadratic above, and

$$g = \rho_x^2 = \sigma_x^2 = \ldots = b_0 x_1^2 + 2b_1 x_1 x_2 + b_2 x_2^3,$$

where ρ is not equivalent to α. Then to find what $J = (\alpha\rho)\alpha_x \rho_x$, which evidently contains the symbols in defined combinations only, represents in terms of the actual coefficients of the forms, we multiply out and find

$$J = (\alpha_1 \rho_2 - \alpha_2 \rho_1)(\alpha_1 x_1 + \alpha_2 x_2)(\rho_1 x_1 + \rho_2 x_2)$$
$$= (\alpha_1^2 \rho_1 \rho_2 - \alpha_1 \alpha_2 \rho_1^2)x_1^2 + (\alpha_1^2 \rho_2^2 - \alpha_2^2 \rho_1^2)x_1 x_2 + (\alpha_1 \alpha_2 \rho_2^2 - \alpha_2^2 \rho_1 \rho_2)x_2^2,$$
$$= (a_0 b_1 - a_1 b_0)x_1^2 + (a_0 b_2 - a_2 b_0)x_1 x_2 + 9a_1 b_2 - a_2 b_1)x_2^2.$$

This is the Jacobian of f and g. Note the simple symbolical form

$$J = (\alpha\rho)\alpha_x \rho_x.$$

3.2.2 Symbolical polars.

We shall now investigate the forms which the standard invariant processes take when expressed in terms of the above symbolism (Aronhold, 1858).

For polars we have, when $f = \alpha_x^m = \beta_x^m = \ldots$,

$$f_y = \frac{1}{m}\left(y\frac{\partial}{\partial x}\right)f = \alpha_x^{m-1}\left(y\frac{\partial}{\partial x}\right)(\alpha_1 x_1 + \alpha_2 x_2) = \alpha_x^{m-1}\alpha_y.$$

Hence

$$f_{y^r} = \alpha_x^{m-r}\alpha_y^r. \tag{75}$$

The *transformed form* of f under T will be

$$f' = [\alpha_1(\lambda_1 x_1' + \mu_1 x_2') + \alpha_2(\lambda_2 x_1' + \mu_2 x_2')]^m$$
$$= [(\alpha_1 \lambda_1 + \alpha_2 \lambda_2)x_1' + \alpha_1 \mu_1 + \alpha_2 \mu_2)x_2']^m,$$

or

$$f' = (a_\lambda x_1' + a_\mu x_2')^m$$
$$= a_\lambda^m x_1'^m + \ldots + \binom{m}{r}a_\lambda^{m-r}a_\mu^r x_1'^{m-r}x_2'^r + \ldots + a_\mu^m x_2'^m. \tag{76}$$

In view of (75) we have here not only the symbolical representation of the transformed form but a very concise proof of the fact, proved elsewhere (Chap. I, (29)), that the transformed coefficients are polars of $a'_0 = f(\lambda_1, \lambda_2) = a^m_\lambda$.

The formula (66) for the polar of a product becomes

$$\alpha^m_x \beta^n_x \Big]_{y^r} = \frac{1}{\binom{m+n}{r}} \sum_{s=0}^{r} \binom{m}{s}\binom{n}{r-s} \alpha^{m-s}_x \alpha^s_y \beta^{n-r+s}_x \beta^{r-s}_y, \qquad (77)$$

where the symbols α, β are not as a rule equivalent.

3.2.3 Symbolical transvectants.

If $f = \alpha^m_x = a^m_x = \ldots, g = \beta^n_x = b^n_x = \ldots$, then

$$(f,g)^1 = \frac{1}{mn}\Omega\alpha^m_x \beta^n_y \Big]_{y=x} = \alpha^{m-1}_x \beta^{n-1}_y \left(\frac{\partial^2}{\partial x_1 \partial y_2} - \frac{\partial^2}{\partial x_2 \partial y_1} \right) \alpha_x \beta_y \Big]_{y=x}$$
$$= (\alpha\beta)\alpha^{m-1}_x \beta^{n-1}_x.$$

Hence the symbolical form for the rth transvectant is

$$(f,g)^r = (\alpha\beta)^r \alpha^{m-r}_x \beta^{n-r}_x. \qquad (78)$$

Several properties of transvectants follow easily from this. Suppose that $g = f$ so that α and β are equivalent symbols. Then obviously we can interchange α and β in any symbolical expression without changing the value of that expression. Also we should remember that $(\alpha\beta)$ is a determinant of the second order, and *formally*

$$(\alpha\beta) = -(\beta\alpha).$$

Suppose now that r is odd, $r = 2k + 1$. Then

$$(f,f)^{2k+1} = (\alpha\beta)^{2k+1}\alpha^{m-2k-1}_x \beta^{n-2k-1} = -(\alpha\beta)^{2k+1}\alpha^{m-2k-1}_x \beta^{n-2k-1}_x$$

Hence this transvectant, being equal to its own negative, vanishes. *Every odd transvectant of a form with itself vanishes.*

If the symbols are not equivalent, evidently

$$(f,g)^r = (-1)^r (g,f)^r. \qquad (79)$$

Also if C is a constant,

$$(Cf,g)^r = C(f,g)^r; \qquad (80)$$
$$(c_1 f_1 + c_2 f_2 + \ldots, d_1 g_1 + d_2 g_2 + \ldots)^r = c_1 d_1 (f_1, g_1)^r + c_1 d_2 (f_1, g_2)^r + \ldots.$$
$$(81)$$

3.2.4   Standard method of transvection.

We may derive transvectants from polars by a simple application of the fundamental postulate. For, as shown in section 1, if $f = a_0 x_1^m + \ldots = a_x^m$,

$$f_{y^r} = \frac{(m-r)!}{m!}\left[\frac{\partial f}{\partial x_1^r}y_1^r + \binom{r}{1}\frac{\partial^r f}{\partial x_1^{r-1}\partial x_2}y_1^{r-1}y_2 + \ldots + \frac{\partial^r f}{\partial x_2^r}y_2^r\right]. \tag{82}$$

Now (y) is cogredient to (x). Hence $\frac{\partial}{\partial x_2}, -\frac{\partial}{\partial x_1}$ are cogredient to y_1, y_2. If we replace the y's by these derivative symbols and operate the result, which we abbreviate as ∂f_{y^r}, upon a second form $g = b_x^n$, we obtain

$$\frac{(n-r)!}{n!}\partial f_{y^r}$$

$$= \left[a_1^r b_2^r - \binom{r}{1}a_1^{r-1}a_2 b_2^{r-1}b_1 + \ldots + (-1)^r a_2^r b_1^r\right]a_x^{m-r}b_x^{n-r}$$

$$= (ab)^r a_x^{m-r}b_x^{n-r} = (f,g)^r. \tag{83}$$

When we compare the square bracket in (82) with a_x^{m-r} times the square bracket in (83), we see that they differ precisely in that y_1, y_2 has been replaced by $b_2, -b_1$. Hence we enunciate the following *standard method of transvection*. Let f be any symbolical form. It may be simple like f in this paragraph, or more complicated like (78), or howsoever complicated. To obtain the rth transvectant of f and $\phi = b_x^n$ we *polarize f r times, change y_1, y_2 into $b_2, -b_1$ respectively in the result and multiply by b_x^{n-r}*. In view of the formula (77) for the polar of a product this is the most desirable method of finding transvectants.

    For illustration, let F be a quartic, $F = a_x^4 = b_x^4$, and f its Hessian,

$$f = (ab)^2 a_x^2 b_x^2.$$

Let

$$g = \alpha_x^3.$$

Then

$$(f,g)^2 = (ab)^2 a_x^2 b_x^2\Big]_{y^2,\, y=a} \times \alpha_x$$

$$= \frac{(ab)^2}{6}\left[\binom{2}{0}\binom{2}{2}a_x^2 b_y^2 + \binom{2}{1}\binom{2}{1}a_x a_y b_x b_y + \binom{2}{2}\binom{2}{0}a_y^2 b_x^2\right]_{y=a} \times \alpha_x$$

$$\tag{84}$$

$$= \frac{1}{6}(ab)^2(b\alpha)^2 a_x^2 \alpha_x + \frac{2}{3}(ab)^2(a\alpha)(b\alpha)a_x b_x \alpha_x + \frac{1}{6}(ab)^2(a\alpha)^2 b_x^2 \alpha_x.$$

    Since the symbols a, b are equivalent, this may be simplified by interchanging a, b in the last term, which is then identical with the first,

$$(f,g)^2 = \frac{1}{3}(ab)^2(b\alpha)^2 a_x^2 \alpha_x + \frac{2}{3}(ab)^2(a\alpha)(b\alpha)a_x b_x \alpha_x.$$

By the fundamental existence theorem this is a joint covariant of F and g.

Let f be as above and $g = (\alpha\beta)\alpha_x^2\beta_x$, where α and β are not equivalent. To find $(f, g)^2$, say, in a case of this kind we first let

$$g = (\alpha\beta)\alpha_x^2\beta_x = \sigma_x^3,$$

introducing a new symbolism for the cubic g. Then we apply the method just given, obtaining

$$(f, g)^2 = \frac{1}{3}(ab)^2(b\sigma)^2 a_x^2\sigma_x + \frac{2}{3}(ab)^2(a\sigma)(b\sigma)a_x b_x\sigma_x.$$

We now examine this result term by term. We note that the first term could have been obtained by polarizing g twice changing y_1, y_2 into $b_2, -b_1$ and multiplying the result by $(ab)^2 a_x^2$. Thus

$$\frac{1}{3}(ab)^2(b\sigma)^2 a_x^2\sigma_x = \frac{1}{3}(\alpha\beta)\alpha_x^2\beta_x\Big]_{y^2;y=b}(ab)^2 a_x^2. \tag{85}$$

Consider next the second term. It could have been obtained by polarizing g once with regard to y, and then the result once with regard to z; then changing y_1, y_2 into $a_2, -a_1$, and z_1, z_2 into $b_2, -b_1$, and multiplying this result by $(ab)^2 a_x b_x$;

$$\frac{2}{3}(ab)^2(a\sigma)(b\sigma)a_x b_x\sigma_x$$

$$= \frac{2}{3}(\alpha\beta)\alpha_x^2\beta_x\Big]_{y;y=a}\Big]_{z;z=b} \times (ab)^2 a_x b_x. \tag{86}$$

From (85),

$$\frac{1}{9}(\alpha\beta)\left[\binom{2}{1}\binom{1}{1}\alpha_x\alpha_y\beta_y + \binom{2}{2}\binom{1}{0}\alpha_y^2\beta_x\right]_{y=b}(ab)^2 a_x^2$$

$$= \frac{2}{9}(ab)^2(\alpha\beta)(ab)(\beta b)a_x^2\alpha_x + \frac{1}{9}(ab)^2(\alpha\beta)(ab)^2 a_x^2\beta_x.$$

From (86),

$$\frac{2}{9}(\alpha\beta)\left[\binom{2}{0}\binom{1}{1}\alpha_x^2\beta_y + \binom{2}{1}\binom{1}{0}\alpha_x\alpha_y\beta_x\right]_{y=a}\Big]_{z;z=b}(ab)^2 a_x b_x$$

$$= \frac{2}{9}\alpha_x^2(\beta a) + \frac{4}{9}\alpha_x\beta_x(\alpha a)\Big]_{z;z=b} \times (ab)^2(\alpha\beta)a_x b_x$$

$$= \frac{2}{9}(ab)^2(\alpha\beta)(ab)(\beta a)\alpha_x a_x b_x + \frac{2}{9}(ab)^2(\alpha\beta)(\alpha a)(\alpha b)\beta_x a_x b_x$$

$$+ \frac{2}{9}(ab)^2(\alpha\beta)(\beta b)(\alpha a)\alpha_x a_x b_x.$$

Hence we have in this case

$$(f,g)^2 = \frac{2}{9}(ab)^2(\alpha\beta)(\alpha b)(\beta b)a_x^2 a_x + \frac{1}{9}(ab)^2(\alpha\beta)(ab)^2 a_x^2 \beta_x$$

$$+\frac{4}{9}(ab)^2(\alpha\beta)(\alpha b)(\beta a)\alpha_x a_x b_x + \frac{2}{9}(ab)^2(\alpha\beta)(\alpha a)(\alpha b)\beta_x a_x b_x. \qquad (87)$$

3.2.5 Formula for the rth transvectant.

The most general formulas for f, g respectively are

$$f = \alpha_x^{(1)}\alpha_x^{(2)} \cdots \alpha_x^{(m)}, g = \beta_y^{(1)}\beta_y^{(2)} \cdots \beta_y^{(n)},$$

in which

$$\alpha_x^{(i)} = \alpha_1^{(i)}x_1 + \alpha_x^{(i)}x_2, \beta_x^{(i)} = \beta_1^{(i)}x_1 + \beta_2^{(i)}x_2.$$

We can obtain a formula of complete generality for the transvectant $(f,g)^r$ by applying the operator Ω directly to the product fg. We have

$$\frac{\partial^2}{\partial x_1 \partial y_2}fg = \sum \alpha_1^{(q)}\beta_2^{(r)}\frac{fg}{\alpha_x^{(q)}\beta_y^{(r)}},$$

$$\frac{\partial^2}{\partial x_2 \partial y_1}fg = \sum \alpha_2^{(q)}\beta_1^{(r)}\frac{fg}{\alpha_x^{(q)}\beta_y^{(r)}}.$$

Subtracting these we obtain

$$(f,g)^1 = \frac{(m-1)!(n-1)!}{m!n!}\sum(\alpha^{(q)}\beta^{(r)})\frac{fg}{\alpha_x^{(q)}\beta_x^{(r)}}.$$

Repetitions of this process, made as follows:

$$(f,g)^2 = \frac{(m-2)!(n-2)!}{m!n!}\sum(\alpha^{(q)}\beta^{(r)})\Omega\left[\frac{fg}{\alpha_x^{(q)}\beta_y^{(r)}}\right]_{y=x}, \qquad (88)$$

lead to the conclusion that the rth transvectant of f and g, as well as the mere result of applying the operator Ω to fg r times, is a sum of terms each one of which contains the product of r determinant factors $(\alpha\beta)$, $m-r$ factors α_x, and $n-r$ factors β_x. We can however write $(f,g)^r$ in a very simple explicit form. Consider the special case

$$f = \alpha_x^{(1)}\alpha_x^{(2)}\alpha_x^{(3)}, \quad g = \beta_y^{(1)}\beta_y^{(2)}.$$

Here, by the rule of (88),

$$
\begin{aligned}
(f,g)^2 = \{ &(\alpha^{(1)}\beta^{(1)})(\alpha^{(2)}\beta^{(2)})\alpha_x^{(3)} + (\alpha^{(1)}\beta^{(1)})(\alpha^{(3)}\beta^{(2)})\alpha_x^{(2)} \\
+ &(\alpha^{(1)}\beta^{(2)})(\alpha^{(2)}\beta^{(1)})\alpha_x^{(3)} + (\alpha^{(1)}\beta^{(2)})(\alpha^{(3)}\beta^{(1)})\alpha_x^{(2)} \\
+ &(\alpha^{(2)}\beta^{(1)})(\alpha^{(3)}\beta^{(2)})\alpha_x^{(1)} + (\alpha^{(2)}\beta^{(1)})(\alpha^{(1)}\beta^{(2)})\alpha_x^{(3)} \\
+ &(\alpha^{(2)}\beta^{(2)})(\alpha^{(3)}\beta^{(1)})\alpha_x^{(1)} + (\alpha^{(2)}\beta^{(2)})(\alpha^{(1)}\beta^{(1)})\alpha_x^{(3)} \\
+ &(\alpha^{(3)}\beta^{(1)})(\alpha^{(1)}\beta^{(2)})\alpha_x^{(2)} + (\alpha^{(3)}\beta^{(1)})(\alpha^{(2)}\beta^{(2)})\alpha_x^{(1)} \\
+ &(\alpha^{(3)}\beta^{(2)})(\alpha^{(1)}\beta^{(1)})\alpha_x^{(2)} + (\alpha^{(3)}\beta^{(2)})(\alpha^{(2)}\beta^{(1)})\alpha_x^{(1)} \div 2!3!,
\end{aligned}
\tag{89}
$$

in which occur only six distinct terms, there being a repetition of each term. Now consider the general case, and the rth transvectant. In the first transvectant one term contains $t_1 = (\alpha^{(1)}\beta^{(1)})\alpha_x^{(2)}\cdots\alpha_x^{(m)}\beta_y^{(2)}\cdots\beta_y^{(n)}$. In the second transvectant there will be a term $u_1 = (\alpha^{(1)}\beta^{(1)})(\alpha^{(2)}\beta^{(2)})\alpha_x^{(3)}\cdots\beta_y^{(3)}\cdots$ arising from Ωt_1, and another term u_1 arising from Ωt_2, where $t_2 = (\alpha^{(2)}\beta^{(2)})\alpha_x^{(1)}\alpha_x^{(3)}\cdots\alpha_x^{(m)}\beta_y^{(1)}\beta_y^{(3)}\cdots\beta_y^{(n)}$. Thus $u_1(y = x)$ and likewise any selected term occurs just twice in $(f,g)^2$. Again the term $v_1 = (\alpha^{(1)}\beta^{(1)})(\alpha^{(2)}\beta^{(2)})(\alpha^{(3)}\beta^{(3)})\alpha_x^{(4)}\cdots\beta_x^{(4)}\cdots$ will occur in $(f,g)^3$ as many times as there are ways of permuting the three superscripts $1,2,3$ or $3!$ times. Finally in $(f,g)^r$, written by (88) in the form (89), each term will be repeated $r!$ times. We may therefore write $(f,g)^r$ as the following summation, in which all terms are distinct and equal in number to $\binom{m}{r}\binom{n}{r}r!$:

$$
(f,\phi)^r = \frac{1}{\binom{m}{r}\binom{n}{r}r!} \sum \left[\frac{(\alpha^{(1)}\beta^{(1)})(\alpha^{(2)}\beta^{(2)})\cdots(\alpha^{(r)}\beta^{(r)})}{\alpha_x^{(1)}\alpha_x^{(2)}\cdots\alpha_x^{(m)}\beta_y^{(1)}\beta_y^{(2)}\cdots\beta_y^{(n)}} fg \right]_{y=x} .
\tag{90}
$$

3.2.6 Special cases of operation by Ω upon a doubly binary form, not a product.

In a subsequent chapter Gordan's series will be developed. This series has to do with operation by Ω upon a doubly binary form which is neither a polar nor a simple product. In this paragraph we consider a few very special cases of such a doubly binary form and in connection therewith some results of very frequent application.

We can establish the following formula:

$$
\Omega^r (xy)^r = constant = (r+1)(r!)^2.
\tag{91}
$$

In proof (74),

$$
\Omega^r = \sum_{i=0}^{r}(-1)^i \binom{r}{i} \frac{\partial^r}{\partial x_1^{r-i}\partial x_2^i} \frac{\partial^r}{\partial y_1^i\partial y_2^{r-i}},
$$

and

$$
(xy)^r = \sum_{i=0}^{r}(-1)^i \binom{r}{i} x_1^{r-i}x_2^i y_1^i y_2^{r-i}.
$$

Hence it follows immediately that

$$\Omega^r (xy)^r = \sum_{i=0}^{r} \binom{r}{i}^2 ((r-i)!)^2 (i!)^2$$

$$= \sum_{i=0}^{r} (r!)^2 = (r+1)(r!)^2.$$

A similar doubly binary form is

$$F = (xy)^j \xi_x^{m-j} \xi_y^{n-j}.$$

If the second factor of this is a polar of ξ_x^{m+n-2j}, we may make use of the fact, proved before, that Ω on a polar is zero. An easy differentiation gives

$$\Omega F = j(m+n-j+1)(xy)^{j-1} \xi_x^{m-j} \xi_y^{n-j},$$

and repetitions of this formula give

$$\Omega^i F = \frac{j!}{(j-1)!} \frac{(m+n-j+1)!}{(m+n-j-i+1)!} (xy)^{j-i} \xi_x^{m-j} \xi_y^{n-j} \left(\begin{array}{c} \text{If } i \leqq j; \\ = 0 \text{ if } i > j \end{array} \right) \qquad (91_1)$$

This formula holds true if $m = n = j$, that is, for $\Omega^i (xy)^j$.

3.2.7 Fundamental theorem of symbolical theory.

Theorem. *Every monomial expression ϕ which consists entirely of symbolical factors of two types, e.g. determinants of type $(\alpha\beta)$ and linear factors of the type α_x and which is a defined expression in terms of the coefficients and variables of a set of forms $f, g, \ldots$ is a concomitant of those forms. Conversely, every concomitant of the set is a linear combination of such monomials.*

Examples of this theorem are given in (78), (84), (87).
In proof of the first part, let

$$\phi = (\alpha\beta)^p (\alpha\gamma)^q \ldots \alpha_x^\rho \beta_x^\sigma \gamma_x^\tau \ldots,$$

where $f = \alpha_x^m$; and $\beta, \gamma, \ldots$ may or may not be equivalent to α, depending upon whether or not ϕ appertains to a single form f or to a set $f, g, \ldots$. Transform the form f, that is, the set, by T. The transformed of f is (76)

$$f' = (\alpha_\lambda x_1' + \alpha_\mu x_2')^m.$$

Hence on account of the equations of transformation,

$$\phi' = (\alpha_\lambda \beta_\mu - \alpha_\mu \beta_\lambda)^p (\alpha_\lambda \gamma_\mu - \alpha_\mu \gamma_\lambda)^q \ldots \alpha_x^\rho \beta_x^\sigma \ldots$$

But

$$\alpha_\lambda \beta_\mu - \alpha_\mu \beta_\lambda = (\lambda\mu)(\alpha\beta). \qquad (92)$$

Hence

$$\phi' = (\lambda\mu)^{p+q+\cdots}\phi,$$

which proves the invariancy of ϕ. Of course if all factors of the second type, α_x, are missing in ϕ, the latter is an *invariant*.

To prove the converse of the theorem let ϕ be a concomitant of the set $f, g, \ldots$ and let the corresponding invariant relation be written

$$\phi(a_0', a_1', \ldots; x_1', x_2') = (\lambda\mu)^k \phi(a_0, a_1, \ldots; x_1, x_2). \tag{93}$$

Now $a_j' = \alpha_\lambda^{m-j}\alpha_\mu^j (j = 0, 1, \ldots m)$. Hence if we substitute these symbolical forms of the transformed coefficients, the left-hand side of (93) becomes a summation of the type

$$\sum PQx_1'^{\omega_1} x_2'^{\omega_1} = (\lambda\mu)^k \phi(a_0, \ldots; x_1, x_2) \quad (\omega_1 + \omega_2 = \omega), \tag{94}$$

where P is a monomial expression consisting of factors of the type α_λ only and Q a monomial whose factors are of the one type α_μ. But the inverse of the transformation T (cf. (10)) can be written

$$x_1' = \frac{\xi_\mu}{(\lambda\mu)}, \quad x_2' = \frac{\xi_\lambda}{(\lambda\mu)},$$

where $\xi_1 = -x_2, \xi_2 = x_1$. Then (94) becomes

$$\sum (-1)^{\omega_2} PQ\xi_\mu^{\omega_1} \xi_\lambda^{\omega_2} = (\lambda\mu)^{k+\omega}\phi \tag{95}$$

We now operate on both sides of (95) by $\Omega^{k+\omega}$, where

$$\Omega = \frac{\partial^2}{\partial\lambda_1\partial\mu_2} - \frac{\partial^2}{\partial\lambda_2\partial\mu_1}.$$

We apply (90) to the left-hand side of the result and (91) to the right-hand side. The left-hand side accordingly becomes a sum of terms each term of which involves necessarily $\omega + k$ determinants $(\alpha\beta)$, $(\alpha\xi)$. In fact, since the result is evidently still of order ω in x_1, x_2 there will be in each term precisely ω determinant factors of type $(\alpha\xi)$ and k of type $(\alpha\beta)$. There will be no factors of type α_λ or ξ_λ remaining on the left since by (91) the right-hand side becomes a constant times ϕ, and ϕ does not involve λ, μ. We now replace, on the left, $(\alpha\xi)$ by its equivalent α_x, $(\beta\xi)$ by β_x, etc. Then (95) gives, after division by the constant on the right,

$$\phi = \Sigma a(\alpha\beta)^p(\alpha\gamma)^q \ldots \alpha_x^\rho \beta_x^\sigma \ldots, \tag{96}$$

where a is a constant; which was to be proved.

This theorem is sometimes called the fundamental theorem of the symbolical theory since by it any binary invariant problem may be studied under the Aronhold symbolical representation.

3.3 Reducibility. Elementary Complete Irreducible Systems

Illustrations of the fundamental theorem proved at the end of Section 2 will now be given.

3.3.1 Illustrations.

It will be recalled that in (96) each symbolical letter occurs to the precise degree equal to the *order of the form* to which it appertains. Note also that $k + \omega$, the index plus the order of the concomitant, used in the proof of the theorem, equals the *weight* of the concomitant. This equals the number of symbolical determinant factors of the type $(\alpha\beta)$ plus the number of linear factors of the type α_x in any term of ϕ. The *order ω of the concomitant* equals the number of symbolical factors of the type α_x in any term of ϕ. The *degree* of the concomitant equals the number of distinct symbols $\alpha, \beta, \ldots$ occurring in its symbolical representation.

Let

$$\phi = (\alpha\beta)^p (\alpha\gamma)^q (\beta\gamma)^r \ldots \alpha_x^\rho \beta_x^\sigma \ldots$$

be any concomitant formula for a set of forms $f = \alpha_x^m, g = \beta_x^n, \ldots$. No generality will be lost in the present discussion by assuming ϕ to be monomial, since each separate term of a sum of such monomials is a concomitant. In order to write down all *monomial concomitants of the set of a given degree i* we have only to construct all symbolical products ϕ involving precisely i symbols which fulfill the laws

$$p + q + \ldots + \rho = m,$$
$$p + r + \ldots + \sigma = n, \qquad\qquad (97)$$
$$\cdots\cdots\cdots\cdots$$

where, as stated above, m is the order of f and equal therefore to the degree to which α occurs in ϕ, n, the order of g, and so on.

In particular let the set consist of $f = \alpha_x^2 = \beta_x^2$ merely. For the concomitant of degree 1 only one symbol may be used. Hence $f = \alpha_x^2$ itself is the only concomitant of degree 1. If $i = 2$, we have for ϕ,

$$\phi = (\alpha\beta)^p \alpha_x^\rho \beta_x^\sigma,$$

and from (97)

$$p + \rho = p + \sigma = 2.$$

Or

p	ρ	σ
0	2	2
1	1	1
2	0	0

Thus the only monomial concomitants of degree 2 are

$$\alpha_x^2\beta_x^2 = f^2, (\alpha\beta)\alpha_x\beta_x \equiv -(\alpha\beta)\alpha_x\beta_x \equiv 0, (\alpha\beta)^2 = \frac{1}{2}D.$$

For the degree 3

$$\phi = (\alpha\beta)^p(\alpha\gamma)^q(\beta\gamma)^r\alpha_x^\rho\beta_x^\sigma\gamma_x^\tau,$$
$$p+q+\rho = 2, p+r+\sigma = 2, q+r+\tau = 2.$$

It is found that all solutions of these three linear Diophantine equations lead to concomitants expressible in the form f^sD^t, or to identically vanishing concomitants.

DEFINITION.

Any concomitant of a set of forms which is expressible as a rational integral function of other concomitants of equal or of lower degree of the set is said to be *reducible* in terms of the other concomitants.

It will be seen from the above that the only irreducible concomitants of a binary quadratic f of the first three degrees are f itself and D, its discriminant. It will be proved later that f, D form a *complete irreducible system* of f. By this we mean a system of concomitants such that every other concomitant of f is reducible in terms of the members of this system. Note that this system for the quadratic is finite. In another chapter we shall prove the celebrated *Gordan's theorem* that a complete irreducible system of concomitants exists for every binary form or set of forms and the system consists always of a finite number of concomitants. All of the concomitants of the quadratic f above which are not monomial are reducible, but this is not always the case as it will be sometimes preferable to select as a member of a complete irreducible system a concomitant which is not monomial (cf. (87)). As a further illustration let the set of forms be $f = \alpha_x^2 = \beta_x^2 = \ldots, g = a_x^2 = b_x^2 = \ldots$; let $i = 2$. Then employing only two symbols and avoiding $(\alpha\beta)^2 = \frac{1}{2}D$, etc.

$$\phi = (\alpha a)^p\alpha_x^\rho a_x^\sigma,$$
$$p+\rho = p+\sigma = 2.$$

The concomitants from this formula are,

$$\alpha_x^2 a_x^2 = f\cdot g, (\alpha a)\alpha_x a_x = J, (\alpha a)^2 = h,$$

J being the Jacobian, and h the bilinear invariant of f and ϕ.

3.3.2   Reduction by identities.

As will appear subsequently the standard method of obtaining complete irreducible systems is by transvection. There are many methods of proving concomitants reducible more powerful than the one briefly considered above, and the interchange of equivalent symbols. One method is reduction by symbolical identities.

Fundamental identity. One of the identities frequently employed in reduction is one already frequently used in various connections, viz. formula (92). We write this

$$a_x b_y - a_y b_x \equiv (ab)(xy). \tag{98}$$

Every reduction formula to be introduced in this book, including Gordan's series and Stroh's series, may be derived directly from (98). For this reason this formula is called the fundamental reduction formula of binary invariant theory (cf. Chap. IV).

If we change y_1 to c_2, y_2 to $-c_1$, (98) becomes

$$(bc)a_x + (ca)b_x + (ab)c_x \equiv 0. \tag{99}$$

Replacing x by d in (99),

$$(ad)(bc) + (ca)(bd) + (ab)(cd) \equiv 0. \tag{100}$$

From (99) by squaring,

$$2(ab)(ac)b_x c_x \equiv (ab)^2 c_x^2 + (ac)^2 b_x^2 - (bc)^2 a_x^2. \tag{101}$$

If ω is an imaginary cube root of unity, and

$$u_1 = (bc)a_x, u_2 = (ca)b_x, u_3 = (ab)c_x,$$

we have

$$(u_1 + u_2 + u_3)(u_1 + \omega u_2 + \omega^2 u_3)(u_1 + \omega^2 u_2 + \omega u_3)$$
$$= (ab)^3 c_x^3 + (bc)^3 a_x^3 + (ca)^3 b_x^3 - 3(ab)(bc)(ca)a_x b_x c_x \equiv 0. \tag{102}$$

Other identities may be similarly obtained.

In order to show how such identities may be used in performing reductions, let $f = a_x^3 = b_x^3 = \cdots$ be the binary cubic form. Then

$$\Delta = (f, f)^2 = (ab)^2 a_x b_x,$$
$$Q = (f, \Delta) = (ab)^2 (cb) a_x c_x^2.$$

$$-(f, Q)^2 = \frac{1}{3}(ab)^2 (bc)[a_x c_y^2 + 2c_x c_y a_y]_{y=d} \times d_x \tag{102_1}$$
$$= \frac{1}{3}[(ab)^2 (cd)^2 (bc)a_x d_x + 2(ab)^2 (ad)(cd)(bc)c_x d_x].$$

But by the interchanges $a \sim d, b \sim c$

$$(ab)^2 (cd)^2 (bc)a_x d_x = (dc)^2 (ba)^2 (cb)a_x d_x \equiv 0.$$

By the interchange $c \sim d$ the second term in the square bracket equals

$$(ab)^2(cd)c_x d_x[(ad)(bc) + (ca)(bd)],$$

or, by (100) this equals

$$(ab)^3(cd)^2 c_x d_x \equiv 0.$$

Hence $(f, Q)^2$ vanishes.

We may note here the result of the transvection $(\Delta, \Delta)^2$;

$$R = (\Delta, \Delta)^2 = (ab)^2(cd)^2(ac)(bd).$$

3.3.3 Concomitants of binary cubic.

We give below a table of transvectants for the binary cubic form. It shows which transvectants are reducible in terms of other concomitants. It will be inferred from the table that the complete irreducible system for the binary cubic f consists of

$$f, \Delta, Q, R,$$

one invariant and three covariants, and this is the case as will be proved later. Not all of the reductions indicated in this table can be advantageously made by the methods introduced up to the present, but many of them can. All four of the irreducible concomitants have previously been derived in this book, in terms of the actual coefficients, but they are given here for convenient reference:

$$f = a_0 x_1^3 + 3a_1 x_1^2 x_2 + 3a_2 x_1 x_2^2 + a_3 x_2^3,$$
$$\Delta = 2(a_0 a_2 - a_1^2)x_1^2 + 2(a_0 a_3 - a_1 a_2)x_1 x_2 + 2(a_1 a_3 - a_2^2)x_2^2, \qquad \text{(cf. (35))}$$
$$Q = (a_0^2 a_3 - 3a_0 a_1 a_2 + 2a_1^3)x_1^3 + 3(a_0 a_1 a_3 - 2a_0 a_2^2 + a_1^2 a_2)x_1^2 x_2$$
$$\quad - 3(a_0 a_2 a_3 - 2a_1^2 a_3 + a_1 a_2^2)x_1 x_2^2 - (a_0 a_3^2 - 3a_1 a_2 a_3 + 2a_2^3)x_2^3, \qquad \text{(cf. (39))}$$
$$R = 8(a_0 a_2 - a_1^2)(a_1 a_3 - a_2^2) - 2(a_0 a_3 - a_1 a_2)^2. \qquad \text{(cf. (74}_1\text{))}$$

The symbolical forms are all given in the preceding Paragraph.

TABLE I

FIRST TRANSV.	SECOND TRANSV.	THIRD TRANSV.
$(f, f) = 0$	$(f, f)^2 = \Delta$	$(f, f)^3 = 0$
$(f, \Delta) = Q$	$(f, \Delta)^2 = 0$	
$(\Delta, \Delta) = 0$	$(\Delta, \Delta)^2 = R$	
$(f, Q) = -\frac{1}{2}\Delta^2$	$(f, Q)^2 = 0$	$(f, Q)^3 = R$
$(\Delta, Q) = \frac{1}{2}Rf$	$(\Delta, Q)^2 = 0$	
$(Q, Q) = 0$	$(Q, Q)^2 = \frac{1}{2}R\Delta$	$(Q, Q)^3 = 0$

3.4 Concomitants in Terms of the Roots

Every binary form $f = a_x^m = b_x^m = \ldots$ is linearly factorable in some field of rationality. Suppose

$$f = (r_2^{(1)} x_1 - r_1^{(1)} x_2)(r_2^{(2)} x_1 - r_1^{(2)} x_2) \ldots (r_2^{(m)} x_1 - r_1^{(m)} x_2).$$

Then the coefficients of the form are the elementary symmetric functions of the m groups of variables (homogeneous)

$$P_j(r_1^{(j)}, r_2^{(j)})(j = 1, 2, \ldots, m).$$

These functions are given by

$$a_j = (01)^j \sum r_1^{(1)} \tau_1^{(2)} \ldots \tau_1^{(j)} \tau_2^{(j+1)} \ldots \tau_2^{(m)} (j = 0, \ldots, m). \tag{103}$$

The number of terms in $\sum$ evidently equals the number of distinct terms obtainable from its leading term by permuting all of its letters after the superscripts are removed. This number is, then,

$$N = (m/)! j! (m - j)! =_m C_i.$$

3.4.1 Theorem on linear factors.

Theorem. *Any concomitant of f is a simultaneous concomitant of the linear factors of f, i.e. of the linear forms*

$$(\tau^{(1)} x), (\tau^{(2)} x), \ldots, (\tau^{(m)} x).$$

For,

$$f' = (-1)^m (\tau'^{(1)} x')(\tau'^{(2)} x') \ldots (\tau'^{(m)} x'), \tag{104}$$

and

$$a_j' = (-1)^i \sum \tau_1'^{(1)} \tau_1'^{(2)} \ldots \tau_1'^{(j)} \tau_2'^{(j+1)} \ldots \tau_2'^{(m)}. \tag{103_1}$$

Let ϕ be a concomitant of f, and let the corresponding invariant relation be

$$\phi' = (a_0', \ldots, a_m')^i (x_1', x_2')^\omega = (\lambda \mu)^k (a_0, \ldots, a_m)^i (x_1, x_2)^\omega = (\lambda \mu)^k \phi.$$

When the primed coefficients in ϕ' are expressed in terms of the roots from (103_1) and the unprimed coefficients in ϕ in this invariant relation are expressed in terms of the roots from (103), it is evident that ϕ' is the same function of the primed τ's that ϕ is of the unprimed τ's. This proves the theorem.

3.4.2 Conversion operators.

In this Paragraph much advantage results in connection with formal manipulations by introducing the following notation for the factored form of f:

$$f = \alpha_x^{(1)}\alpha_x^{(2)} \cdots \alpha_x^{(m)}. \tag{105}$$

Here $\alpha_x^{(j)} = \alpha_1 + \alpha_2^{(j)}x_2 (j = 1,\cdots,m)$. The α's are related to the roots $(r_1^{(j)}, r_2^{(j)})$ of the previous Paragraph by the equations

$$\alpha_1^{(j)} = r_2^{(j)}, \alpha_2^{(j)} = -r_1^{(j)};$$

that is, the roots are $(+\alpha_2^{(j)}, -\alpha_1^{(j)})(j = 1,\cdots,m)$. The umbral expressions a_1, a_2 are now cogredient to $\alpha_1^{(j)}, \alpha_2^{(j)}$ (Chap. I, §2, VII, and Chap. Ill, (76)). Hence,

$$\left(\alpha^{(j)}\frac{\partial}{\partial a}\right) = \alpha_1^{(j)}\frac{\partial}{\partial a_1} + \alpha_2^{(j)}\frac{\partial}{\partial a_2}$$

is an invariantive operator by the fundamental postulate. In the same way

$$[D_a] = \left(\alpha^{(1)}\frac{\partial}{\partial a}\right)\left(\alpha^{(2)}\frac{\partial}{\partial a}\right)\cdots\left(\alpha^{(m)}\frac{\partial}{\partial a}\right)$$

and

$$[D_{abc}] = [D_a][D_b][D_c]\cdots$$

If the transformation T is looked upon as a change of reference points, the multiplier λ undergoes a homographic transformation under T. are invariantive operators. If we recall that the only degree to which any umbral pair a_1, a_2 can occur in a symbolical concomitant,

$$\phi = \Sigma\Pi\kappa(ab)(ac)\cdots,$$

of f is the precise degree m, it is evident that $[D_{abc...}]$ operated upon ϕ gives a concomitant which is expressed entirely in terms of the roots $(\alpha_2^{(j)}, -\alpha_1^{(j)})$ of f. Illustrations follow. Let $2\,\phi$ be the discriminant of the quadratic

$$f = a_x^2 = b_x^2 = \cdots, \phi = (ab)^2.$$

Then

$$\left(\alpha^{(1)}\frac{\partial}{\partial a}\right)\phi = 2(\alpha^{(1)}b)(ab); [D_a]\phi = 2(\alpha^{(1)}b)(\alpha^{(2)}b).$$

Hence

$$[D_{ab}]\phi = -2(\alpha^{(1)}\alpha^{(2)})^2. \tag{106}$$

This result is therefore some concomitant of f expressed entirely in terms of the roots of f. It will presently appear that it is, except for a numerical factor, the invariant ϕ itself expressed in terms of the roots. Next let ϕ be the covariant Q of the cubic $f = a_x^3 = \dots\,.$ Then

$$Q = (ab)^2(ac)b_x c_x^2,$$

$$\frac{1}{2}[D_a]\,Q = (\alpha^{(1)}b)(\alpha^{(2)}b)(c\alpha^{(3)})b_x c_x^2 + (\alpha^{(01)}b)(\alpha^{(3)}b)(c\alpha^{(2)})b_x c_x^2$$
$$+ (\alpha^{(3)}b)(\alpha^{(2)}b)(x\alpha^{(1)}b_x c_x^2,$$

$$\frac{1}{4}[D_{ab}]\,Q = (\alpha^{(1)}b)(\alpha^{(2)}b)(c\alpha^{(3)})\alpha_x^{(3)} c_x^2$$
$$+(\alpha^{(1)}\alpha^{(3)})(\alpha^{(2)}\alpha^{(1)})(c\alpha^{(3)})\alpha_x^{(2)} c_x^2 + (\alpha^{(1)}\alpha^{(2)})(\alpha^{(2)}\alpha^{(3)})(c\alpha^{(3)})\alpha_x^{(1)} c_x^2$$
$$+(\alpha^{(1)}\alpha^{(2)})(\alpha^{(3)}\alpha^{(1)})(c\alpha^{(3)})\alpha_x^{(3)} c_x^2 + (\alpha^{(1)}\alpha^{(3)})(\alpha^{(3)}\alpha^{(1)})(c\alpha^{(2)})\alpha_x^{(2)} c_x^2$$
$$+(\alpha^{(1)}\alpha^{(3)})(\alpha^{(3)}\alpha^{(2)})(c\alpha^{(2)})\alpha_x^{(1)} c_x^2 + (\alpha^{(3)}\alpha^{(1)})(\alpha^{(2)}\alpha^{(3)})(c\alpha^{(1)})\alpha_x^{(2)} c_x^2$$
$$+(\alpha^{(3)}\alpha^{(2)})(\alpha^{(2)}\alpha^{(1)})(c\alpha^{(2)})\alpha_x^{(3)} c_x^2 + (\alpha^{(3)}\alpha^{(2)})(\alpha^{(2)}\alpha^{(3)})(c\alpha^{(1)})\alpha_x^{(1)} c_x^2$$

$$[D_{abc}]\,Q = -2^5 \sum (\alpha^{(1)}\alpha^{(2)})^2 (\alpha^{(1)}\alpha^{(3)})\alpha_x^{(3)2}\alpha_x^{(2)}, \tag{107}$$

wherein the summation covers the permutations of the superscripts. This is accordingly a covariant of the cubic expressed in terms of the roots.

Now it appears from (104) that each coefficient of $f = a_x^m = \dots$ is of degree m in the α's of the roots $(\alpha_2^{(j)} - \alpha_1^{(j)})$. Hence any concomitant of degree i will be of degree im in these roots. Conversely, any invariant or covariant which is of degree im in the root letters α will, when expressed in terms of the coefficients of the form, be of degree i in these coefficients. This is a property which invariants enjoy in common with all symmetric functions. Thus $[D_{ab}]\phi$ above is an invariant of the quadratic of degree 2 and hence it must be the discriminant ϕ itself, since the latter is the only invariant of f of that degree (cf. §3). Likewise it appears from Table I that Q is the only covariant of the cubic of degree-order $(3, 3)$, and since by the present rule $[D_{abc}]\,Q$ is of degree-order $(3, 3)$, (107) is, aside from a numerical multiplier, the expression for Q itself in terms of the roots.

It will be observed generally that $[D_{ab\dots}]$ preserves not only the degree-order (i, ω) of ϕ, but also the weight since $w = \frac{1}{2}(im + \omega)$. If then in any case ϕ happens to be the only concomitant of f of that given degree-order (i, w), the expression $[D_{ab\dots}]\phi$ is precisely the concomitant ϕ expressed in terms of the roots. This rule enables us to derive easily by the method above the expressions for the irreducible system of the cubic f in terms of the roots. These are

$$f = a_x^{(1)} a_x^{(2)} a_x^{(3)}; \quad a_x^3.$$
$$\Delta = \sum (a^{(1)}a^{(2)})^2 a_x^{(3)2}; \quad (ab)^2 a_x b_x.$$
$$Q = \sum (a^{(1)}a^{(2)})^2 (a^{(1)}a^{(3)})a_x^{(3)2} a_x^{(2)}; \quad (ab)^2 (ac) b_x c_x^2.$$
$$R = (a^{(1)}a^{(2)})^2 (a^{(2)}a^{(3)})^2 (a^{(3)}a^{(1)})^2; \quad (ab)^2 (cd)^2 (ac)(bd).$$

Consider now the explicit form of Q:

$$Q = \left(a^{(1)}a^{(2)}\right)^2 \left(a^{(1)}a^{(3)}\right)^2 a_x^{(3)2}a_x^{(2)} + \left(a^{(2)}a^{(3)}\right)^2 \left(a^{(2)}a^{(1)}\right)^2 a_x^{(1)2}a_x^{(3)}$$

$$+ \left(a^{(3)}a^{(1)}\right)^2 \left(a^{(3)}a^{(2)}\right)^2 a_x^{(2)2}a_x^{(1)} + \left(a^{(3)}a^{(2)}\right)^2 \left(a^{(3)}a^{(1)}\right)^2 a_x^{(1)2}a_x^{(2)}$$

$$+ \left(a^{(2)}a^{(1)}\right)^2 \left(a^{(2)}a^{(3)}\right)^2 a_x^{(3)2}a_x^{(1)} + \left(a^{(1)}a^{(3)}\right)^2 \left(a^{(1)}a^{(2)}\right)^2 a_x^{(2)2}a_x^{(3)}$$

It is to be noted that this is symmetric in the two groups of letters $(a_1^{(j)}, a_2^{(j)})$. Also each root (value off) occurs in the same number of factors as any other root in a term of Q. Thus in the first term the superscript (1) occurs in three factors. So also does (2).

3.4.3   Principal theorem.

We now proceed to prove the principal theorem of this subject (Cayley).

Definition.

In Chapter I, Section 1, II, the length of the segment joining $C(x_1 x_2)$, and $D(y_1, y_2)$; real points, was shown to be

$$CD = \frac{\lambda\mu(yx)}{(\lambda y_1 + y_2)(\lambda x_1 + x_2)},$$

where λ is the multiplier appertaining to the points of reference P, Q, and μ is the length of the segment PQ. If the ratios $x_1 : x_2$, $y_1 : y_2$ are not real, this formula will not represent a real segment CD. But in any case if $(r_a^{(j)}, r_2^{(j)})$, $(r_a^{(k)}, r_2^{(k)})$, are any two roots of a binary form $f = a_x^m$, real or imaginary, we define the difference of these two roots to be the number

$$[\tau^{(j)}\tau^{(k)}] = \frac{\lambda\mu(\tau^{(j)}\tau^{(k)})}{(\lambda\tau_1^{(j)} + \tau_2^{(j)})(\lambda\tau_1^{(k)} + \tau_2^{(k)})}.$$

We note for immediate use that the expression

$$\Pi(\tau) = (\lambda\tau_1^{(1)} + \tau_2^{(1)})(\lambda\tau_1^{(2)})\ldots(\lambda\tau_1^{(m)} + \tau_2^{(m)})$$

is symmetric in the roots. That is, it is a symmetric function of the two groups of variables $(\tau_1^{(j)}, \tau_2^{(j)})(j = 1, \ldots, m)$. In fact it is the result of substituting $(1, -\lambda)$ for (x_1, x_2) in

$$f = (-1)^m (\tau^{(1)}x)(\tau^{(2)}x)\ldots(\tau^{(m)}x),$$

and equals

$$\Pi(\tau) = (a_0 - ma_1\lambda + \ldots + (-1)^m a_m\lambda^m).$$

Obviously the reference points P, Q can be selected[1] so that $(1, -\lambda)$ is not a root, *i.e.* so that $\Pi(\tau) \neq 0$.

Theorem. *Let f be any binary form, then any function of the two types of differences*

$$[\tau^{(j)}\tau^{(k)}], \, [\tau^{(j)}x] = \lambda\mu(\tau^{(f)}x)/(\lambda\tau_1^{(f)} + \tau_2^{(j)})(\lambda x_1 + x_2),$$

which is homogenous in both types of differences and symmetric in the roots $(\tau_1^{(j)}, \tau_2^{(j)})(j = 1, \ldots, m)$ will, when expressed in terms of x_1, x_2 and the coefficients of f, and made integral by multiplying by a power of $\Pi(\tau)$ times a power of $(\lambda x_1 + x_2)$, be a concomitant if and only if every one of the products of differences of which it consists involves all roots $(\tau_1^{(j)}, \tau_2^{(j)})$ (values of j) in equal numbers of its factors. Moreover all concomitants of f are functions ϕ defined in this way. If only the one type of difference $[\tau^{(j)}\tau^{(k)}]$ occurs in ϕ, it is an invariant, if only the type $[\tau^{(j)}x]$, it is an identical covariant,–a power of f itself, and if both types occur, ϕ is a covariant. [Cf. theorem in Chap. III, §2, VII.]

In proof of this let the explicit form of the function ϕ described in the theorem be

$$\phi = \sum_k [r^{(1)}r^{(2)}]^{\alpha_k} [r^{(1)}r^{(3)}]^{\beta_k} \ldots [r^{(1)}x]^{\rho_k} [r^{(2)}x]^{\sigma_k} \ldots,$$

where

$$\alpha_1 + \beta_1 + \ldots = \alpha_2 + \beta_2 + \ldots = \ldots,$$
$$\rho_1 + \sigma_1 + \ldots = \rho_2 + \sigma_2 + \ldots = \ldots,$$

and ϕ is symmetric in the roots. We are to prove that ϕ is invariantive when and only when each superscript occurs in the same number of factors as every other superscript in a term of ϕ. We note first that if this property holds and we express the differences in ϕ in explicit form as defined above, the terms of Σ will, without further algebraical manipulation, have a common denominator, and this will be of the form

$$\prod(r)^u(\lambda x_1 + x_2)^v.$$

Hence $\prod(r)^u(\lambda x_1 + x_2)^v\phi$ is a sum of monomials each one of which is a product of *determinants* of the two types $(r^{(j)}r^{(k)}), (r^{(j)}x)$. But owing to the cogrediency of the roots and variables these determinants are separately invariant under T, hence $\prod(r)^u(\lambda x_1 + x_2)^v\phi$ is a concomitant. Next assume that in ϕ it is not true that each superscript occurs the same number of times in a term as every other superscript. Then although when the above explicit formulas for differences are introduced $(\lambda x_1 + x_2)$ occurs to the same power v in every denominator in Σ,

---

[1] If the transformation T is looked upon as a change of reference points, the multiplier λ undergoes a homographic transformation under T.

64

this is not true of a factor of the type $(\lambda r_1^{(j)} + r_2^{(j)})$. Hence the terms of Σ must be reduced to a common denominator. Let this common denominator be $\prod(r)^u(\lambda x_1 + x_2)^v$. Then $\prod(r)^u(\lambda x_1 + x_2)^v\phi$ is of the form

$$\phi_1 = \sum_k \prod_j (\lambda r_1^{(j)} + r_2^{(j)})^{u_{jk}} (r^{(1)}r^{(2)})^{\alpha_k} (r^{(1)}r^{(3)})^{\beta_k} \ldots \times (r^{(1)}x)^{\rho_k} (r^{(2)}x)^{\sigma_k} \ldots,$$

where not all of the positive integers u_{jk} are zero. *Now ϕ is invariantive under T. Hence it must be unaltered under the special case of T; $x_1 = -x_2', x_2 = x'$. From this $\tau_1^{(j)} = -\tau_2'^{(j)}, \tau_2^{(j)} = \tau_1'^{(j)}$. Hence

$$\phi_1' = \sum_\kappa \prod_j (\lambda \tau_2^{(j)} - \tau_1^{(j)})^{u_{j\kappa}} (\tau^{(1)}\tau^{(2)})^{\alpha_\kappa} (\tau^{(1)}\tau^{(3)})^{\beta_\kappa} \ldots (\tau^{(1)}x)^{\rho_\kappa} \ldots,$$

and this is obviously not identical with ϕ_1 on account of the presence of the factor Π. Hence ϕ_1 is not a concomitant.

All parts of the theorem have now been proved or are self-evident except that *all* concomitants of a form are expressible in the manner stated in the theorem. To prove this, note that any concomitant ϕ of f, being rational in the coefficients of f, is symmetric in the roots. To prove that ϕ need involve the roots in the form of differences only, before it is made integral by multiplication by $\Pi(\tau)^u(\lambda x_1 + x_2)^v$, it is only necessary to observe that it must remain unaltered when f is transformed by the following transformation of determinant unity:

$$x_1 = x_1' + cx_2', x_2 = x_2',$$

and functions of determinants $(\tau^{(j)}\tau^{(k)}), (\tau^{(j)}x)$ are the only symmetric functions which have this property.

As an illustration of the theorem consider concomitants of the quadratic $f = (\tau^{(1)}x^{(2)})(\tau^{(2)}x)$. These are of the form

$$\phi = \sum_\kappa [\tau^{(1)}\tau^{(2)}]^{\alpha_\kappa} [\tau^{(1)}x]^{\rho_\kappa} [\tau^{(2)}x]^{\sigma_\kappa}.$$

Here owing to homogeneity in the two types of differences,

$$\alpha_1 = \alpha_2 = \ldots; \rho_1 + \sigma_1 = \rho_2 + \sigma_2 = \ldots.$$

Also due to the fact that each superscript must occur as many times in a term as every other superscript,

$$\alpha_1 + \rho_1 = \alpha_1 + \sigma_1, \alpha_2 + \rho_2 = \alpha_2 + \sigma_2, \ldots.$$

Also owing to symmetry α_k must be even. Hence $\alpha_k = 2\alpha$, $\rho_\kappa = \sigma_\kappa = \beta$, and

$$\Pi(\tau)^{2\alpha+\beta}(\lambda x_1 + x_2)^{2\beta}\phi = c\{(\tau^{(1)}\tau^{(2)})^2\}^\alpha \{(\tau^{(1)}x)(\tau^{(2)}x)\}^\beta = CD^\alpha f^\beta,$$

where C is a numerical multiplier. Now α and β may have any positive integral values including zero. Hence the concomitants of f consist of the discriminant

$D = -(r^{(1)}r^{(2)})^2$, the form $f = (r^{(1)}x)(r^{(2)}x)$ itself, and products of powers of these two concomitants. In other words we obtain here a proof that f and D form a complete irreducible system for the quadratic. We may easily derive the irreducible system of the cubic by the same method, and it may also be applied with success to the quartic although the work is there quite complicated. We shall close this discussion by determining by this method all of the invariants of a binary cubic $f = -(r^{(1)}x)(r^{(2)}x)(r^{(3)}x)$. Here

$$\phi = \sum_k [r^{(1)}r^{(2)}]^{a_k}[r^{(2)}r^{(3)}]^{\beta_k}[r^{(3)}r^{(1)}]^{\gamma^k}$$

and

$$a_k + \gamma_k = \alpha_k + \beta_k = \beta_k + \gamma_k.$$

That is,

$$a_k = \beta_k = \gamma_k = 2\alpha.$$

Hence

$$\Pi(r)^{4a}\phi = c\{(r^{(1)}r^{(2)})^2(r^{(2)}r^{(3)})^2(r^{(3)}r^{(1)})^2\}^a = CR^{\alpha}.$$

Thus the discriminant R and its powers are the only invariants.

3.4.4 Hermite's Reciprocity Theorem.

Theorem. *If a form $f = a_x^m = b_x^m = \cdots$ of order m has a concomitant of degree n and order ω, then a form $g = \alpha_x^n = \ldots$ of order n has a concomitant of degree m and order ω.*

To prove this theorem let the concomitant of f be

$$I = \sum k(ab)^p(ac)^q \cdots a_x^r b_x^s \cdots (r + s + \cdots = \omega),$$

where the summation extends over all terms of I and k is numerical. In this the number of distinct symbols $a, b, \ldots$ is n. This expression I if not symmetric in the n letters $a, b, c, \ldots$ can be changed into an equivalent expression in the sense that it represents the same concomitant as I, and which is symmetric. To do this, take a term of I, as

$$k(ab)^p(ac)^q \cdots a_x^r b_x^s \cdots ,$$

and in it permute the equivalent symbols $a, b, \ldots$ in all $n!$ possible ways, add the $n!$ resulting monomial expressions and divide the sum by $n!$. Do this for all terms of I and add the results for all terms. This latter sum is an expression J equivalent to I and symmetric in the n symbols. Moreover each symbol occurs to the same degree in every term of J as does every other symbol, and this degree is precisely m. Now let

$$g = \alpha_x^{(1)}\alpha_x^{(2)} \cdots \alpha_x^{(n)},$$

and in a perfectly arbitrary manner make the following replacements in J:

$$\begin{pmatrix} a, & b, & c, & \ldots, & l \\ \alpha^{(1)}, & \alpha^{(2)}, & \alpha^{(3)}, & \ldots, & \alpha^{(n)} \end{pmatrix}.$$

The result is an expression in the roots $(\alpha_2^{(j)}, -\alpha_1^{(j)})$ of g,

$$J_\alpha = \sum C(\alpha^{(1)}\alpha^{(2)})^p (\alpha^{(1)}\alpha^{(3)})^q \cdots \alpha_x^{(1)^r} \alpha_x^{(2)^s} \cdots ,$$

which possesses the following properties: It is symmetric in the roots, and of order ω. In every term each root (value of (j)) occurs in the same number of factors as every other root. Hence by the principal theorem of this section J_α is a concomitant of g expressed in terms of the roots. It is of degree m in the coefficients of g since it is of degree m in each root. This proves the theorem.

As an illustration of this theorem we may note that a quartic form f has an invariant J of degree 3 (cf. (70_1)); and, reciprocally, a cubic form g has an invariant R of degree 4, viz. the discriminant of g (cf. (39)).

3.5   Geometrical Interpretations. Involution

In Chapter I, Section 1, II, III, it has been shown how the roots $(r_1^{(i)}, r_2^{(i)})(i = 1, \ldots, m)$ of a binary form

$$f = (a_0, a_1, \ldots, a_m)(x_1, x_2)^m$$

may be represented by a range of m points referred to two fixed points of reference, on a straight line EF. Now the evanescence of any invariant of f implies, in view of the theory of invariants in terms of the roots, a definite relation between the points of this range, and this relation is such that it holds true likewise for the range obtained from $f = 0$ by transforming f by T. A property of a range $f = 0$ which persists for $f' = 0$ is called a *projective property*. Every property represented by the vanishing of an invariant I of f is therefore projective in view of the invariant equation

$$I(a_0', \ldots) = (\lambda\mu)^k I(a_0, \ldots).$$

Any covariant of f equated to zero gives rise to a "derived" point range connected in a definite manner with the range $f = 0$, and this connecting relation is projective. The identical evanescence of any covariant implies projective relations between the points of the original range $f = 0$ such that the derived point range obtained by equating the covariant to zero is absolutely indeterminate. The like remarks apply to covariants or invariants of two or more forms, and the point systems represented thereby.

3.5.1 Involution.

If

$$f = (a_0, a_1, \cdots \,\backslash\!\backslash\, x_1, x_2)^m, g = (b_0, b_1, \cdots \,\backslash\!\backslash\, x_1, x_2)^m$$

are two binary forms of the same order, then

$$f + kg = (a_0 + kb_0, a_1 + kb_1, \cdots \,\backslash\!\backslash\, x_1, x_2)^m,$$

where k is a variable parameter, denotes a system of qualities which are said to form, with f and g, an *involution*. The * single infinity of point ranges given by k, taken with the ranges $f = 0$, $y = 0$ are said to form an involution of point ranges.

In Chapter I, Section 1, V, we proved that a point pair $((u), (v))$ can be found harmonically related to any two given point pairs $((p), (r))$, $((q), (s))$. If the latter two pairs are given by the respective quadratic forms f, g, the pair $((u), (v))$ is furnished by the Jacobian C of f, g. If the eliminant of three quadratics f, g, h vanishes identically, then there exists a linear relation

$$f + kg + lh = 0,$$

and the pair $h = 0$ belongs to the involution defined by the two given pairs.

Theorem. *There are, in general, $2(m-1)$ quantics belonging to the involution $f + kg$ which contain a squared linear factor, and the set comprising all double roots of these quantics is the set of roots of the Jacobian of f and g.*

In proof of this, we have shown in Chapter I that the discriminant of a form of order m is of degree $2(m-1)$. Hence the discriminant of $f+kg$ is a polynomial in k of order $2(m-1)$. Equated to zero it determines $2(m-1)$ values of k for which $f + kg$ has a double root.

We have thus proved that an involution of point ranges contains $2(m-1)$ ranges each of which has a double point. We can now show that the $2(m-1)$ roots of the Jacobian of f and g are the double points of the involution. For if $x_1 u_2 - x_2 u_1$ is a double factor of $f + kg$, it is a simple factor of the two forms

$$\frac{\partial f}{\partial x_1} + k\frac{\partial g}{\partial x_1}, \frac{\partial f}{\partial x_2} + k\frac{\partial g}{\partial x_2},$$

and hence is a simple factor of the k eliminant of these forms, which is the Jacobian of f, g. By this, for instance, the points of the common harmonic pair of two quadratics are the double points of the involution defined by those quadratics. The square of each linear factor of C belongs to the involution $f + kg$.

In case the Jacobian vanishes identically the range of double points of the involution becomes indeterminate. This is to be expected since f is then a multiple of g and the two fundamental ranges $f = 0, g = 0$ coincide.

3.5.2 Projective properties represented by vanishing co-variants.

The most elementary irreducible covariants of a single binary form $f = (a_0, a_1, \ldots \, \emptyset \, x_1, x_2)^m$ are the Hessian H, and the third-degree covariant T, viz.

$$H = (f, f)^2, T = (f, H).$$

We now give a geometrical interpretation of each of these.

Theorem. *A necessary and sufficient condition in order that the binary form f may be the mth power of a linear form is that its Hessian H should vanish identically.*

If we construct the Hessian determinant of $(r_2 x_1 - r_1 x_2)^m$, it is found to vanish. Conversely, assume that $H = 0$. Since H is the Jacobian of the two first partial derivatives $\frac{\partial f}{\partial x_1}, \frac{\partial f}{\partial x_2}$, the equation $H = 0$ implies a linear relation

$$\kappa_2 \frac{\partial f}{\partial x_1} - \kappa_1 \frac{\partial f}{\partial x_2} = 0.$$

Also by Euler's theorem

$$x_1 \frac{\partial f}{\partial x_1} + x_2 \frac{\partial f}{\partial x_2} = mf,$$

and

$$\frac{\partial f}{\partial x_1} dx_1 + \frac{\partial f}{\partial x_2} dx_2 = df.$$

Expansion of the eliminant of these three equations gives

$$\frac{df}{f} = m \frac{d(\kappa_1 x_1 + \kappa_2 x_2)}{\kappa_1 x_1 + \kappa_2 x_2},$$

and by integration

$$f = (\kappa_1 x_1 + \kappa_2 x_2)^m,$$

and this proves the theorem.

Theorem. *A necessary and sufficient condition in order that a binary quartic form $f = a_0 x_1^4 + \cdots$ should be the product of two squared linear factors is that its sextic covariant T should vanish identically.*

To give a proof of this we need a result which can be most easily proved by the methods of the next chapter (cf. Appendix (29)) *e.g.* if i and J are the respective invariants of f,

$$i = 2(a_0 a_4 - 4 a_1 a_3 + 3 a_2^2),$$

$$J = 6 \begin{vmatrix} a_0 & a_1 & a_2 \\ a_1 & a_2 & a_3 \\ a_2 & a_3 & a_4 \end{vmatrix},$$

then
$$(T,T)^6 = \frac{1}{24}(i^3 - 6J^2).$$

We also observe that the discriminant of f is $\frac{1}{27}(i^3 - 6J^2)$. Now write α_x^2 as the square of a linear form, and

$$f = \alpha_x^2 q_x^2 = a_x^4 = b_x^4 = \cdots .$$

Then

$$H = (\alpha_x^2 q_x^2, a_x^4)^2$$
$$= \frac{1}{6}[(\alpha a)^2 q_x^2 + (qa)^2 \alpha_x^2 + 4(\alpha a)(qa)\alpha_x q_x]a_x^2$$
$$= \frac{1}{6}[3(\alpha a)^2 q_x^2 + 3(qa)^2 \alpha_x^2 - 2(\alpha q)^2 a_x^2]a_x^2.$$

But

$$(\alpha a)^2 a_x^2 = (f, \alpha_x^2)^2 = \frac{1}{6}(\alpha q)^2 \alpha_x^2,$$
$$(qa)^2 a_x^2 = (f, q_x^2)^2 = \frac{1}{6}[(\alpha q)^2 q_x^2 + 3(qq)^2 \alpha_x^2].$$

Hence
$$H = -\frac{1}{6}(\alpha q)^2 f + \frac{1}{4}(qq)^2 \alpha_x^4. \tag{108}$$

This shows that when $H = 0$, f is a fourth power since $(\alpha q)^2, (qq)^2$ are constants.
It now follows immediately that

$$T = (f, H) = \frac{1}{4}(qq)^2(f, \alpha_x)\alpha_x^3.$$

Next if f contains two pairs of repeated factors, q_x^2 is a perfect square, $(qq)^2 = 0$, and $T = 0$. Conversely, without assumption that α_x^2 is the square of a linear form, if $T = 0$, then
$$(T,T)^6 = \frac{1}{24}(i^3 - 6J^2) = 0,$$

and f has at least one repeated factor. Let this be a_x. Then from

$$T = \frac{1}{4}(qq)^2(f, \alpha_x)\alpha_x^3 = 0,$$

we have either $(qq)^2 = 0$, when q_x^2 is also a perfect square, or $(f, \alpha_x) = 0$, when $f = \alpha_x^4$. Hence the condition $T = 0$ is both necessary and sufficient.

Chapter 4

REDUCTION

4.1 Gordan's Series. The Quartic

The process of making reductions by means of identities, illustrated in Chapter III, Section 3, is tedious. But we may by a generalizing process, prepare such identities in such a way that the prepared identity will reduce certain extensive types of concomitants with great facility. Such a prepared identity is the series of Gordan.

4.1.1 Gordan's series.

This is derived by rational operations upon the fundamental identity

$$a_x b_y = a_y b_x + (ab)(xy).$$

From the latter we have

$$
\begin{aligned}
a_x^m b_y^n &= \quad [a_y b_x + (ab)(xy)]^m b_y^{n-m} \, (n \geqq m) \\
&= \textstyle\sum_{k=0}^{m} \binom{m}{k} a_y^{m-k} b_x^{m-k} b_y^{n-m} (ab)^k (xy) k.
\end{aligned}
\tag{109}
$$

Since the left-hand member can represent any doubly binary form of degree-order $(m,\, n)$, we have here an expansion of such a function as a power series in (xy). We proceed to reduce this series to a more advantageous form. We construct the $(n{-}k)$th y-polar of

$$(a_x^m, b_x^n)^k = (ab)^k a_x^{m-k} b_x^{n-k},$$

by the formula for the polar of a product (66). This gives

$$(a_x^m, b_x^n)_{y^{n-k}}^k$$

$$
= \frac{(ab)^k}{\binom{m+n-2k}{n-k}} \sum_{h=0}^{m-k} \binom{m-k}{m-k-h} \binom{n-k}{n-m+h} a_y^{m-k-h} a_x^h b_x^{m-k-h} b_y^{n-m+h}.
$$

$$\tag{110}$$

Subtracting $(ab)^k a_y^{m-k} b_x^{m-k} b_y^{n-m}$ from each term under the summation and remembering that the sum of the numerical coefficients in the polar of a product is unity we immediately obtain

$$(ab)^k a_y^{m-k} b_x^{m-k} b_y^{n-m}$$

$$= (a_x^m, b_x^n)_{y^{n-k}}^k - \frac{(ab)^k}{\binom{m+n-2k}{n-k}} \sum_{h=1}^{m-k} \binom{m-k}{m-k-h}\binom{n-k}{n-m+h}$$

$$\times\, a_y^{m-k-h} b_x^{m-k-h} b_y^{n-m}(a_x^h b_y^h - a_y^h b_x^h). \tag{111}$$

Aside from the factor $\binom{m}{k}$ the left-hand member of (111) is the coefficient of $(xy)^k$ in (109). Thus this coefficient is the $(n-k)$th polar of the kth transvectant of a_x^m, b_x^n minus terms which contain the factor $(ab)^{k+1}(xy)$. We now use (111) as a recursion formula, taking $k = m, m-1, \dots$. This gives

$$(ab)^m b_y^{n-m} = (a_x^m, b_x^n)_{y^n-m}^m,$$

$$(ab)^{m-1} a_y b_x b_y^{n-m} = (a_x^m, b_x^n)_{y^{n-m+1}}^{m-1} - \frac{1}{n-m+2}(a_x^m, b_x^n)_{y^{n-m}}^m(xy). \tag{112}$$

We now proceed to prove by induction that

$$(ab)^{k+1} a_y^{m-k-1} b_x^{m-k-1} b_y^{n-m} = \alpha_0(a_x^m, b_x^n)_{y^{n-k-1}}^{k+1}$$

$$+ \alpha_1(a_x^m, b_x^n)_{y^{n-k-2}}^{k+2}(xy) + \dots$$

$$+ \alpha_j(a_x^m, b_x^n)_{y^{n-k-j-1}}^{k+j+1}(xy)^i + \dots \tag{113}$$

$$+ \alpha_{m-k-1}(a_x^m, b_x^n)_{y^{n-m}}^m(xy)^{m-k-1},$$

where the α's are constants. The first steps of the induction are given by (112). Assuming (113) we prove that the relation is true when k is replaced by $k-1$. By Taylor's theorem

$$\xi^{h-1} + \xi^{h-2} + \dots + \xi + 1 = t_{h-1}(\xi-1)^{h-1} + t_{h-2}(\xi-1)^{h-2} + \dots + t_1(\xi-1) + t_0.$$

Hence

$$(a_x^h b_y^h - a_y^h b_x^h) = t_{h-1}(ab)^h(xy)^h + t_{h-2}(ab)^{h-1}(xy)^{h-1} a_y b_x + \dots$$

$$+ t_{h-i}(ab)^{h-i+1}(xy)^{h-i+1} a_y^{i-1} b_x^{i-1} + \dots + t_0(ab)(xy)a_y^{h-1} b_x^{h-1}. \tag{114}$$

Hence (111) may be written

$$(ab)^k a_y^{m-k} b_{x'}^{m-k} b_y^{n-m} = (a_x^m, b_x^n)_{y^{n-k}}^k$$

$$+ \sum_{h=1}^{m-k} \sum_{i=1}^{h} A_{hi}(ab)^{h-i+k+1} a_y^{m-k-h+i-1} b_x^{m-k-h+i-1} b_y^{n-m}(xy)^{h-i+1}, \tag{115}$$

in which the coefficients A_{hi} are numerical. But the terms

$$T_{hi} = (ab)^{h-i+k+l} a_y^{m-k-h+i-1} b_x^{m-k-h+i-1} b_y^{n-m} \quad (m-k \geq h \geq 1, i \leq h)$$

for all values of h, i are already known by (112), (113) as linear combinations of polars of transvectants; the type of expression whose proof we seek. Hence since (115) is linear in the T_{hi} its terms can immediately be arranged in a form which is precisely (113) with k replaced by $k-1$. This proves the statement.

We now substitute from (113) in (109) for all values of k. The result can obviously be arranged in the form

$$a_x^m b_y^n = C_0(a_x^m, b_x^n)_{y^n}^0 + C_1(a_x^m, b_x^n)_{y^{n-1}}^1 (xy) + \cdots \tag{116}$$
$$+ C_j(a_x^m, b_x^n)_{y^{n-j}}^j (xy)^j + \cdots + C_m(a_x^m, b_x^n)_{y^{n-m}}^m (xy)^m.$$

It remains to determine the coefficients C_j. By (91_1) of Chapter III we have, after operating upon both sides of (116) by Ω^j and then placing $y = x$,

$$\frac{m!n!}{(m-j)!(n-j)!}(ab)^j a_x^{m-j} b_x^{n-j} = C_j \frac{j!(m+n-j+1)!}{(m+n-2j+1)!}(ab)^j a_x^{m-j} b_x^{n-j}.$$

Solving for C_j, placing the result in (116) ($j = 0, 1, \ldots, m$), and writing the result as a summation,

$$a_x^m b_y^n = \sum_{j=0}^{m} \frac{\binom{m}{j}\binom{n}{j}}{\binom{m+n-j+1}{j}} (xy)^j (a_x^m, b_x^n)_{y^n-j}^j. \tag{117}$$

This is Gordan's series.

To put this result in a more useful, and at the same time a more general form let us multiply (117) by $(ab)^r$ and change m, n into $m-r$, $n-r$ respectively. Thus

$$(ab)^r a_x^{m-r} b_y^{n-r}$$
$$= \sum_{j=0}^{m-r} \frac{\binom{m-r}{j}\binom{n-r}{j}}{\binom{m+n-2r-j+1}{j}} (xy)^j (a_x^m, b_x^n)_{y^n-j-r}^{j+r}. \tag{118}$$

If we operate on this equation by $(x\frac{\partial}{\partial y})^k, (y\frac{\partial}{\partial x})^k$, we obtain the respective formulas

$$(ab)^r a_x^{m-r} b_x^k b_y^{n-r-k}$$
$$= \sum_j \frac{\binom{m-r}{j}\binom{n-r-k}{j}}{\binom{m+n-2r-j+1}{j}} (xy)^j (a_x^m, b_x^n)_{y^n-j-r-k}^{j+r}, \tag{119}$$
$$(ab)^r a_x^{m-r-k} a_y^k b_y^{n-r}$$
$$= \sum_j \frac{\binom{m-r-k}{j}\binom{n-r}{j}}{\binom{m+n-2r-j+1}{j}} (xy)^j (a_x^m, b_x^n)_{y^n-j-r+k}^{j+r}. \tag{120}$$

It is now desirable to recall the standard method of transvection; replace y_1 by

c_2, y_2 by $-c_1$ in (119) and multiply by $c_x^{p-n+r+k}$, with the result

$$(ab)^r (bc)^{n-r-k} a_x^{m-r} b_x^k c_x^{p-n+r+k}$$

$$= \sum_j (-1)^j \frac{\binom{m-r}{j}\binom{n-r-k}{j}}{\binom{m+n-2r-j+1}{j}} ((a_x^m, b_x^n)^{j+r}, c_x^p)^{n-j-r-k}. \qquad (121)$$

Likewise from (120)

$$(ab)^r (bc)^{n-r} (ac)^k a_x^{m-r-k} c_x^{p-n+r-k}$$

$$= \sum_j (-1)^j \frac{\binom{m-r-k}{j}\binom{m-r}{j}}{\binom{m+n-2r-j+1}{j}} ((a_x^m, b_x^n)^{j+r}, c_x^p)^{n-j-r+k}. \qquad (122)$$

The left-hand member of equation (121) is unaltered in value except for the factor $(-1)^{n-k}$ by the replacements $a \sim c, m \sim p, r \sim n - r - k$; and likewise (122) is unaltered except for the factor $(-1)^{n+k}$ by the replacements $a \sim c, m \sim p, r \sim n - r$. The right-hand members are however altered in *form* by these changes. If the changes are made in (121) and if we write $f = b_x^n, g = a_x^m, h = c_x^p, \alpha_1 = 0, \alpha_2 = n - r - k, \alpha_3 = r$, we obtain

$$\sum_j \frac{\binom{m-\alpha_1-\alpha_3}{j}\binom{\alpha_2}{j}}{\binom{m+n-2\alpha_3-j+1}{j}} ((f,g)^{\alpha_3+j}, h)^{\alpha_1+\alpha_2-j}$$

$$= (-1)^{\alpha_1} \sum_j \frac{\binom{p-\alpha_1-\alpha_2}{j}\binom{\alpha_3}{j}}{\binom{n+p-2\alpha_2-j+1}{j}} ((f,h)^{\alpha_2+j}, g)^{\alpha_1+\alpha_3-j}, \qquad (123)$$

where we have

$$\alpha_2 + \alpha_3 \not> n, \alpha_3 + \alpha_1 \not> m, \alpha_1 + \alpha_2 \not> p, \qquad (124_1)$$

together with $\alpha_1 = 0$.

If the corresponding changes, given above, are made in (122) and if we write $\alpha_1 = k, \alpha_2 = n - r, \alpha_3 = r$, we obtain the equation (123) again, precisely. Also relations (124_1) reproduce, but there is the additional restriction $\alpha_2 + \alpha_3 = n$. Thus (123) holds true in two categories of cases, viz. (1) $\alpha_1 = 0$ with (124_1), and (2) $\alpha_2 + \alpha_3 = n$ with (124_1). We write series (123) under the abbreviation

$$\begin{bmatrix} f & g & h \\ n & m & p \\ \alpha_1 & \alpha_2 & \alpha_3 \end{bmatrix} ; \alpha_2 + \alpha_3 \not> n, \alpha_3 + \alpha_1 \not> m, \alpha_1 + \alpha_2 \not> p,$$

    (i) $\alpha_1 = 0$,

    (ii) $\alpha_1 + \alpha_2 = n$.

It is of very great value as an instrument in performing reductions. We proceed to illustrate this fact by proving certain transvectants to be reducible.

Consider (Δ, Q) of Table I.

$$(\Delta, Q) = ((\Delta, f), \Delta).$$

Here $n = p = 2$, $m = 3$, and we may take $\alpha_1 = 0$, $\alpha_2 = \alpha_3 = 1$, giving the series

$$\begin{vmatrix} \Delta & f & \Delta \\ 2 & 3 & 2 \\ 0 & 1 & 1 \end{vmatrix},$$

that is,

$$((\Delta, f), \Delta) + \frac{2}{3}((\Delta, f)^2, \Delta)^0 = ((\Delta, \Delta), f) + \frac{1}{2}((\Delta, \Delta)^2, f)^0.$$

But

$$(\Delta, \Delta) = 0, (\Delta, f)^2 = 0, (\Delta, \Delta)^2 = R.$$

Hence

$$(\Delta, Q) = ((\Delta, f), \Delta) = \frac{1}{2} Rf,$$

which was to be proved.

Next let $f = a_x^m$ be any binary form and $H = (f, f)^2$ its Hessian. We wish to show that $((f, f)^2, f)^2$ is always reducible and to perform the reduction by Gordan's series. Here we may employ

$$\begin{pmatrix} f & f & f \\ m & m & m \\ 0 & 3 & 1 \end{pmatrix},$$

and since $(f, f)^{2\kappa+1} = 0$, this gives at once

$$\frac{\binom{m-1}{1}\binom{3}{1}}{\binom{2m-2}{1}}((f, f)^2, f)^2 + \frac{\binom{m-1}{3}\binom{3}{3}}{\binom{2m-4}{3}}((f, f)^4, f)^0 = \frac{\binom{m-3}{1}\binom{1}{1}}{\binom{2m-6}{1}}((f, f)^4, f)^0.$$

Solving we obtain

$$((f, f)^2, f)^2 = \frac{m-3}{2(2m-5)}((f, f)^4, f)^0 = \frac{m-3}{2(2m-5)} if, \tag{124}$$

where $i = (f, f)^4$.

Hence when $m \geqq 4$ this transvectant is always reducible.

4.1.2   The quartic.

By means of Gordan's series all of the reductions indicated in Table I and the corresponding ones for the analogous table for the quartic, Table II below, can be very readily made. Many reductions for forms of higher order and indeed for a general order can likewise be made (Cf. (124)). It has been shown by Stroh[1] that certain classes of transvectants cannot be reduced by this series but the simplest members of such a class occur for forms of higher order than the

---

[1] Stroh; Mathematische Annalen, vol. 31.

fourth. An example where the series will fail, due to Stroh, is in connection with the decimic $f = a_x^{10}$. The transvectant

$$((f, f)^6, f)^4$$

is not reducible by the series in its original form although it is a reducible covariant. A series discovered by Stroh will, theoretically, make all reductions, but it is rather difficult to apply, and moreover we shall presently develop powerful methods of reduction which largely obviate the necessity of its use. Stroh's series is derived by operations upon the identity $(ab)c_x + (bc)a_x + (ca)b_x = 0$.

TABLE II

	$r = 1$	$r = 2$	$r = 3$	$r = 4$
$(f, f)^\tau$	0	H	0	i
$(f, H)^\tau$	T	$\frac{1}{6}if$	0	J
$(f, T)^\tau$	$\frac{1}{12}(if^2 - 6H^2)$	0	$\frac{1}{4}(Jf - iH)$	0
$(H, H)^\tau$	0	$\frac{1}{6}(2Jf - iH)$	0	$\frac{1}{6}i^2$
$(H, T)^\tau$	$\frac{1}{6}(Jf^2 - ifH)$	0	$\frac{1}{24}(i^2f - 6JH)$	0
$(T, T)^\tau$	0	$\frac{1}{72}(i^2f^2 + 6iH^2 - 12JfH)$	0	0

We infer from Table II that the complete irreducible system of the quartic consists of

$$f, H, T, i, J.$$

This will be proved later in this chapter. Some of this set have already been derived in terms of the actual coefficients (cf. (70_1)). They are given below. These are readily derived by non-symbolical transvection (Chap. III) or by the method of expanding their symbolical expressions and then expressing the symbols in terms of the actual coefficients (Chap. III, Section 2).

$$f = a_0 x_1^4 + 4a_1 x_1^3 x_2 + 6a_2 x_1^2 x_2^2 + 4a_3 x_1 x_2^3 + a_4 x_2^4,$$
$$H = 2[(a_0 a_2 - a_1^2)x_1^4 + 2(a_0 a_3 - a_1 a_2)x_1^3 x_2$$
$$+ (a_0 a_4 + 2a_1 a_3 - 3a_2^2)x_1^2 x_2^2 + 2(a_1 a_4 - a_2 a_3)x_1 x_2^3 + (a_2 a_4 - a_3^2)x_2^4],$$
$$T = (a_0^2 a_3 - 3a_0 a_1 a_2 + 2a_1^3)x_1^6 + (a_0^2 a_4 + 2a_0 a_1 a_3 - 9a_0 a_2^2 + 6a_1^2 a_2)x_1^5 x_2$$
$$+ 5(a_0 a_1 a_4 - 3a_0 a_2 a_3 + 2a_1^2 a_3)x_1^4 x_2^2 + 10(a_1^2 a_4 - a_0 a_3^2)x_1^3 x_2^3$$
$$+ 5(-a_0 a_3 a_4 + 3a_1 a_2 a_4 - 2a_1 a_3^2)x_1^2 x_2^4 \tag{125}$$
$$+ (9a_4 a_2^2 - a_4^2 a_0 - 2a_1 a_3 a_4 - 6a_3^2 a_2)x_1 x_2^5$$
$$+ (3a_2 a_3 a_4 - a_1 a_4^2 - 2a_3^3)x_2^6,$$
$$i = 2(a_0 a_4 - 4a_1 a_3 + 3a_2^2),$$
$$J = 6 \begin{vmatrix} a_0 & a_1 & a_2 \\ a_1 & a_2 & a_3 \\ a_2 & a_3 & a_4 \end{vmatrix} = 6(a_0 a_2 a_4 + 2a_1 a_2 a_3 - a_2^3 - a_0 a_3^2 - a_1^2 a_4).$$

These concomitants may be expressed in terms of the roots by the methods of Chapter III, Section 4, and in terms of the Aronhold symbols by the standard method of transvection. To give a fresh illustration of the latter method we select $T = (f, H) = -(H, f)$. Then

$$(H, f) = ((ab)^2 a_x^2 b_x^2, c_x^4)$$

$$= \frac{(ab)^2}{4} \left[\binom{2}{0}\binom{2}{1} a_x^2 b_x b_y + \binom{2}{1}\binom{2}{0} a_x a_y b_x^2 \right]_{y \sim c} c_x^3$$

$$= \frac{1}{2}(ab)^2 (bc) a_x^2 b_x c_x^3 + \frac{1}{2}(ab)^2 (ac) a_x b_x^2 x_x^3$$

$$= (ab)^2 (ac) a_x b_x^2 c_x^3.$$

Similar processes give the others. We tabulate the complete totality of such results below. The reader will find it very instructive to develop these results in detail.

$$f = a_x^4 = b_x^4 = \ldots,$$
$$H = (ab)^2 a_x^2 b_x^2,$$
$$T = (ab)^2 (ca) a_x b_x^2 c_x^3,$$
$$i = (ab)^4,$$
$$J = (ab)^2 (bc)^2 (ca)^2.$$

Except for numerical factors these may also be written

$$f = \alpha_x^{(1)} \alpha_x^{(2)} \alpha_x^{(3)} \alpha_x^{(4)},$$
$$H = \sum (\alpha_x^{(1)} \alpha_x^{(2)})^2 \alpha_x^{(3)2} \alpha_x^{(4)2},$$
$$T = \sum (\alpha_x^{(1)} \alpha_x^{(2)})^2 (\alpha_x^{(1)} \alpha_x^{(3)}) \alpha_x^{(2)} \alpha_x^{(3)2} \alpha_x^{(4)3}, \tag{126}$$
$$i = \sum (\alpha_x^{(1)} \alpha_x^{(2)})^2 (\alpha_x^{(3)} \alpha_x^{(4)})^2,$$
$$J = \sum (\alpha_x^{(1)} \alpha_x^{(2)})^2 (\alpha_x^{(3)} \alpha_x^{(4)})^2 (\alpha_x^{(3)} \alpha_x^{(1)})(\alpha_x^{(2)} \alpha_x^{(4)}).$$

It should be remarked that the formula (90) for the general rth transvectant of Chapter III, Section 2 may be employed to great advantage in representing concomitants in terms of the roots.

With reference to the reductions given in Table II we shall again derive in detail only such as are typical, to show the power of Gordan's series in performing reductions. The reduction of $(f, H)^2$ has been given above (cf. (124)).

We have

$$(-T, H)^3 = ((H, f), H)^3 = (H, T)^3.$$

Here we employ the series

$$\begin{pmatrix} H & f & H \\ 4 & 4 & 4 \\ 0 & 3 & 1 \end{pmatrix}.$$

This gives

$$\sum_{j=0}^{3} \frac{\binom{3}{j}\binom{3}{j}}{\binom{7-j}{j}} ((H,f)^{1+j}, H)^{3-j} = \sum_{j=0}^{1} \frac{\binom{1}{j}\binom{1}{j}}{\binom{3-j}{j}} ((H,H)^{3+j}, f)^{1-j}.$$

Substitution of the values of the transvectants $(H,f)^r$, $H,H)^4$ gives

$$(H,T)^3 = \frac{1}{24}(-6JH + i^2 f).$$

The series for $(T,T)^2 = ((f,H),T)^2$ is

$$\begin{vmatrix} f & H & T \\ 4 & 4 & 6 \\ 0 & 2 & 1 \end{vmatrix},$$

or

$$((f,H),T)^2 + ((f,H)^2,T) = ((f,T)^2,H) + \frac{2}{3}((f,T)^8,h)^0.$$

But

$$(T,T)^2 = -\frac{1}{72}(i^2 f^2 + 6iH^2 - 12JHf),$$

Hence, making use of the third line in Table II,

$$(T,T)^2 = -\frac{1}{72}(i^2 f^2 + 6iH^2 - 12JHf),$$

which we wished to prove. The reader will find it profitable to perform all of the reductions indicated in Table II by these methods, beginning with the simple cases and proceeding to the more complicated.

4.2 Theorems on Transvectants

We shall now prove a series of very far-reaching theorems on transvectants.

4.2.1 Monomial concomitant a term of a transvectant

Every monomial expression, ϕ, in Aronhold symbolical letters of the type peculiar to the invariant theory, i.e. involving the two types of factors (ab), a_x;

$$\phi = \prod (ab)^p ac^q \dots a_x^\rho b_x^\sigma c_x^\tau \dots,$$

is a term of a determinate transvectant.

In proof let us select some definite symbolical letter as a and in all *determinant* factors of ϕ which involve a set $a_1 = -y_2$, $a_2 = y_1$. Then ϕ may be separated into three factors, *i.e.*

$$\phi' = PQa_x^\rho,$$

78

where Q is an aggregate of factors of the one type b_y, $Q = b_y^3 c_y^t ...$, and P is a symbolical expression of the same general type as the original ϕ but involving one less symbolical letter,

$$p = (bc)^u (bd)^v ... b_x^\sigma c_x^\tau ...$$

Now PQ does not involve a. It is, moreover, a term of some polar whose index r is equal to the order of Q in y. To obtain the form whose rth polar contains the term PQ it is only necessary to let $y = x$ in PQ since the latter will then go back into the original polarized form (Chap. Ill, Section 1, I). Hence ϕ is a term of the result of polarizing $(PQ)_{y=x}r$ times, changing y into a and multiplying this result by a_x^p. Hence by the standard method of transvection ϕ is a term of the transvectant

$$((PQ)_{y=x}, a_x^{r+p})^r \quad (r + p = m). \tag{127}$$

For illustration consider

$$\phi = (ab)^2 (ac)(bc) a_x b_x c_x^2$$

Placing $a \sim y$ in $(ab)^2(ac)$ we have

$$\phi' = -b_y^2 c_y^2 (bc) b_x c_x^2 \cdot a_x$$

Placing $y \sim x$ in ϕ' we obtain

$$\phi'' = -(bc) b_x^3 c_x^3 a_x.$$

Thus ϕ is a term of

$$A = (-(bc) b_x^3 c_x^3, a_x^4)^3.$$

In fact the complete transvectant A is

$$+A = -\frac{1}{20}(bc)(ca)^3 a_x b_x^3 - \frac{9}{20}(bc)(ca)^2(ba) a_x b_x^2 c_x - \frac{9}{20}(bc)(ca)(ba)^2 a_x b_x c_x^2 - \frac{1}{20}(bc)(ba)^3 a_x c_x^3$$

and ϕ is its third term.

DEFINITION.

The mechanical rule by which one obtains the transvectant $(ab)a_x^{m-1} b_x^{m-1}$ from the product $a_x^m b_x^m$, consisting of folding one letter from each symbolical form a_x^m, b_x^m into a determinant (ab) and diminishing exponents by unity, is called *convolution*. Thus one may obtain $(ab)^2(ac)a_x b_x^2 c_x^3$ from $(ab)a_x^3 b_x^3 c_x^4$ by convolution.

4.2.2 Theorem on the difference between two terms of a transvectant.

Theorem. *(1) The difference between any two terms of a transvectant is equal to a sum of terms each of which is a term of a transvectant of lower index of forms obtained from the forms in the original transvectant by convolution.*

(2) The difference between the whole transvectant and one of its terms is equal to a sum of terms each of which is a term of a transvectant of lower index of forms obtained from the original forms by convolution (Gordan).

In proof of this theorem we consider the process of constructing the formula for the general rth transvectant in Chapter III, Section 5. In particular we examine the structure of a transvectant-like formula (89). Two terms of this or of any transvectant are said to be *adjacent* when they differ only in the arrangement of the letters in a pair of symbolical factors. An examination of a formula such as (89) shows that two terms can be adjacent in any one of three ways, viz.:

$$(1)\ P(\alpha^{(i)}\beta^{(j)})(\alpha^{(h)}\beta^{(k)}) \text{ and } P(\alpha^{(t)}\beta^{(k)})(\alpha^{(h)}\beta^{(j)}),$$
$$(2)\ P(\alpha^{(i)}\beta^{(j)})\alpha_x^{(h)} \text{ and } P(\alpha^{(h)}\beta^{(j)})\alpha_x^{(i)},$$
$$(3)\ P(\alpha^{(i)}\beta^{(j)})\beta_x^{(k)} \text{ and } P(\alpha^{(i)}\beta^{(k)})\beta_x^{(j)},$$

where P involves symbols from both forms f, g as a rule, and both types of symbolical factors.

The differences between the adjacent terms are in these cases respectively

$$(1)\ P(\alpha^{(i)}\alpha^{(h)})(\beta^{(j)}\beta^{(k)}),$$
$$(2)\ P(\alpha^{(i)}\alpha^{(h)})\beta_x^{(j)},$$
$$(3)\ P(\beta^{(k)}\beta^{(j)})\alpha_x^{(i)}.$$

These follow directly from the reduction identities, *i.e.* from formulas (99), (100).

Now, taking f, g to be slightly more comprehensive than in (89), let

$$f = A\alpha_x^{(1)}\alpha_x^{(2)}\ldots\alpha_x^{(m)},$$
$$g = B\beta_x^{(1)}\beta_x^{(2)}\ldots\beta_x^{(n)},$$

where A and B involve only factors of the first type $(\gamma\delta)$. Then formula (90) holds true;

$$(f,g)^\tau = \frac{1}{\tau!\binom{m}{\tau}\binom{n}{\tau}}\sum\left[\frac{(\alpha^{(1)}\beta^{(1)})(\alpha^{(2)}\beta^{(2)})\ldots(\alpha^{(\tau)}\beta^{(\tau)})}{\alpha_x^{(1)}\alpha_x^{(2)}\ldots\alpha_x^{(\tau)}\beta_x^{(1)}\beta_x^{(2)}\ldots\beta_x^{(\tau)}}fg\right].$$

and the difference between any two adjacent terms of $(f,g)^\tau$ is a term in which at least one factor of type $(\alpha\beta)$ is replaced by one of type $(\alpha\alpha')$ or of type $(\beta\beta')$. There then remain in the term only $\tau - 1$ factors of type $(\alpha\beta)$. Hence this difference is a term of a transvectant of lower index of forms obtained from the original forms f, g by convolution.

For illustration, two adjacent terms of $((ab)^2 a_x^2 b_x^2, c_x^4)^2$ are

$$(ab)^2(ac)^2 b_x^2 c_x^2, (ab)^2(ac)(bc)a_x b_x c_x^2.$$

The difference between these terms, viz. $(ab)^3(ac)b_x c_x^3$, is a term of

$$((ab)^3 a_x b_x, c_x^4),$$

and the first form of this latter transvectant may be obtained from $(ab)^2 a_x^2 b_x^2$ by convolution.

Now let t_1, t_2 be any two terms of $(f, g)^\tau$. Then we may place between t_1, t_2 a series of terms of $(f, g)^\tau$ such that any term of the series,

$$t_1, t_{11}, t_{12}, \ldots, t_{1i}, t_2$$

is adjacent to those on either side of it. For it is always possible to obtain t_2 from t_1 by a finite number of interchanges of pairs of letters,–a *pair* being composed either of two α's or else of two β's. But

$$t_1 - t_2 = (t_1 - t_{11}) + (t_{11} - t_{12}) + \ldots + (t_1 - t_2),$$

and all differences on the right are differences between *adjacent* terms, for which the theorem was proved above. Thus the part (1) of the theorem is proved for all types of terms.

Next if t is any term of $(f, g)^\tau$, we have, since the number of terms of this transvectant is

$$r! \binom{m}{r}\binom{n}{r},$$

$$(f, g)^\tau - t = \frac{1}{r!\binom{m}{r}\binom{n}{r}} \sum t' - t \tag{128}$$

$$= \frac{1}{r!\binom{m}{r}\binom{n}{r}} \sum (t' - t),$$

and by the first part of the theorem and on account of the form of the right-hand member of the last formula this is equal to a linear expression of terms of transvectants of lower index of forms obtained from f, g by convolution.

4.2.3 Difference between a transvectant and one of its terms.

The difference between any transvectant and one of its terms is a linear combination of transvectants of lower index of forms obtained from the original forms by convolution.

Formula (128) shows that any term equals the transvectant of which it is a term plus terms of transvectants of lower index. Take one of the latter terms and apply the same result (128) to it. It equals the transvectant of index $s < \tau$ of which it is a term plus terms of transvectant of index $< s$ of forms obtained from the original forms by convolution. Repeating these steps we arrive at transvectants of index 0 between forms derived from the original forms by convolution, and so after not more than τ applications of this process the right-hand side of (128) is reduced to the type of expression described in the theorem.

Now on account of the Theorem I of this section we may go one step farther. As proved there *every* monomial symbolical expression is a term of a determinate transvectant one of whose forms is the simple $f = a_x^m$ of degree-order $(1, m)$. Since the only convolution applicable to the form a_x^m is the vacuous convolution producing a_x^m itself, Theorem III gives the following result:

Let ϕ be any monomial expression in the symbols of a single form f, and let some symbol a occur in precisely r determinant factors. Then ϕ equals a linear combination of transvectants of index $\leqq r$ of a_x^m and forms obtained from $(PQ)_{x=y}$ (cf. (127)) by convolution.

For illustration

$$\phi = (ab)^2 (bc)^2 a_x^2 c_x^2 = ((ab)^2 a_x^2 b_x^2 c_x^4)^2 - ((ab)^3 a_x b_x, c_x^4) + \frac{1}{3}((ab)^4, c_x^4)^0.$$

It may also be noted that $(PQ)_{y=x}$ and all forms obtained from it by convolution are of degree one less than the degree of ϕ in the coefficients of f. Hence by reasoning inductively from the degrees 1, 2 to the degree i we have the result:

Theorem. *Every concomitant of degree i of a form f is given by transvectants of the type*

$$(C_{i-1}, f)^i,$$

where the forms C_{i-1} are all concomitants of f of degree $i - 1$. (See Chap. III, §2, VII.)

4.3 Reduction of Transvectant Systems

We proceed to apply some of these theorems.

4.3.1 Reducible transvectants of a special type. $(C_{i-1}, f)^i$.

The theorem given in the last paragraph of Section 2 will now be amplified by another proof. Suppose that the complete set of irreducible concomitants of degrees $< i$ of a single form is known. Let these be

$$f, \gamma_1, \gamma_2, \cdots, \gamma_k,$$

and let it be required to find all irreducible concomitants of degree i. The only concomitant of degree unity is $f = a_x^m$. All of degree 2 are given by

$$(f, f)^\tau = (ab)^\tau a_x^{m-\tau} b_x^{m-\tau},$$

where, of course, τ is even. A covariant of degree i is an aggregate of symbolical products each containing i symbols. Let C_i be one of these products, and a one of the symbols. Then by Section 2 C_i is a term of a transvectant

$$(C_{i-1}, x_x^m)^i,$$

where C_{i-1} is a symbolical monomial containing $i - 1$ symbols, *i.e.* of degree $i - 1$. Hence by Theorem II of Section 2,

$$C_i = (C_{i-1}, f)^i + \sum (\bar{C}_{i-1} f)^{j'} \, (j' < j), \tag{129}$$

where $\bar{C}_{i-1}$ is a monomial derived from C_{i-1} by convolution. Now C_{i-1}, $\bar{C}_{i-1}$ being of degree $i-1$ are rational integral expressions in the irreducible forms $f, \gamma_1, \ldots, \gamma_k$. That is they are polynomials in $f, \gamma_1, \ldots, \gamma_k$, the terms of which are of the type

$$\phi_{i-1} = f^a \gamma_1^{a_1} \cdots \gamma_k^{a_k}.$$

Hence C_i is a sum of transvectants of the type

$$(\phi_{i-1}, f)^i (j \leqq m),$$

and since any covariant of f, of degree i is a linear combination of terms of the type of C_i, all concomitants of degree i are expressible in terms of transvectants of the type

$$(\phi_{i-1}, f)^i, \tag{130}$$

where ϕ_{i-1} is a monomial expression in $f, \gamma_1, \ldots, \gamma_k$, of degree $i-1$, as just explained.

In order to find all *irreducible* concomitants of a stated degree i we need now to develop a method of finding what transvectants of (130) are reducible in terms of $f, \gamma_1, \ldots, \gamma_k$. With this end in view let $\phi_{i-1} = \rho\sigma$, where ρ, σ are also monomials in $f, \gamma_1, \ldots, \gamma_k$, of degrees $< i-1$. Let ρ be a*form of order n_1; $p = p_x^{n_1}$, and $\sigma = \sigma_x^{n_2}$. Then assume that $j \leqq n_2$, the order of σ. Hence we have

$$(\phi_{i-1}, f)^j = (p_x^{n_1} \sigma_x^{n_2}, a_x^m)^j.$$

Then in the ordinary way by the standard method of transvection we have the following:

$$(\phi_{i-1}, f)_j = K\{p_x^{n_1} \sigma_x^{n_2-j} \sigma_y^j\}_{y=a} a_x^{m-j} + \cdots$$
$$= Kp(\sigma, f)^j + \cdots . \tag{131}$$

Hence if p_2 now represents $(\sigma, f)^j$, then pp_2 is a term of (ϕ_{i-1}, f), so that

$$(\phi_{i-1}, f)^j = pp_2 + \sum (\bar{\phi}_{i-1}, f)^{j_2'} (j' < j). \tag{132}$$

Evidently p, p_2 are both covariants of degree /lti and hence are reducible in terms of $f, \gamma_1, \cdots, \gamma_k$. Now we have the right to assume that we are constructing the irreducible concomitants of degree i by proceeding from transvectants of a stated index to those of the next higher index, *i.e.* we assume these transvectants to be *ordered* according to increasing indices. This being true, all of the transvectants $(\phi_{i-1}, f)^{j'}$ at the stage of the investigation indicated by (132) will be known in terms of $f, \gamma_1, \cdots, \gamma_k$ or known to be irreducible, those that are so, since j'/ltj. Hence (132) shows (ϕ_{i-1}, f) to be reducible since it is a polynomial in $f, \gamma_1, \cdots, \gamma_k$ and such concomitants of degree i as are already known.

The principal conclusion from this discussion therefore is that irreducible concomitants of degree i are obtained only from transvectants $(\phi_{i-1}, f)^j$ for which no factor of order $\geqq j$ occurs in ϕ_{i-1}. Thus for instance if $m = 4$, $(f^2, f)^j$ is reducible for all values of j since f^2 contains the factor f of order 4 and j cannot exceed 4.

We note that if a form γ is an invariant it may be omitted when we form ϕ_{i-1}, for if it is present $(\phi_{i-1}, f)^j$ will be reducible by (80).

83

4.3.2 Fundamental systems of cubic and quartic.

Let $m = 3$ (cf. Table I). Then $f = a_x^3$ is the only concomitant of degree 1. There is one of degree 2, the Hessian $(f, f)^2 = \Delta$. Now all forms ϕ_2 of $(\phi_2, f)^j$ are included in

$$\phi_2 = f^\alpha \Delta^\beta,$$

and either $\alpha = 2, \beta = 0$, or $\alpha = 0, \beta = 1$. But $(f^2, f)^j$ is reducible for all values of j since f^2 contains the factor f of order 3 and $j \not> 3$. Hence the only transvectants which could give irreducible concomitants of degree 3 are

$$(\Delta, f)^j \ (j = 1, 2).$$

But $(\Delta, f)^2 = 0$ (cf. Table I). In fact the series

$$\begin{pmatrix} f & f & f \\ 3 & 3 & 3 \\ 1 & 2 & 1 \end{pmatrix}$$

gives $\frac{1}{2}((f, f)^2, f)^2 = -((f, f)^2, f)^2 \equiv -(\Delta, f)^2 = 0$. Hence there is one irreducible covariant of degree 3, $e.g.$

$$(\Delta, f) = -Q.$$

Proceeding to the degree 4, there are three possibilities for ϕ_3 in $(\phi_3, f)^j$. These are $\phi_3 = f^3, f\Delta, Q$. Since $j \not> 3$ $(f^3, f)^j, (f\Delta, f)^j (j = 1, 2, 3)$ are all reducible by Section 3, I. Of $(Q, f)^j (j = 1, 2, 3), (Q, f)^2 = 0$, as has been proved before (cf. (102)), and $(Q, f) = \frac{1}{2}\Delta^2$ by the Gordan series (cf. Table I)

$$\begin{pmatrix} f & \Delta & f \\ 3 & 2 & 3 \\ 0 & 1 & 1 \end{pmatrix}.$$

Hence $(Q, f)^3 = -R$ is the only irreducible case. Next the degree 5 must be treated. We may have

$$\phi_4 = f^4, f^2\Delta, fQ, R, \Delta^2.$$

But R is an invariant, Δ is of order 2, and Q of order 3. Hence since $j \not> 3$ in $(\phi_4, f)^j$ the only possibility for an irreducible form is $(\Delta^2, f)^j$, and this is reducible by the principle of I if $j < 3$. But

$$(\Delta^2, f)^3 = (\delta_x^2 \delta_x'^2, a_x^3)^3 = (\delta a)^2 (\delta' a)\delta_x' = (\delta_x'^2, (\delta a)^2 a_x) = 0.$$

For $(\delta a)^2 a_x = (\Delta, f)^2 = 0$, as shown above. Hence there are no irreducible concomitants of degree 5. It immediately follows that there are none of degree > 5, either, since ϕ_5 in $(\phi_5, f)^j$ is a more complicated monomial than ϕ_4 in the same forms f, Δ, Q and all the resulting concomitants have been proved reducible.

Consequently the complete irreducible system of concomitants of f, which may be called the *fundamental system* (Salmon) of f is

$$f, \Delta, Q, R.$$

Next let us derive the system for the quartic f; $m = 4$. The concomitants of degree 2 are $(f, f)^2 = H, (f, f)^4 = i$. Those of degree 3 are to be found from

$$(H, f)^j \, (j = 1, 2, 3, 4).$$

Of these $(f, H) = T$ and is irreducible; $(f, H)^4 = J$ is irreducible, and, as has been proved, $(H, f)^2 = \frac{1}{6} i f$ (cf. (124)). Also from the series

$$\begin{pmatrix} f & f & f \\ 4 & 4 & 4 \\ 1 & 3 & 1 \end{pmatrix},$$

$(H, f)^3 = 0$. For the degree four we have in $(\phi_3, f)^j$

$$\phi_3 = f^3, fH, T,$$

all of which contain factors of order $\geqq j \not> 4$ except T. From Table II all of the transvectants $(T, f)^j \, (j = 1, 2, 3, 4)$ are reducible or vanish, as has been, or may be proved by Gordan's series. Consider one case; $(T, f)^4$. Applying the series

$$\begin{pmatrix} f & H & f \\ 4 & 4 & 4 \\ 1 & 3 & 1 \end{pmatrix},$$

we obtain

$$((f, H), f)^4 = -((f, H)^2, f)^3 - \frac{3}{10}((f, H)^3, f)^2.$$

But $((f, H)^2, f)^3 = \frac{1}{6} i(f, f)^3 = 0$; and $(f, H)^3 = 0$ from the proof above. Hence

$$((f, H), f)^4 = (T, f)^4 = 0.$$

There are no other irreducible forms since ϕ_4 in $(\phi_4, f)^i$ will be a monomial in f, H, T more complicated than ϕ_3. Hence the fundamental system of f consists of

$$f, H, T, i, J;$$

It is worthy of note that this has been completely derived by the principles of this section together with Gordan's series.

4.3.3 Reducible transvectants in general.

In the transvectants studied in (I) of this section, e.g. $(\phi_{i-1}, f)^i$, the second form is simple, $f = a_x^m$, of the first degree. It is possible and now desirable to extend those methods of proving certain transvectants to be reducible to the more general case where both forms in the transvectants are monomials in other concomitants of lesser degree.

Consider two systems of binary forms, an (A) system and a (B) system. Let the forms of these systems be

(A): $A_1, A_2, \ldots, A_k$, of orders $a_1, a_2, \ldots, a_k$ respectively;

and

(B): $B_1, B_2, \ldots, B_l$, of orders $b_1, b_2, \ldots, b_k$ respectively.

Suppose these forms expressed in the Aronhold symbolism and let

$$\phi = A_1^{\alpha_1} A_2^{\alpha_2} \ldots A_k^{\alpha_k}, \psi = B_1^{\beta_1} B_2^{\beta_2}, \ldots B_l^{\beta_l}.$$

Then a system (C) is said to be the system derived by transvection from (A) and (B) when it includes all terms in all transvectants of the type

$$(\phi, \psi)^i. \tag{133}$$

Evidently the problem of reducibility presents itself for analysis immediately. For let

$$\phi = \rho\sigma, \psi = \mu\nu,$$

and suppose that j can be separated into two integers,

$$j = j_1 + j_2,$$

such that the transvectants

$$(\rho, \mu)^{i_1}, (\sigma, \nu)^{i_2}$$

both exist and are different from zero. Then the process employed in proving formula (132) shows directly that $(\phi, \psi)^i$ contains terms which are products of terms of $(\rho, \mu)^{i_1}$ and terms of $(\sigma, \nu)^{i_2}$, that is, contains reducible terms.

In order to discover what transvectants of the (C) system contain reducible terms we employ an extension of the method of Paragraph (I) of this section. This may be adequately explained in connection with two special systems

$$(A) = f, (B) = i,$$

where f is a cubic and i is a quadratic. Here

$$(C) = (\phi, \psi)^i = (f^\alpha, i^\beta)^i.$$

Since f^α must not contain a factor of order $\geq j$, we have

$$3\alpha - 3 < j \leq 3\alpha; j = 3\alpha, 3\alpha - 1, 3\alpha - 2.$$

Also

$$2\beta - 2 < j \leq 2\beta; j = 2\beta, 2\beta - 1.$$

Consistent with these conditions we have

$$(f, i), (f, i)^2, (f, i^2)^3, (f^2, i^2)^4, (f^2, i^3)^5, (f^2, i^3)^6, (f^3, i^4)^7, (f^3, i^4)^8, (f^3, i^5)^9, \ldots.$$

Of these, $(f^2, i^2)^4$ contains terms of the product $(f, i)^2(f, i)^2$, that is, reducible terms. Also $(f^2, i^3)^5$ is reducible by $(f, i)^2\ (f, i^2)^3$. In the same way $(f^3, i^4)^7$, ...all contain reducible terms. Hence the transvectants of (C) which do not contain reducible terms are six in number, viz.

$$f, i, (f, i), (f, i)^2, (f, i^2)^3, (f^2, i^3)^6.$$

The reader will find it very instructive to find for other and more complicated (A) and (B) systems the transvectants of (C) which do not contain reducible terms. It will be found that the irreducible transvectants are in all cases finite in number. This will be proved as a theorem in the next chapter.

4.4 Syzygies

We can prove that m is a superior limit to the number of functionally independent invariants and covariants of a single binary form $f = a_x^m$ of order m. The totality of independent relations which can and do subsist among the quantities

$$x_1, x_2, x_1', x_2', \alpha_i', \alpha_i(i = 0, \ldots, m), \lambda_1, \lambda_2, \mu_1, \mu_2, M = (\lambda\mu)$$

are $m + 4$ in number. These are

$$\alpha_i' = \alpha_\lambda^{m-i}\alpha_\mu^i(i = 0, \ldots, m); x_1 = \lambda_1 x_1' + \mu_1 x_2', x_2 = \lambda_2 x_1' + \mu_2 x_2';$$

$$M = \lambda_1\mu_2 - \lambda_2\mu_1.$$

When one eliminates from these relations the four variables $\lambda_1, \lambda_2, \mu_1, \mu_2$ there result at most m relations. This is the maximum number of equations which can exist between $\alpha_i', \alpha_i(i = 0, \ldots, m), x_1, x_2, x_1', x_2'$, and M. That is, if a greater number of relations between the latter quantities are assumed, extraneous conditions, not implied in the invariant problem, are imposed upon the coefficients and variables. But a concomitant relation

$$\phi(\alpha_0', \ldots, \alpha_m', x_1', x_2') = M^k\phi(\alpha_0, \ldots, \alpha_m, x_1, x_2)$$

is an equation in the transformed coefficients and variables, the untransformed coefficients and variables and M. Hence there cannot be more than m algebraically independent concomitants as stated.

Now the fundamental system of a cubic contains four concomitants which are such that no one of them is a rational integral function of the remaining three. The present theory shows, however, that there must be a relation between the four which will give one as a function of the other three although this function is not a rational integral function. Such a relation is called a syzygy (Cayley). Since the fundamental system of a quartic contains five members these must also be connected by one syzygy. We shall discover that the fundamental system of a quintic contains twenty-three members. The number of syzygies for a form of high order is accordingly very large. In fact it is possible to deduce a complete set of syzygies for such a form in several ways. There is, for instance, a class of theorems on Jacobians which furnishes an advantageous method of constructing syzygies. We proceed to prove these theorems.

4.4.1   Reducibility of $((f,g),h)$.

Theorem. *If f, g, h are three binary forms, of respective orders n, m, p all greater than unity, the iterated Jacobian $((f,g),h)$ is reducible.*

The three series

$$\begin{pmatrix} f & g & h \\ n & m & p \\ 0 & 1 & 1 \end{pmatrix},$$

$$\begin{pmatrix} h & f & g \\ p & n & m \\ 0 & 1 & 1 \end{pmatrix},$$

$$\begin{pmatrix} g & h & f \\ m & p & n \\ 0 & 1 & 1 \end{pmatrix}$$

give the respective results

$$((f,g),h) = ((f,h),g) + \frac{p-1}{n+p-2}(f,h)^2 g - \frac{m-1}{m+n-2}(f,g)^2 h,$$

$$-((h,f),g) = -((h,g),f) - \frac{m-1}{m+p-2}(h,g)^2 f + \frac{n-1}{n+p-2}(h,f)^2 g,$$

$$((g,h),f) = ((g,f),h) + \frac{n-1}{m+n-2}(g,f)^2 h - \frac{p-1}{m+p-2}(g,h)^2 f.$$

We add these equations and divide through by 2, noting that $(f,g) = -(g,f)$, and obtain

$$((f,g),h) = \frac{n-m}{2(m+n-2)}(f,g)^2 h + \frac{1}{2}(f,h)^2 g - \frac{1}{2}(g,h)^2 f. \tag{134}$$

This formula constitutes the proof of the theorem. It may also be proved readily by transvection and the use of reduction identity (101).

4.4.2   Product of two Jacobians.

Theorem. *If $e = a_x^m, f = b_x^n, g = c_x^p, h = d_x^q$ are four binary forms of orders greater than unity, then*

$$(e,f)(g,h) = -\frac{1}{2}(e,g)^2 fh + \frac{1}{2}(e,h)^2 fg + \frac{1}{2}(f,g)^2 eh - \frac{1}{2}(f,g)^2 eg. \tag{135}$$

We first prove two new symbolical identities. By an elementary rule for expanding determinants

$$\begin{vmatrix} a_1^2 & a_1 a_2 & a_2^2 \\ b_1^2 & b_1 b_2 & b_2^2 \\ c_1^2 & c_1 c_2 & c_2^2 \end{vmatrix} = -(ab)(bc)(ca).$$

Hence

$$\begin{vmatrix} a_1^2 & a_1 a_2 & a_2^2 \\ b_1^2 & b_1 b_2 & b_2^2 \\ c_1^2 & c_1 c_2 & c_2^2 \end{vmatrix} \begin{vmatrix} d_2^2 & -2d_2 d_2 & d_1^2 \\ e_2^2 & -2e_2 e_1 & e_1^2 \\ f_2^2 & -2f_2 f_1 & f_1^2 \end{vmatrix}$$

$$= 2(ab)(bc)(ca)(de)(ef)(fd)$$

$$= \begin{vmatrix} (ad)^2 & (ae)^2 & (af)^2 \\ (bd)^2 & (be)^2 & (bf)^2 \\ (cd)^2 & (ce)^2 & (cf)^2 \end{vmatrix}. \tag{136}$$

In this identity set $c_1 = -x_2, c_2 = x_1, f_1 = -x_2, f_2 = x_1$.

Then (136) gives the identity.

$$2(ab)(de)a_x b_x d_x e_x = \begin{vmatrix} (ad)^2 & (ae)^2 & a_x^2 \\ (bd)^2 & (be)^2 & b_x^2 \\ d_x^2 & e_x^2 & 0 \end{vmatrix}. \tag{137}$$

We now have

$$(e,f)(g,h) = (a,b)(c,d)a_x^{m-1} b_x^{n-1} c_x^{p-1} d_x^{q-1}$$

$$= \frac{1}{2} a_x^{m-2} b_x^{n-2} c_x^{p-2} d_x^{q-2} \begin{vmatrix} (ac)^2 & (ad)^2 & a_x^2 \\ (bc)^2 & (bd)^2 & b_x^2 \\ c_x^2 & d_x^2 & 0 \end{vmatrix}$$

by (137). Expanding the right-hand side we have formula (135) immediately.

4.5 The square of a Jacobian.

The square of a Jacobian $J = (f, g)$ is given by the formula

$$-2J^2 = (f,f)^2 g^2 + (g,g)^2 f^2 - 2(f,g)^2 fg. \tag{138}$$

This follows directly from (135) by the replacements

$$e = f, f = g, g = f, h = g.$$

4.5.1 Syzygies for the cubic and quartic forms.

In formula (138) let us make the replacements $J = Q, f = f, g = \Delta$, where f is a cubic, Δ is its Hessian, and Q is the Jacobian (f, Δ). Then by Table I

$$S = 2Q^2 + \Delta^3 + RF^2 = 0. \tag{139}$$

This is the required syzygy connecting the members of the fundamental system of the cubic.

Next let f, H, T, i, J be the fundamental system of a quartic f. Then, since T is a Jacobian, let $J = T, f = f, g = H$ in (138), and we have

$$-2T^2 = H^3 - 2(f,H)^2 fH + (H,H)^2 f^2.$$

But by Table II

$$(f, H)^2 = \frac{1}{6}if, (H, H)^2 = \frac{1}{6}(2Jf - iH).$$

Hence we obtain

$$S = 2T^2 + H^3 - \frac{1}{2}if^2 H + \frac{1}{3}Jf^3 = 0. \tag{140}$$

This is the syzygy connecting the members of the fundamental system of the quartic.

Of the twenty-three members of a system of the quintic nine are expressible as Jacobians (cf. Table IV, Chap. VI). If these are combined in pairs and substituted in (135), and substituted singly in (138), there result 45 syzygies of the type just derived. For references on this subject the reader may consult Meyer's "Bericht ueber den gegenwärtigen Stand der Invariantentheorie" in the Jahresbericht der Deutschen Mathematiker-Vereinigung for 1890-91.

4.5.2 Syzygies derived from canonical forms.

We shall prove that the binary cubic form,

$$f = a_0 x_1^3 + 3a_1 x_1^2 x_2 + 3a_2 x_1 x_2^2 + a_3 x_2^3,$$

may be reduced to the form,

$$f = X^3 + Y^3,$$

by a linear transformation with non-vanishing modulus. In general a binary quantic f of order m has $m + 1$ coefficients. If it is transformed by

$$T : x_1 = \lambda_1 x_1' + \mu_1 x_2', x2 = \lambda_2 x_1' + \mu_2 x_2',$$

four new quantities $\lambda_1, \mu_1, \lambda_2, \mu_2$ are involved in the coefficients of f'. Hence no binary form of order m with less than $m - 3$ arbitrary coefficients can be the transformed of a general quantic of order TO by a linear transformation. Any quantic of order m having just $m - 3$ arbitrary quantities involved in its coefficients and which can be proved to be the transformed of the general form f by a linear transformation of non-vanishing modulus is called a canonical form of f. We proceed to reduce the cubic form f to the canonical form $X^3 + Y^3$. Assume

$$f = a_0 x_1^3 + \ldots = p_1(x_1 + \alpha_1 x_2)^3 + p_2(x_1 + \alpha_2 x_2)^3 = X^3 + Y^3. \tag{140$_1$}$$

This requires that f be transformable into its canonical form by the inverse of the transformations

$$S : X = p_1^{\frac{1}{3}}\chi_1 + p_1^{\frac{1}{3}}\alpha_1\chi_1, Y = p_2^{\frac{1}{3}}\chi_1 + p_2^{\frac{1}{3}}\alpha_2\chi_2.$$

We must now show that $p_1, p_2, \alpha_1, \alpha_2$ may actually be determined, and that the determination is unique. Equating coefficients in (140_1) we have

$$\begin{aligned}
p_1 + p_2 &= \alpha_0, \\
\alpha_1 p_1 + \alpha_2 p_2 &= \alpha_1, \\
\alpha_1^2 p_1 + \alpha_2^2 p_2 &= \alpha_2, \\
\alpha_1^3 p_1 + \alpha_2^3 p_2 &= \alpha_3.
\end{aligned} \tag{140_2}$$

Hence the following matrix, M, must be of rank 2:

$$M = \begin{vmatrix} 1 & \alpha_1 & \alpha_1^2 & \alpha_1^3 \\ 1 & \alpha_2 & \alpha_2^2 & \alpha_2^3 \\ \alpha_0 & \alpha_1 & \alpha_2 & \alpha_3 \end{vmatrix}$$

From $M = 0$ result

$$\begin{vmatrix} 1 & \alpha_1 & \alpha_1^2 \\ 1 & \alpha_2 & \alpha_2^2 \\ \alpha_0 & \alpha_1 & \alpha_2 \end{vmatrix} = 0, \qquad \begin{vmatrix} 1 & \alpha_1 & \alpha_1^2 \\ 1 & \alpha_2 & \alpha_2^2 \\ \alpha_1 & \alpha_2 & \alpha_3 \end{vmatrix} = 0.$$

Expanding the determinants we have

$$\begin{aligned}
P\alpha_0 + Q\alpha_1 + R\alpha_2 &= 0, \\
P\alpha_1 + Q\alpha_2 + R\alpha_3 &= 0,
\end{aligned}$$

Also, evidently

$$P + Q\alpha_i + R\alpha_i^2 = 0 \,(i = 1, 2)$$

Therefore our conditions will all be consistent if α_1, α_2 are determined as the roots, $\xi_1 \div \xi_2$, of

$$\frac{1}{2}\Delta \equiv \begin{vmatrix} \alpha_0 & \alpha_1 & \alpha_2 \\ \alpha_1 & \alpha_2 & \alpha_3 \\ \xi_2^2 & -\xi_1\xi_2 & \xi_1^2 \end{vmatrix} = 0.$$

This latter determinant is evidently the Hessian of f, divided by 2. Thus the complete reduction of f to its canonical form is accomplished by solving its Hessian covariant for the roots α_1, α_2, and then solving the first two equations of (140_2) for p_1, p_2. The inverse of S will then transform f into $X^3 + Y^3$. The determinant of S is

$$D = (p_1 \cdot p_2)^{\frac{1}{3}} (\alpha_2 - \alpha_1),$$

and $D \neq 0$ unless the Hessian has equal roots. Thus the necessary and sufficient condition in order that the canonical reduction be possible is that the discriminant of the Hessian (which is also the discriminant, R, of the cubic f) should not vanish. If $R = 0$, a canonical form of f is evidently $X^2 Y$.

Among the problems that can be solved by means of the canonical form are, (a) the determination of the roots of the cubic $f = 0$ from

$$X^3 + Y^3 = (X + Y)(X + \omega Y)(X + \omega^2 Y).$$

ω being an imaginary cube root of unity, and (b) the determination of the syzygy among the concomitants of f. We now solve problem (b). From Table I, by substituting $\alpha_0 = \alpha_3 = 1, \alpha_1 = \alpha_2 = 0$, we have the fundamental system of the canonical form:

$$X^3 + Y^3, 2XY, X^3 - Y^3, -2.$$

Now we may regard the original form f to be the transformed form of $X^3 + Y^3$ under S. Hence, since the modulus of S is D, we have the four invariant relations

$$f = X^3 + Y^3,$$
$$\Delta = 2D^2 XY,$$
$$Q = D^3(X^3 - Y^3),$$
$$R = -D^6 \cdot 2.$$

It is an easy process to eliminate D, X, Y from these four equations. The result is the required syzygy:

$$f^2 R + 2Q^2 + \Delta^3 = 0$$

A general binary quartic can be reduced to the canonical form (Cayley)

$$X^4 + Y^4 + 6mX^2 Y^2;$$

a ternary cubic to the form (Hesse)

$$X^3 + Y^3 + Z^3 + 6mXYZ.$$

An elegant reduction of the binary quartic to its canonical form may be obtained by means of the provectant operators of Chapter III, Section 1, V. We observe that we are to have identically

$$f = (a_0, a_1, \ldots, a_4)(x_1, x_2)^4 = X_1^4 + X_2^4 + 6mX_1^2 X_2^2,$$

where X_1, X_2 are linear in x_1, x_2;

$$X_1 = \alpha_1 x_1 + \alpha_2 x_2, X_2 = \beta_1 x_1 + \beta_2 x_2.$$

Let the quadratic $X_1 X_2$ be $q = (A_0, A_1, A_2)(x_1, x_2)^2$. Then

$$\partial q \cdot X_j^4 = (A_0, A_1, A_2) \left(\frac{\partial}{\partial x_2}, -\frac{\partial}{\partial x_1} \right)^2 X_j^4 = 0 \ (j = 1, 2).$$

$$6m\partial q \cdot X_1^2 X_2^2 = 12 \cdot 2(4A_0 A_2 - A_1^2)mX_1 X_2 = 12\lambda X_1 X_2.$$

Equating the coefficients of $x_1^2, x_1 x_2, x_2^2$ in the first equation above, after operating on both sides by ∂q, we now have

$$A_0 a_2 - A_1 a_1 + A_2 a_0 = \lambda A_0,$$

$$A_0 a_3 - A_1 a_2 + A_2 a_1 = \frac{1}{2}\lambda A_0,$$

$$A_0 a_4 - A_1 a_3 + A_2 a_2 = \lambda A_2.$$

Forming the eliminant of these we have an equation which determines λ, and therefore m, in terms of the coefficients of the original quartic f. This eliminant is

$$\begin{vmatrix} a_0 & a_1 & a_2 - \lambda \\ a_1 & a_2 + \frac{1}{2}\lambda & a_3 \\ a_2 - \lambda & a_3 & a_4 \end{vmatrix} = 0,$$

or, after expanding it,

$$\lambda^3 - \frac{1}{2}i\lambda - \frac{1}{3}J = 0,$$

where i, J are the invariants of the quartic f determined in Chapter III, §1, V. It follows that the proposed reduction of f to its canonical form can be made in three ways.

A problem which was studied by Sylvester,[2] the reduction of the binary sextic to the form

$$X_1^6 + x_2^6 + X_3^6 + 30m X_1^2 X_2^2 X_3^2,$$

has been completely solved very recently by E. K. Wakeford.[3]

4.6 Hilbert's Theorem

We shall now prove a very extraordinary theorem due to Hilbert on the reduction of systems of quantics, which is in many ways closely connected with the theory of syzygies. The proof here given is by Gordan. The original proof of Hilbert may be consulted in his memoir in the Mathematische Annalen, volume 36.

4.6.1 Theorem

Theorem. *If a homogeneous algebraical function of any number of variables be formed according to any definite laws, then, although there may be an infinite number of functions F satisfying the conditions laid down, nevertheless a finite number $F_1, F_2, \ldots, F_r$ can always be found so that any other F can be written in the form*

$$F = A_1 F_1 + A_2 F_2 + \cdots + A_r F_r,$$

where the A's are homogeneous integral functions of the variables but do not necessarily satisfy the conditions for the F's.

An illustration of the theorem is the particular theorem that the equation of any curve which passes through the intersections of two curves $F_1 = 0$, $F_2 = 0$ is of the form

$$F = A_1 F_1 + A_2 F_2 = 0.$$

Here the law according to which the F's are constructed is that the corresponding curve shall pass through the stated intersections. There are an infinite number of functions satisfying this law, all expressible as above, where A_1, A_2

---

[2]Cambridge and Dublin Mathematical Journal, vol. 6 (1851), p. 293.
[3]Messenger of Mathematics, vol. 43 (1913-14), p. 25.

are homogeneous in x_1, x_2, x_3 but do not, as a rule, represent curves passing through the intersections.

We first prove a lemma on monomials in n variables.

Lemma 1. *If a monomial* $x_1^{k_1} x_2^{k_2} \ldots x_n^{k_n}$, *where the k's are positive integers, be formed so that the exponents $k_1 \ldots, k_n$ satisfy prescribed conditions, then, although the number of products satisfying the given conditions may be infinite, nevertheless a finite number of them can be chosen so that every other is divisible by one at least of this finite number.*

To first illustrate this lemma suppose that the prescribed conditions are

$$2k_1 + 3k_2 - k_3 - k_4 = 0, \tag{141}$$
$$k_1 + k_4 = k_2 + k_3.$$

Then monomials satisfying these conditions are

$$x_1^2 x_2^2 x_3^5 x_4^5, \; x_1^2 x_3^3 x_4, \; x_2 x_3 x_4^2, \; x_1^2 x_2 x_3^4 x_4^3, \ldots$$

and all are divisible by at least one of the set $x_1^2 x_3^3 x_4, x_2 x_3 x_4^2$.

Now if $n = 1$, the truth of the lemma is self-evident. For all of any set of positive powers of one variable are divisible by that power which has the least exponent. Proving by induction, assume that the lemma is true for monomials of $n - 1$ letters and prove it true for n letters.

Let $K = x_1^{k_1} x_2^{k_2} \ldots x_n^{k_n}$ be a representative monomial of the set given by the prescribed conditions and let $P = x_1^{a_1} x_2^{a_2} \ldots x_n^{a_n}$ be a specific product of the set. If K is not divisible by P, one of the numbers k must be less than the corresponding number a. Let $k_r < a_r$. Then k_r has one of the series of values

$$0, 1, 2, \ldots, a_r - l,$$

that is, the number of ways that this can occur for a single exponent is finite and equal to

$$N = a_1 + a_2 + \ldots + a_n.$$

The cases are

    k_1 equals one of the series $0, 1, \cdots, a_1 - 1$; (a_1 cases),

    k_2 equals one of the series $0, 1, \cdots, a_2 - 1$; (a_2 cases), (142)

    etc.

Now let $k_r = m$ and suppose this to be case number p of (142). Then the $n - 1$ remaining exponents $k_1, k_2, \cdots, k_{\tau-1}, k_{\tau+1}, \cdots, k_n$ satisfy definite conditions which could be obtained by making $k_r = m$ in the original conditions. Let

$$K_p = x_1^{k_1} x_2 =^{k_2} \cdots x_\tau^m \cdots x_n^{k_n} = x_\tau^m K_p'$$

be a monomial of the system for which $k_r = m$. Then K_p' contains only $m - 1$ letters and its exponents satisfy definite conditions which are such that $x_\tau^m K_p'$ satisfies the original conditions. Hence by hypothesis a finite number of monomials of the type K_p', say,

$$L_1, L_2, \cdots, L_{a_p},$$

exist such that all monomials K'_p are divisible by at least one L. Hence $K_p = x_\tau^m K'_p$ is divisible by at least one L, and so by at least one of the monomials

$$M_p^{(1)} = x_\tau^m L_1, M_p^{(2)} = x_\tau^m L_2, \cdots, M_p^{(a_p)} = x_\tau^m L_{a_p}.$$

Also all of the latter set of monomials belong to the original system. Thus in the case number p in (142) K is divisible by one of the monomials

$$M_p^{(1)}, M_p^{(2)}, \cdots, M_p^{(a_p)},$$

Now suppose that K is not divisible by P. Then one of the cases (142) certainly arises and so K is *always* divisible by one of the products

$$M_1^{(1)}, M_1^{(2)}, \cdots, M_1^{(\alpha_1)}, M_2^{(1)}, M_2^{(2)}, \cdots, M_2^{(\alpha_2)}, \cdots, M_N^{(\alpha_N)},$$

or else by P. Hence if the lemma holds true for monomials in $n - 1$ letters, it holds true for n letters, and is true universally.

We now proceed to the proof of the main theorem. Let the variables be $\chi_1, \ldots, \chi_n$ and let F be a typical function of the system described in the theorem. Construct an auxiliary system of functions η of the same variables under the law that a function is an η function when it can be written in the form

$$\eta = \Sigma A F \tag{143}$$

where the A's are integral functions rendering η homogeneous, but not otherwise restricted except in that the number of terms in η must be finite.

Evidently the class of η functions is closed with respect to linear operations. That is,

$$\Sigma B \eta = B_1 \eta_1 + B_2 \eta_2 + \ldots = \Sigma B A F = \Sigma A' F$$

is also an η function. Consider now a typical η function. Let its terms be ordered in a normal order. The terms will be defined to be in normal order if the terms of any pair,

$$S = \chi_1^{a_1} \chi_2^{a_2} \cdots \chi_n^{a_n}, T = \chi_1^{b_1} \chi_2^{b_2} \cdots \chi_n^{b_n}.$$

are ordered so that if the exponents a, b of S and T are read simultaneously from left to right the term first to show an exponent less than the exponent in the corresponding position in the other term occurs farthest to the right. If the normal order of S, T is (S, T), then T is said to be of lower rank than S. That is, the terms of η are assumed to be arranged according to descending rank and there is a term of highest and one of lowest rank. By hypothesis the η functions are formed according to definite laws, and hence their first terms satisfy definite laws relating to their exponents. By the lemma just proved we can choose a finite number of η functions, $\eta_1, \eta_2, \ldots \eta_p$ such that the first term of any other η is divisible by the first term of at least one of this number. Let the first term of a definite η be divisible by the first term of η_{m_1} and let the quotient be P_1.

Then $\eta - P_1\eta_{m_1}$ is an η function, and its first term is of lower rank than the first term of η. Let this be denoted by

$$\eta = P_1\eta_{m_1} + \eta^{(1)}.$$

Suppose next that the first term of $\eta^{(1)}$ is divisible by η_{m_2}; thus,

$$\eta^{(1)} = P_2\eta_{m_2} + \eta^{(2)},$$

and the first term of $\eta^{(2)}$ is of lower rank than that of $\eta^{(1)}$. Continuing, we obtain

$$\eta^{(r-1)} = P_r\eta_{m_r} + \eta^{(r)}.$$

Then the first terms of the ordered set

$$\eta, \eta^{(1)}, \eta^{(2)}, \ldots, \eta^{(r)}, \ldots$$

are in normal order, and since there is a term of lowest rank in η we must have for some value of r

$$\eta^{(r)} = P_{r+1}\eta m_{r+1}.$$

That is, we must eventually reach a point where there is no η function $\eta^{(r+1)}$ of the same order as η and whose first term is of lower rank than the first term of $\eta^{(r)}$. Hence

$$\eta = P_1\eta_{m_1} + P_2\eta_{m_2} + \ldots + P_{r+1}\eta_{m_{r+1}} \tag{144}$$

and all η's on the right-hand side are members of a definite finite set

$$\eta_1, \eta_2, \ldots, \eta_p.$$

But by the original theorem and (143), every F is itself an η function. Hence by (144)

$$F = A_1 F_1 + A_2 F_2 + \ldots + A_r F_r \tag{145}$$

where $F_i (i = 1, \ldots, r)$ are the F functions involved linearly in $\eta_1, \eta_2, \ldots, \eta_p$. This proves the theorem.

4.6.2 Linear Diophantine equations.

If the conditions imposed upon the exponents k consist of a set of linear Diophantine equations like (141), the lemma proved above shows that *there exists a set of solutions finite in number by means of which any other solution can be reduced*. That is, this fact follows as an evident corollary.

Let us treat this question in somewhat fuller detail by a direct analysis of the solutions of equations (141). The second member of this pair has the solutions

	$k_1,$	$k_2,$	$k_3,$	$k_4,$
(1)	0	0	1	1
(2)	0	1	0	1
(3)	1	0	1	0
(4)	1	1	0	0
(5)	2	1	1	0
(6)	0	0	1	1
...	...	...	...	...

Of these the fifth is obtained by adding the first and the fourth; the sixth is reducible as the sum of the third and the fourth, and so on. The sum or difference of any two solutions of any such linear Diophantine equation is evidently again a solution. Thus solutions (1), (2), (3), (4) of $k_1 + k_4 = k_2 + k_3$ form the complete set of irreducible solutions. Moreover, combining these, we see at once that the general solution is

$$\text{(I)} \quad k_1 = x + y, \, k_2 = x + z, \, k_3 = y + w, \, k_4 = z + w.$$

Now substitute these values in the first equation of (141)

$$2k_1 + 3k_2 - 3k_3 - k_4 = 0.$$

There results

$$5x + y + 2z = 2w$$

By the trial method illustrated above we find that the irreducible solutions of the latter are

$$x = 2, w = 5, y = 2, w = 1; z = 1, w = 1; x = 1, y = 1, w = 3,$$

where the letters not occurring are understood to be zero. The general solution is here

$$\text{(II)} \quad x = 2a + d, \, y = 2b + d, \, z = c, \, w = 5a + b + c + 3d,$$

and if these be substituted in (I) we have

$$k_1 = 2a + 2b + 2dk_2 = 2a + c + dk_3 = 5a + 3b + c + 4dk_4 = 5a + b + 2c + 3d$$

Therefore the only possible irreducible simultaneous solutions of (141) are

	$k_1,$	$k_2,$	$k_3,$	k_4
(1)	2	2	5	5
(2)	2	0	3	1
(3)	0	1	1	2
(4)	2	1	4	3

But the first is the sum of solutions (3) and (4); and (4) is the sum of (2) and (3). Hence (2) and (3) form the complete set of irreducible solutions referred to in the corollary. The general solution of the pair is

$$k_1 = 2\alpha, k_2 = \beta, k_3 = 3\alpha, k_4 = \alpha + 2\beta.$$

The corollary may now be stated thus:

Corollary 1. *Every simultaneous set of linear homogeneous Diophantine equations possesses a set of irreducible solutions, finite in number.*

A direct proof without reference to the present lemma is not difficult.[4] Applied to the given illustration of the above lemma on monomials the above analysis shows that if the prescribed conditions on the exponents are given by (141) then the complete system of monomials is given by

$$x_1^{2\alpha} x_2^6 x_3^{3\alpha+\beta} x_4^{\alpha+2\beta},$$

where α and β range through all positive integral values independently. Every monomial of the system is divisible by at least one of the set

$$x_1^2 x_3^3 x_4, x_2 x_3 x_4^2,$$

which corresponds to the irreducible solutions of the pair (141).

4.6.3 Finiteness of a system of syzygies.

A syzygy S among the members of a fundamental system of concomitants of a form (cf. (140)) f,

$$I_1, I_2, \ldots, I_\mu$$

is a polynomial in the I's formed according to the law that it will vanish identically when the I's are expressed explicitly in terms of the coefficients and variables of f. The totality of syzygies, therefore, is a system of polynomials (in the invariants I) to which Hilbert's theorem applies. It therefore follows at once that there exists a finite number of syzygies,

$$S_1, S_2, \ldots, S_\nu$$

such that any other syzygy S is expressible in the form

$$S = C_1 S_1 + C_2 S_2 + \cdots + C_\nu S_\nu \tag{146}$$

Moreover the C's, being also polynomials in the I's are themselves invariants of f. Hence

Theorem. *The number of irreducible syzygies among the concomitants of a form f is finite, in the sense indicated by equation (146).*

---

[4]Elliott, Algebra of Qualities, Chapter IX.

4.7 Jordan's Lemma

Many reduction problems in the theory of forms depend for their solution upon a lemma due to Jordan which may be stated as follows:

Lemma 2. *If $u_1 + u_2 + u_3 = 0$, then any product of powers of u_1, u_2, u_3 of order n can be expressed linearly in terms of such products as contain one exponent equal to or greater than $\frac{2}{3}n$.*

We shall obtain this result as a special case of a considerably more general result embodied in a theorem on the representation of a binary form in terms of other binary forms.

Theorem. *If $a_x, b_x, c_x, \ldots$ are r distinct linear forms, and $A, B, C, \ldots$ are binary forms of the respective orders $\alpha, \beta, \gamma, \ldots$ where*

$$\alpha + \beta + \gamma + \ldots = n - r + 1$$

then any binary form f of order n can be expressed in the form

$$f = a_x^{n-\alpha} A + b_x^{n-\beta} B + c_x^{n-\gamma} C + \ldots,$$

and the expression is unique.

As an explicit illustration of this theorem we cite the case $n = 3, r = 2$. Then $\alpha + \beta = 2, \alpha = \beta = 1$.

$$f = a_x^2 (p_{00}x_1 + p_{01}x_2) + b_x^2 (p_{10}x_1 + p_{11}x_2) \tag{147}$$

Since f, a binary cubic, contains four coefficients it is evident that this relation (147) gives four linear nonhomogeneous equations for the determination of the four unknowns $p_{00}, p_{01}, p_{10}, p_{11}$. Thus the theorem is true for this case provided the determinant representing the consistency of these linear equations does not vanish. Let $a_x = a_1 x_1 + a_2 x_2, b_x = b_1 x_1 + b_2 x_2$, and $D = a_1 b_2 - a_2 b_1$. Then the aforesaid determinant is

$$\begin{vmatrix} a_1^2 & 0 & b_1^2 & 0 \\ 2a_1 a_2 & a_1^2 & 2b_1 b_2 & b_1^2 \\ a_2^2 & 2a_1 a_2 & b_2^2 & 2b_1 b_2 \\ 0 & a_2^2 & 0 & b_2^2 \end{vmatrix}$$

This equals D^4, and $D \neq O$ on account of the hypothesis that a_x and b_x are distinct. Hence the theorem is here true. In addition to this we can solve for the p_y and thus determine A, B explicitly. In the general case the number of unknown coefficients on the right is

$$\alpha + \beta + \gamma + \ldots + r = n + 1$$

Hence the theorem itself may be proved by constructing the corresponding consistency determinant in the general case;[5] but it is perhaps more instructive to proceed as follows:

---

[5] Cf. Transactions Amer. Math. Society, Vol. 15 (1914), p. 80.

It is impossible to find r binary forms $A, B, C, \ldots$ of orders $\alpha, \beta, \gamma, \ldots$ where

$$\alpha + \beta + \gamma + \ldots = n - r + 1,$$

such that, identically,

$$E = a_x^{n-\alpha} A + b_x^{n-\beta} B + c_x^{n-\gamma} C + \ldots \equiv 0.$$

In fact suppose that such an identity exists. Then operate upon both sides of this relation $\alpha + 1$ times with

$$\Delta = a_2 \frac{\partial}{\partial x_1} - a_1 \frac{\partial}{\partial x_2} \qquad (a_x = a_1 x_1 + a_2 x_2).$$

Let g_x^n be any form of order n and take $a_2 = 0$. Then

$$
\begin{aligned}
\Delta^{\alpha+1} g_x^n &= k(a_1 \cdot g_2)^{\alpha+1} g_x^{n-\alpha-a} \\
&= k_1 a_1^{\alpha+1} g_1^{n-\alpha-1} g_2^{\alpha+1} x^{n-\alpha-1} - 2 + k_2 a_1^{\alpha+1} g_1^{n-\alpha-2} g_2^{\alpha+2} x_2^{n-\alpha-2} \\
&\quad + \ldots + k_{n-\alpha} a_1^{\alpha+1} g_2^n x_2^{n-\alpha-1},
\end{aligned}
$$

where the k's are numerical. Hence $\Delta^{\alpha+1} g_x^n$ cannot vanish identically in case $a_2 = 0$, and therefore not in the general case $a_2 \neq 0$, except when the last $n - \alpha$ coefficients of g_x^n vanish: that is, unless g_x^n contains $a_x^{n-\alpha}$ as a factor. Hence

$$\Delta^{\alpha+1} E = b_x^{n-\alpha-\beta-1} B' + c_x^{n-\alpha-\gamma-1} C' + \ldots,$$

where B', C' are of orders $\beta, \gamma, \ldots$ respectively. Now $\Delta^{\alpha+1} E$ is an expression of the same type as E, with r changed into $r-1$ and n into $n-\alpha-1$, as is verified by the equation

$$\beta + \gamma + \ldots = (n - \alpha - 1) - (r - 1) + 1 = n - r + 1 - \alpha$$

Thus if there is no such relation as $E \equiv 0$ for $r - 1$ linear forms $a_x, b_x, \ldots$, there certainly are none for r linear forms. But there is no relation for one form ($r = 1$) save in the vacuous case (naturally excluded) where A vanishes identically. Hence by induction the theorem is true for all values of r.

Now a count of coefficients shows at once that any binary form f of order n can be expressed linearly in terms of $n + 1$ binary forms of the same order. Hence f is expressible in the form

$$f = a_x^{n-\alpha} A + b_x^{n-\beta} B + c_x^{n-\gamma} D + \cdots.$$

That the expression is unique is evident. For if two such were possible, their difference would be an identically vanishing expression of the type $E \equiv 0$, and, as just proved, none such exist. This proves the theorem.

100

4.7.1 Jordan's lemma.

Proceeding to the proof of the lemma, let $u_3 = -(u_1 + u_2)$, supposing that u_1, u_2 replace the variables in the Theorem I just proved. Then u_3, u_1, u_2 are three linear forms and the Theorem I applies with $r = 3$, $\alpha + \beta + \gamma = n - 2$. Hence any homogeneous expression f in u_1, u_2, u_3 can be expressed in the form

$$u_1^{n-\alpha} A + u_2^{n-\beta} B + u_3^{n-\gamma} C,$$

or, if we make the interchanges

$$\begin{pmatrix} n - \alpha & n - \beta & n - \gamma \\ \lambda & \mu & \nu \end{pmatrix}$$

in the form

$$u_1^{\lambda} A + u_2^{\mu} B + u_3^{\nu} C, \tag{148}$$

where

$$\lambda + \mu + \nu = 2n + 2. \tag{149}$$

Again integers λ, μ, ν may always be chosen such that (149) is satisfied and

$$\lambda \geqq \frac{2}{3}n, \mu \geqq \frac{2}{3}n, \nu \geqq \frac{2}{3}n.$$

Hence Jordan's lemma is proved.

A case of three linear forms u_i for which $u_1 + u_2 + u_3 = 0$ is furnished by the identity

$$(ab)c_x + (bc)a_x + (ca)b_x = 0.$$

If we express A in (148) in terms of u_1, u_2 by means of $u_1 + u_2 + u_3 = 0$, B in terms of u_2, u_3, and C in terms of u_3, u_1, we have the conclusion that any product of order n of $(ab)c_x, (bc)a_x, (ca)b_x$ can be expressed linearly in terms of

$$(ab)^n c_x^n, (ab)^{n-1}(bc)c_x^{n-1}a_x, (ab)^{n-2}(bc)^2 c_x^{n-2}a_x^2, \ldots,$$
$$(ab)^{\lambda}(bc)^{n-\lambda}c_x^{\lambda}a_x^{n-\lambda},$$
$$(bc)^n a_x^n, (bc)^{n-1}(ca)a_x^{n-1}b_x, (bc)^{n-2}(ca)^2 a_x^{n-2}b_x^2, \ldots,$$
$$(bc)^{\mu}(ca)^{n-\mu}a_x^{\mu}b_x^{n-\mu} \tag{150}$$
$$(ca)^n b_x^n, (ca)^{n-1}(ab)b_x^{n-1}c_x, (ca)^{n-2}(ab)^2 b_x^{n-2}c_x^2, \ldots,$$
$$(ca)^{\nu}(ab)^{n-\nu}b_x^{\nu}c_x^{n-\nu},$$

where

$$\lambda \geqq \frac{2}{3}n, \mu \geqq \frac{2}{3}n, \nu \geqq \frac{2}{3}n.$$

It should be carefully noted for future reference that this monomial of order n in the three expressions $(ab)c_x, (bc)a_x, (ca)b_x$ is thus expressed linearly in terms of symbolical products in which there is always present a power of a determinant of type (ab) equal to or greater than $\frac{2}{3}n$. The weight of the coefficient of the leading term of a covariant is equal to the number of determinant factors of the type (ab) in its symbolical expression. Therefore (150) shows that if this weight w of a covariant of f does not exceed the order of the form f all covariants having leading coefficients of weight w and degree 3 can be expressed linearly in terms of those of *grade* not less than $\frac{2}{3}w$. The same conclusion is easily shown to hold for covariants of arbitrary weight.

4.8   Grade

The process of finding fundamental systems by passing step by step from those members of one degree to those of the next higher degree, illustrated in Section 3 of this chapter, although capable of being applied successfully to the forms of the first four orders fails for the higher orders on account of its complexity. In fact the fundamental system of the quintic contains an invariant of degree 18 and consequently there would be at least eighteen successive steps in the process. As a proof of the finiteness of the fundamental system of a form of order n the process fails for the same reason. That is, it is impossible to tell whether the system will be found after a finite number of steps or not.

In the next chapter we shall develop an analogous process in which it is proved that the fundamental system will result after a finite number of steps. This is a process of passing from the members of a given *grade* to those of the next higher *grade*.

4.8.1   Definition.

The highest index of any determinant factor of the type (ab) in a monomial symbolical concomitant is called the *grade* of that concomitant. Thus $(ab)^4(ac)^2 b_x^2 c_x^4$ is of grade 4. The terms of covariants (84), (87) are each of grade 2.

Whereas there is no upper limit to the degree of a concomitant of a form f order n, it is evident that the maximum grade is n by the theory of the Aronhold symbolism. Hence if we can find a method of passing from all members of the fundamental system of f of one grade to all those of the next higher grade, this will prove the finiteness of the system, since there would only be a finite number of steps in this process. This is the plan of the proof of Gordan's theorem in the next chapter.

4.8.2   Grade of a covariant.

Theorem. *Every covariant of a single form f of odd grade $2\lambda - 1$ can be transformed into an equivalent covariant of the next higher even grade 2λ.*

We prove, more explicitly, that if a symbolical product contains a factor $(ab)^{2\lambda-1}$ it can be transformed so as to be expressed in terms of products each containing the factor $(ab)^{2\lambda}$. Let A be the product. Then by the principles of Section 2 A is a term of

$$((ab)^{2\lambda-1}a_x^{n+1-2\lambda}b_x^{n+1-2\lambda}, \phi)^{\gamma}.$$

Hence by Theorem III of Section 2.

$$A = ((ab)^{2\lambda-1}a_x^{n+1-2\lambda}b_x^{n+1-2\lambda}, \phi)^{\gamma} + \sum K(((ab)^{2\lambda-1}a_x^{n+\bar{1}-2\lambda}b_x^{n+1-2\lambda}, \bar{\phi})^{\gamma'},$$

$$(151)$$

where $\gamma' < \gamma$ and $\bar{\phi}$ is a concomitant derived from ϕ by convolution, K being numerical. Now the symbols are equivalent. Hence

$$\psi = (ab)^{2\lambda-1}a_x^{n+1-2\lambda}b_x^{n+1-2\lambda} = -(ab)^{2\lambda-1}a_x^{n+1-2\lambda}b_x^{n+1-2\lambda} = 0.$$

Hence all transvectants on the right-hand side of (151), in which no convolution in ψ occurs, vanish. All remaining terms contain the symbolical factor $(ab)^{2\lambda}$, which was to be proved.

DEFINITION. A terminology borrowed from the theory of numbers will now be introduced. A symbolical product, A, which contains the factor $(ab)^r$ is said to be congruent to zero modulo $(ab)^r$;

$$A \equiv 0(\mathrm{mod}\ (ab)^r).$$

Thus the covariant (84)

$$C = \frac{1}{3}(ab)^2(ba)^2 a_x^2 \alpha_x + \frac{2}{3}(ab)^2(a\alpha)(b\alpha)a_x b_x \alpha_x$$

gives

$$C \equiv \frac{2}{3}(ab)^2(a\alpha)(b\alpha)a_x b_x \alpha_x(\mathrm{mod}(b\alpha)^2).$$

4.8.3 Covariant congruent to one of its terms

Theorem. *Every covariant of $f = a_x^n = b_x^n = \ldots$ which is obtainable as a covariant of $(f, f)^{2k} = g_{1x}^{2n-4k} = (ab)^{2k}a_x^{n-2k}b_x^{n-2k}$ (Chap. II, §4) is congruent to any definite one of its own terms modulo $(ab)^{2k+1}$.*

The form of such a concomitant monomial in the g symbols is

$$A = (g_1 g_2)^P (g_1 g_3)^q \cdots g_{1x}^\rho g_{2x}^\sigma \cdots$$

Proceeding by the method of Section 2 of this chapter change g_1 into y; i.e. $g_{11} = y_2, g_{12} = -y_1$. Then A becomes a form of order $2n-4k$ in y, viz. $\alpha_y^{2n-4k} = \beta_y^{2n-4k} = \ldots$. Moreover

$$A = (\alpha_y^{2n-4k}, g_{1y}^{2n-4k})^{2n-4k} = (\alpha_y^{2n-4k}, (ab)^{2k}a_y^{n-2k}b_y^{n-2k})^{2n-4k},$$

by the standard method of transvection. Now this transvectant A is free from y. Hence there are among its terms expressed in the symbols of f only two types of adjacent terms, viz. (cf. §2, II)

$$(da)(eb)P, \quad (db)(ea)P.$$

The difference between A and one of its terms can therefore be arranged as a succession of differences of adjacent terms of these two types and since P involves $(ab)^{2k}$ any such difference is congruent to zero modulo $(ab)^{2k+1}$, which proves the theorem.

4.8.4   Representation of a covariant of a covariant.

Theorem. *If $n \geq 4k$, any covariant of the covariant*

$$g_x^{2n-4k} = (ab)^{2k} a_x^{n-2k} b_x^{n-2k}$$

is expressible in the form

$$\sum C_{2k+1} + (ab)^{\frac{n}{2}} (bc)^{\frac{n}{2}} (ca)^{\frac{n}{2}} \Gamma, \tag{152}$$

where C_{2k+1} represents a covariant of grade $2k+1$ at least, the second term being absent ($\Gamma = 0$) if n is odd.

Every covariant of g_x^{2n-4k} of a stated degree is expressible as a linear combination of transvectants of g_x^{2n-4k} with covariants of the next lower degree (cf. §2, III). Hence the theorem will be true if proved for $T = (g_x^{2n-4k}, g_x^{2n-4k})^\sigma$ the covariants of second degree of this form. By the foregoing theorem T is congruent to any one of its own terms mod $(ab)^{2k+1}$. Hence if we prove the present theorem for a stated term of T, the conclusion will follow. In order to select a term from T we first find T by the standard transvection process (cf. Chap. III, §2). We have after writing $s = n - 2k$ for brevity, and $a_x^s b_x^s = \alpha_x^{2s}$

$$T = (ab)^{2k}(cd)^{2k} \sum_{t=0}^{\sigma} \frac{\binom{s}{t}\binom{s}{\sigma-t}}{\binom{2s}{\sigma}} c_x^{s-t} d_x^{s-\sigma+t} \cdot (ca)^t (da)^{\sigma-t} \alpha_x^{2t-\sigma}. \tag{153}$$

Now the terms of this expression involving α may be obtained by polarizing α_x^{2s} t times with respect to y, $\sigma - t$ times with respect to z, and changing y into c and z into d. Performing these operations upon $a_x^s b_x^s$ we obtain for T,

$$T = \sum_{t=0}^{\sigma} \sum_{u=0}^{t} \sum_{v=0}^{\sigma-t} K_{tuv} (ab)^{2k} (cd)^{2k} (ac)^u (ad)^v (bc)^{t-u} (bd)^{\sigma-t-v}$$

$$\times a_x^{s-u-v} b_x^{s-\sigma+u+v} c_x^{s-t} d_x^{s-\sigma+t}, \tag{154}$$

where K_{tuv} is numerical. Evidently σ is even.

We select as a representative term the one for which $t = \sigma$, $u = v = 0$.

This is

$$\phi = (ab)^{2k}(bc)^{\sigma}(cd)^{2k}a_x^{n-2k}b_x^{n-2k-\sigma}c_x^{n-2k-\sigma}d_x^{n-2k}.$$

Assume $n \geqq 4k$. Then by Section 6,

$$\psi = (ab)^{2k}(bc)^{\sigma}(ca)^{2k}a_x^{n-4k}b_x^{n-2k-\sigma}c_x^{n-2k-\sigma}$$

can be expressed in terms of covariants whose grade is greater than $2k$ unless $\sigma = 2k = \frac{n}{2}$. Also in the latter case ψ is the invariant

$$\psi = (ab)^{\frac{n}{2}}(bc)^{\frac{n}{2}}(ca)^{\frac{n}{2}}.$$

It will be seen at once that n must then be divisible by 4. Next we transform ϕ by $(cd)a_x = (ad)c_x - (ac)d_x$. The result is

$$\phi' = \sum_{i=0}^{2k}\binom{2\kappa}{i}(ab)^{2k}(bc)^{\sigma}(ca)^{i}(ad)^{2k-i}a_x^{n-4k}b_x^{n-2k-\sigma}c_x^{n-\sigma-i}d_x^{n-2k+i}.$$

(I) Now if $\sigma > k$, we have from Section 6 that ϕ is of grade $> \frac{2}{3} \cdot 3k$, i.e. $> 2k$, or else contains $(ab)^{\frac{n}{2}}(bc)^{\frac{n}{2}}(ca)^{\frac{n}{2}}$ i.e.

$$\phi = \sum C_{2k+1} + (ab)^{\frac{n}{2}}(bc)^{\frac{n}{2}}(ca)^{\frac{n}{2}}T. \tag{155}$$

(II) Suppose then $\sigma leqq k$. Then in ϕ', since $i = 2k$ has been treated under ψ above, we have either

$$(a)i \geqq k,$$

or

$$(b)2k - i > k.$$

In case (a) (155) follows directly from Section 6. In case (b) the same conclusion follows from the argument in (I). Hence the theorem is proved.

Chapter 5

GORDAN'S THEOREM

We are now in position to prove the celebrated theorem that every concomitant of a binary form f is expressible as a rational and integral algebraical function of a definite finite set of the concomitants of f. Gordan was the first to accomplish the proof of this theorem (1868), and for this reason it has been called Gordan's theorem. Unsuccessful attempts to prove the theorem had been made before Gordan's proof was announced.

The sequence of introductory lemmas, which are proved below, is that which was first given by Gordan in his third proof (cf. Vorlesungen uber Invariantentheorie, Vol. 2, part 3). [1] The proof of the theorem itself is somewhat simpler than the original proof. This simplification has been accomplished by the theorems resulting from Jordan's lemma, given in the preceding chapter.

5.1 Proof of the Theorem

We proceed to the proof of a series of introductory lemmas followed by the finiteness proof.

5.1.1 Lemma

Lemma 3. *If* $(A) : A_1, A_2, \ldots, A_k$ *is a system of binary forms of respective orders* $a_1, a_2, \ldots, a_k$, *and* $(B) : B_1, B_2, \ldots, B_l$, *a system of respective orders by* $b_1, b_2, \ldots, b_l$, *and if*

$$\phi = A_1^{\alpha_1} A_2^{\alpha_2} \ldots A_k^{\alpha_k}, \quad \psi = B_1^{\beta_1} B_2^{\beta_2} \ldots B_l^{\beta_l}$$

denote any two products for which the a's and the β's are all positive integers (or zero), then the number of transvectants of the type of

$$\tau = (\phi, \psi)^j$$

which do not contain reducible terms is finite.

---

[1] Cf. Grace and Young; Algebra of Invariants (1903).

To prove this, assume that any term of τ contains ρ symbols of the forms A not in second order determinant combinations with a symbol of the B forms, and σ symbols of the B's not in combination with a symbol of the A's. Then evidently we have for the total number of symbols in this term, from (A) and (B) respectively,

$$a_1\alpha_1 + a_2\alpha_2 + \ldots + a_k\alpha_k = \rho + j,$$
$$b_1\beta_1 + b_2\beta_2 + \ldots + b_l\beta_l = \sigma + j. \tag{156}$$

To each positive integral solution of the equations (156), considered as equations in the quantities $\alpha, \beta, \rho, \sigma, j$, will correspond definite products ϕ, ψ and a definite index j, and hence a definite transvectant τ. But as was proved (Chap. IV, Section 3, III), if the solution corresponding to $(\phi, \psi)^j$ is the sum of those corresponding to $(\phi_1, \psi_1)^{j_1}$ and $(\phi_2, \psi_2)^{j_2}$, then τ certainly contains reducible terms. In other words transvectants corresponding to reducible solutions contain reducible terms. But the number of irreducible solutions of (156) is finite (Chap. IV, Section 5, II). Hence the number of transvectants of the type τ which do not contain reducible terms is finite. A method of finding the irreducible transvectants was given in Section 3, III of the preceding chapter.

Definitions.

A system of forms (A) is said to be *complete* when any expression derived by convolution from a product ϕ of powers of the forms (A) is itself a rational integral function of the forms (A).

A system (A) will be called *relatively complete for the modulus G* consisting of the product of a number of symbolical determinants when any expression derived by convolution from a product ϕ is a rational integral function of the forms (A) together with terms containing G as a factor.

As an illustration of these definitions we may observe that

$$f = a_x^3 = \cdots, \Delta = (ab)^2 x_x b_x, Q = (ab)^2 (ca) b_x c_x^2,$$
$$R = (ab)^2 (cd)^2 (ac)(bd)$$

is a complete system. For it is the fundamental system of a cubic f, and hence any expression derived by convolution from a product of powers of these four concomitants is a rational integral function of f, Δ, Q, R.

Again f itself forms a system relatively complete modulo $(ab)^2$.

Definition.

A system (A) is said to be *relatively complete for the set of moduli $G_1, G_2, \cdots$* when any expression derived from a product of powers of A forms by convolution is a rational integral function of A forms together with terms containing at least one of the moduli $G_1, G_2, \cdots$ as a factor.

In illustration it can be proved (cf. Chap. IV, §7, IV) that in the complete system derived for the quartic

$$H = (ab)^2 a_x^2 b_x^2,$$

any expression derived by convolution from a power of H is rational and integral in H and

$$G_1 = (ab)^4, G_2 = (bc)^2 (ca)^2 (ab)^2.$$

Thus H is a system which is relatively complete with regard to the two moduli

$$G_1 = (ab)^4, G_2 = (bc)^2 (ca)^2 (ab)^2.$$

Evidently a complete system is also relatively complete for any set of moduli. We call such a system absolutely complete.

Definitions.

The system (C) derived by transvection from the systems (A), (B) contains an infinite number of forms. Nevertheless (C) is called a *finite system* when all its members are expressible as rational integral algebraic functions of a finite number of them.

The system (C) is called *relatively finite with respect to a set of moduli* $G_1, G_2, \ldots$ when every form of (C) is expressible as a rational integral algebraic function of a finite number of the forms (C) together with terms containing at least one of the moduli $G_1, G_2, \ldots$ as a factor.

The system of all concomitants of a cubic f is absolutely finite, since every concomitant is expressible rationally and integrally in terms of f, Δ, Q, R.

Lemma 4. *If the systems (A), (B) are both finite and complete, then the system (C) derived from them by transvection is finite and complete.*

We first prove that the system (C) is finite. Let us first arrange the transvectants

$$\tau = (\phi, \psi)^j$$

in an ordered array

$$\tau_1, \tau_2, \cdots, \tau_r, \cdots, (157)$$

the process of ordering being defined as follows:

(a) Transvectants are arranged in order of ascending total degree of the product $\phi\psi$ in the coefficients of the forms in the two systems (A), (B).

(b) Transvectants for which the total degree is the same are arranged in order of ascending indices j; and further than this the order is immaterial.

Now let t, t' be any two terms of τ. Then

$$(t - t') = \Sigma(\bar{\phi}, \bar{\psi})^{j'} (j' < j),$$

where $\bar{\phi}$ is a form derived by convolution from ϕ. But by hypothesis (A), (B) are complete systems. Hence $\bar{\phi}, \bar{\psi}$ are rational and integral in the forms A, B respectively,

$$\bar{\phi} = F(A), \bar{\psi} = G(B).$$

Therefore $(\bar{\phi}, \bar{\psi})^j$ can be expressed in terms of transvectants of the type τ (*i.e.* belonging to (C)) of index less than j and hence coming before τ in the ordered array (157). But if we assume that the forms of (C) derived from all transvectants before τ can be expressed rationally and integrally in terms of a finite number of the forms of (C),

$$C_1, C_2, \ldots, C_r,$$

then all C's up to and including those derived from

$$\tau = (\phi, \psi)^j$$

can be expressed in terms of

$$C_1, C_2, \ldots, C_r, t.$$

But if τ contains a reducible term $t = t_1 t_2$ then since t_1, t_2 must both arise from transvectants before τ in the ordered array no term t need be added and all C's up to and including those derived from τ are expressible in terms of

$$C_1, C_2, \ldots, C_r.$$

Thus in building by this procedure a system of C's in terms of which all forms of (C) can be expressed we need to add a new member only when we come to a transvectant in (157) which contains no reducible term. But the number of such transvectants in (C) is finite. Hence, a finite number of C's can be chosen such that every other is a rational function of these.

The proof that (C) is finite is now finished, but we may note that a set of C's in terms of which all others are expressible may be chosen in various ways, since t in the above is any term of τ. Moreover since the difference between any two terms of τ is expressible in terms of transvectants before τ in the ordered array we may choose instead of a single term t of an irreducible $\tau = (\phi, \psi)^j$, an aggregate of any number of terms or even the whole transvectant and it will remain true that every form of (C) can be expressed as a rational integral algebraic function of the members of the finite system so chosen.

We next prove that the finite system constructed as above is complete.

Let

$$C_1, C_2, \ldots, C_r$$

be the finite system. Then we are to prove that any expression $\bar{X}$ derived by convolution from

$$X = C_1^{\gamma_1} C_2^{\gamma_2} \ldots C_r^{\gamma_r}$$

is a rational integral algebraic function of $C_1, \ldots, C_r$. Assume that $\bar{X}$ contains ρ second-order determinant factors in which a symbol from an (A) form is in combination with a symbol belonging to a (B) form.

Then $\bar{X}$ is a term of a transvectant $(\bar{\phi}, \bar{\psi})^\rho$, where $\bar{\phi}$ contains symbols from system (A) only, and $\bar{\psi}$ contains symbols from (B) only. Then $\bar{\phi}$ must be derivable by convolution from a product ϕ of the A's and $\bar{\psi}$ from a product ψ of B forms. Moreover

$$\dot{\bar{X}} = (\bar{\phi}, \bar{\psi})^\rho + \sum (\bar{\bar{\phi}}, \bar{\bar{\psi}})^{\rho'} \quad (\rho' < \rho),$$

and $\bar{\bar{\phi}}, \bar{\bar{\psi}}$ having been derived by convolution from $\bar{\phi}, \bar{\psi}$, respectively, are ultimately so derivable from ϕ, ψ. But

$$\bar{\phi} = F(A), \quad \bar{\psi} = G(B)$$

and so $\bar{X}$ is expressed as an aggregate of transvectants of the type of

$$\tau = (\phi, \psi)^i.$$

But it was proved above that every term of τ is a rational integral function of

$$C_1, \ldots, C_r.$$

Hence $\bar{X}$ is such a function; which was to be proved.

5.1.2   Lemma

Lemma 5. *If a finite system of forms (A), all the members of which are covariants of a binary form f, includes f and is relatively complete for the modulus G'; and if, in addition, a finite system (B) is relatively complete for the modulus G and includes one form B_1 whose only determinantal factors are those constituting G', then the system (C) derived by transvection from (A) and (B) is relatively finite and complete for the modulus G.*

In order to illustrate this lemma before proving it let (A) consist of one form $f = a_x^3 = \cdots$, and (B) of two forms

$$\Delta = (ab)^2 a_x b_x, \, R = (ab)^2 (ac)(bd)(cd)^2.$$

Then (A) is relatively complete for the modulus $G' = (ab)^2$. Also B is absolutely complete, for it is the fundamental system of the Hessian of f. Hence the lemma states that (C) should be absolutely complete. This is obvious. For (C) consists of the fundamental system of the cubic,

$$f, \Delta, Q, R,$$

and other covariants of f.

We divide the proof of the lemma into two parts.

Part 1. First, we prove the fact that *if P be an expression derived by convolution from a power of f, then any term, t, of $\sigma = (P, \psi)^i$ can be expressed as an aggregate of transvectants of the type*

$$\tau = (\phi, \psi)^i,$$

in which the degree of ϕ is at most equal to the degree of P. Here ϕ and ψ are products of powers of forms $(A), (B)$ respectively, and by the statement of the lemma (A) contains only covariants of f and includes f itself.

This fact is evident when the degree of P is zero. To establish an inductive proof we assume it true when the degree of P is $< r$ and note that

$$t = (P, \psi)^i + \Sigma(\bar{P}, \bar{\psi})^{i'} \ (i' < i),$$

and, inasmuch as P and $\bar{P}$ are derived by convolution from a power of f,

$$P = F(A) + G'Y \equiv F(A) \ (\mathrm{mod}\, G'),$$
$$\bar{P} = F'(A) + G'Y' \equiv F'(A) \ (\mathrm{mod}\, G').$$

Also

$$\bar{\psi} = \Phi(B) + GZ \equiv \Phi(B)(\ \mathrm{mod}\ G).$$

Hence t contains terms of three types $(a), (b), (c)$.

(a) Transvectants of the type $(F(A), \phi(B))^i$, the degree of $F(A)$ being r, the degree of P.

(b) Transvectants of type $(G'Y, \psi)^k$, $G'Y$ being of the same degree as P.

(c) Terms congruent to zero modulo G.

Now for (a) the fact to be proved is obvious. For (b), we note that $G'Y$ can be derived by convolution from $B_1 f^s$, where $s < r$. Hence any term of $(G'Y, \psi)^k$ can be derived by convolution from $B_1 f^s \psi$ and is expressible in the form

$$\sum (P', \overline{B_1 \psi}),$$

where P' is derived by convolution from f^s and is of degree $< r$. But by hypothesis every term in these latter transvectants is expressible as an aggregate

$$\equiv \sum (\phi, \psi)^i (\mathrm{modulo}\ G),$$

inasmuch as

$$\overline{B_1 \psi} \equiv \Phi(B)(\mathrm{modulo}\ G).$$

But in this $(\phi, \psi)^i$ ϕ is of degree $\leq s < r$. Hence

$$t \equiv \sum (\phi, \psi)^i (\mathrm{mod}\ G),$$

and the desired inductive proof is established.

As a *corollary* to the fact just proved we note that *if P contain the factor G', then any term in*

$$(P, \psi)^i$$

can be expressed in the form

$$\sum (\phi, \psi)^i \tag{158}$$

where the degree of ϕ is less than that of P.

Part 2. We now present the second part of the proof of the original lemma, and first to prove that (C) is relatively finite modulo G.

We postulate that the transvectants of the system (C) are arranged in an ordered array defined as follows by (a), (b), (c).

(a) The transvectants of (C) shall be arranged in order of ascending degree of $\phi\psi$, assuming the transvectants to be of the type $\tau = (\phi, \psi)^j$.

(b) Those for which the degree of $\phi\psi$ is the same shall be arranged in order of ascending degree of ϕ.

(c) Transvectants for which both degrees are the same shall be arranged in order of ascending index j; and further than this the ordering is immaterial.

Let t, t' be any two terms of τ. Then

$$t' - t = \Sigma(\overline{\phi}, \overline{\psi})^{\overline{j}}(j' < j).$$

Also by the hypotheses of the lemma

$$\overline{\phi} = F(A) + G'Y, \overline{\psi} \qquad\qquad = \Phi(B) + GZ.$$

Hence

$$t' - t \equiv \Sigma(F(A), \Phi(B))^f + \Sigma(G'Y, \Phi(B))^f \, (mod G).$$

Now transvectants of the type $(F(A), \Phi(B))^f$ belong before τ in the ordered array since $j' < j$ and the degree of $F(A)$ is the same as that of ϕ. Again $(G'Y, \Phi(B))^f$ can by the above corollary (158) be expressed in the form

$$\sum (\phi', \psi')^j,$$

where the degree of ϕ' is less than that of $G'Y$ and hence less than that of ϕ.

Consequently, $t' - t$ can be written

$$t' - t = \sum (\phi'', \psi'')^j + \sum (\phi', \psi')^j \, (\mathrm{mod} \ G),$$

where the degree of ϕ'' is the same as that of ϕ and where j'/ltj, and where the degree of ϕ' is less than that of ϕ. Therefore if all terms of transvectants coming before

$$\tau = (\phi, \psi)^i$$

in the ordered array are expressible rationally and integrally in terms of

$$C_1, C_2, \ldots, C_q,$$

except for terms congruent to zero modulo G, then all terms of transvectants up to and *including* τ can be so expressed in terms of

$$C_1, C_2, \ldots, C_q, t,$$

where t is any term of τ. As in the proof of *lemma 2*, if τ contains a reducible term $t = t_1 t_2$, t does not need to be added to

$$C_1, C_2, \ldots, C_q,$$

since then t_1, t_2 are terms of transvectants coming before $/tau$ in the ordered array. Hence, in building up the system of C's in terms of which all forms of (C) are rationally expressible modulo G, by proceeding from one transvectant τ to the next in the array, we add a new member to the system only when we come to a transvectant containing no reducible term. But the number of such irreducible transvectants in (C) is finite. Hence (C) is relatively finite modulo G. Note that $C_1, \ldots, C_q$ may be chosen by selecting one term from each irreducible transvectant in (C).

Finally we prove that (C) is relatively complete modulo G. Any term $\overline{X}$ derived by convolution from

$$X = C_1^{\gamma_1} C_2^{\gamma} \ldots C_q^{\gamma_q},$$

is a term of a transvectant $(\bar{\phi}, \bar{\psi})^\rho$, where, as previously, $\bar{\phi}$ is derived by convolution from a product of A forms and $\bar{\psi}$ from a product of B forms. Then

$$\overline{X} = (\bar{\phi}, \bar{\psi})^\rho + \Sigma(\bar{\bar{\phi}}, \bar{\bar{\psi}})^{\rho'} \rho' < \rho.$$

That is, $\overline{X}$ is an aggregate of transvectants $(\bar{\phi}, \bar{\psi})^\sigma$, $\bar{\phi} = P$ can be derived by convolution from a power of f, and

$$\bar{\psi} \equiv \Phi(B) \ (\mathrm{mod}\ G).$$

Thus,

$$\ddot{X} \equiv \sum (P, \Phi(B))^\sigma \ (\mathrm{mod}\ G)$$
$$\equiv \sum (P, \psi)^\sigma \ (\mathrm{mod}\ G)$$
$$\equiv \sum (\phi, \psi)^i \ (\mathrm{mod}\ G)$$

where ϕ is of degree not greater than the degree of P, by the first part of the proof. But all transvectants of the last type are expressible as rational integral functions of a finite number of C's modulo G. Hence the system (C) is relatively complete, as well as finite, modulo G.

5.1.3 Corollary

Corollary 2. *If the system (B) is absolutely complete then (C) is absolutely complete.*

Corollary 3. *If (B) is relatively complete for two moduli G_1, G_2 and contains a form whose only determinantal factors are those constituting G', then the system (C) is relatively complete for the two moduli G_1, G_2.*

5.1.4 Theorem

Theorem. *The system of all concomitants of a binary form $f = a_x^n = \ldots$ of order n is finite.*

The proof of this theorem can now be readily accomplished in view of the theorems in Paragraphs III, IV of Chapter IV, Section 7, and lemma 3 just proved.

The system consisting of f itself is relatively complete modulo $(ab)^2$. It is a finite system also, and hence it satisfies the hypotheses regarding (A) in lemma 3. This system $(A) = f$ may then be used to start an inductive proof concerning systems satisfying lemma 3. That is we assume that we know a finite system A_{k-1} which consists entirely of covariants of f, which includes f, and which is relatively complete modulo $(ab)^{2k}$. Since every covariant of f can be derived from f by convolution it is a rational integral function of the forms in A_{k-1} except for terms involving the factor $(ab)^{2k}$. We then seek to construct a subsidiary finite system B_{k-1} which includes one form B_1 whose only determinant factors are $(ab)^{2k} = G'$, and which is relatively complete modulo $(ab)^{2k+2} = G$. Then the system derived by transvection from A_{k-1} and B_{k-1} will be relatively finite and complete modulo $(ab)^{2k+2}$. That is, it will be the system A_k. This procedure, then, will establish completely an inductive process by which we construct the system concomitants of f relatively finite and complete modulo $(ab)^{2k+2}$ from the set finite and complete modulo $(ab)^{2k}$, and since the maximum grade is n we obtain by a finite number of steps an absolutely finite and complete system of concomitants of f. Thus the finiteness of the system of all concomitants of f will be proved.

Now in view of the theorems quoted above the subsidiary system B_{k-1} is easily constructed, and is comparatively simple. We select for the *form B_1* of the lemma

$$B_1 = (ab)^{2k} a_x^{n-2k} b_x^{n-2k} = h_x.$$

Next we set apart for separate consideration the case (c) $n = 4k$. The remaining cases are (a) $n > 4k$, and (b) $n < 4k$.

(a) By Theorem IV of Section 7 in the preceding chapter if $n > 4k$ any form derived by convolution from a power of h_k is of grade $2k + 1$ at least and hence can be transformed so as to be of grade $2k + 2$ (Chap. IV, §7, II). Hence h_k itself forms a system which is relatively finite and complete modulo $(ab)^{2k+2}$ and is the system B_{k-1} required.

(b) If $n < 4k$ then h_k is of order less than n. But in the problem of constructing fundamental systems we may proceed from the forms of lower degree to those of the higher. Hence we may assume that the fundamental system of any form of order $< n$ is known. Hence in this case (b) we know the fundamental system of h_k. But by III of Chapter IV, Section 7 any concomitant of h_k is congruent to any one of this concomitant's own terms modulo $(ab)^{2k+1}$. Hence if we select one term from each member of the known fundamental system of h_k we have a system which is relatively finite and complete modulo $(ab)^{2k+2}$; that is, the required system B_{k-1}.

(c) Next consider the case $n = 4k$. Here by Section 7, IV of the preceding chapter the system $B_{k-1} = h_k$ is relatively finite and complete with respect to two moduli

$$G_1 = (ab)^{2k+2}, G_2 = (ab)^{2k}(bc)^{2k}(cd)^{2k},$$

and G_2 is an invariant of f. Thus by corollary 2 of lemma 3 the system, as C_k derived by transvection from A_{k-1} and B_{k-1} is relatively finite and complete with respect to the two moduli G_1, G_2. Hence, if $\bar{C}_k$ represents any form of the system C_k obtained from a form of C_k by convolution,

$$\bar{C}_k = F_l(C_k) + G_2 P_1 (mod(ab)^{2k+2}).$$

Here P_1 is a *covariant* of degree less than the degree of $\bar{C}_k$. Hence P_1 may be derived by convolution from f, and so

$$P_l = F_2(C_k) + G_2 P_2 (mod(ab)^{2k+2}),$$

and then P_2 is a covariant of degree less than the degree of P_1. By repetitions of this process we finally express $\bar{C}_k$ as a polynomial in

$$G_2 = (ab)^{2k}(bc)^{2k}(ca)^{2k},$$

whose coefficients are all covariants of f belonging to C_k, together with terms containing $G_1 = (ab)^{2k+2}$ as a factor, *i.e.*

$$\bar{C}_k \equiv F_1(C_k) + G_2 F_2(C_k) + G_2^2 F_3(C_k) + \cdots + G_2^\tau F_r(C_k)(mod G_1).$$

Hence if we adjoin G_2 to the system C_k we have a system A_k which is relatively finite and complete modulo $(ab)^{2k+2}$.

Therefore in all cases $(a), (b), (c)$ we have been able to construct a system A_k relatively finite and complete modulo $(ab)^{2k+2}$ from the system A_{k-1} relatively finite and complete modulo $(ab)^{2k}$. Since A_0 evidently consists of f itself the required induction is complete.

Finally, consider what the circumstances will be when we come to the end of the sequence of moduli

$$(ab)^2, (ab)^4, (ab)^6, \cdots .$$

If n is even, $n = 2g$, the system A_{g-1} is relatively finite and complete modulo $(ab)^{2a} = (ab)^n$. The system B_{g-1} consists of the invariant $(ab)^n$ and hence is absolutely finite and complete. Hence, since A_g is absolutely finite and complete, the irreducible transvectants of A_g constitute the fundamental system of f. Moreover A_g consists of A_{g-1} and the invariant $(ab)^n$.

If n is odd, $n = 2g + 1$, then A_{g-1} contains f and is relatively finite and complete modulo $(ab)^{2g}$. The system B_{g-1} is here the fundamental system of the quadratic $(ab)^{2g}a_x b_x$ e.g.

$$B_{g-1} = \{(ab)^{2g}a_x b_x, (ab)^{2g}(ac)(bd)(cd)^{2g}\}.$$

This system is relatively finite and complete modulo $(ab)^{2g+1}$. But this modulus is zero since the symbols are equivalent. Hence B_{g-1} is absolutely finite and complete and by lemma $3 A_g$ will be absolutely finite and complete. Then the set of irreducible transvectants in A_g is the fundamental system of f.

Gordan's theorem has now been proved.

5.2 Fundamental Systems of the Cubic and Quartic by the Gordan Process

It will now be clear that the proof in the preceding section not only establishes the existence of a finite fundamental system of concomitants of a binary form f of order n, but it also provides an inductive procedure by which this system may be constructed.

5.2.1 System of the cubic.

For illustration let $n = 3$,

$$f = a_x^3 = b_x^3 = \cdots .$$

The system A_0 is f itself. The system B_0 is the fundamental system of the single form

$$h_1 = (ab)^2 a_x b_x,$$

since h_1 is of order less than 3. That is,

$$B_0 = \{(ab)^2 a_x b_x, D\}$$

where D is the discriminant of h_1. Then A_1 is the system of transvectants of the type of

$$\tau = (f^\alpha, h_1^\beta, D^\gamma)^j.$$

But B_0 is absolutely finite and complete. Hence A_l is also.

Now D belongs to this system, being given by $\alpha = \beta = j = 0, \gamma = 1$. If $j > 0$ then τ is reducible unless $\gamma = 0$, since D is an invariant. Hence, we have to consider which transvectants

$$\tau = (f^a, h_1^\beta)^j$$

are irreducible. But in Chapter IV, Section 3 II, we have proved that the only one of these transvectants which is irreducible is $Q = (f, h_1)$. Hence, the irreducible members of A_1 consist of

$$A_1 = \{f, h_1, Q, D\},$$

or in the notation previously introduced,

$$A_1 = \{f, \Delta, Q, R\}.$$

But B_0 is absolutely complete and finite. Hence these irreducible forms of A_1 constitute the fundamental system of f.

5.2.2 System of the quartic.

Let $f = a_x^4 = b_x^4 = \cdots$. Then $A_0 = \{f\}$. Here B_0 is the single form

$$h_1 = (ab)^2 a_x^2 b_x^2,$$

and B_0 is relatively finite and complete $(\text{modd}(ab)^4, (ab)^2(bc)^2(ca)^2)$. The system C_1 of transvectants

$$\tau = (f^\alpha, h_1^\beta)^j$$

is relatively finite and complete $(\text{modd}(ab)^4, (ab)^2(bc)^2(ca)^2)$. In τ if $j > 1$, τ contains a term with the factor $(ab)^2(ac)^2$ which is congruent to zero with respect to the two moduli. Hence $j = 1$, and by the theory of reducible transvectants (Chap. IV, Section 3, III)

$$4\alpha - 4 < j \leq 4\alpha,$$

or $\alpha = 1, \beta = 1$. The members of C_1 which are irreducible with respect to the two moduli are therefore

$$f, h_1, (f, h_1).$$

Then

$$A_1 = \{f, h_1, (f, h_1), J = (ab)^2(bc)^2(ca)^2\}.$$

Next B_1 consists of $i = (ab)^4$ and is absolutely complete. Hence, writing $h_1 = H, (f, h_1) = T$, the fundamental system of f is

$$f, H, T, i, J.$$

Chapter 6

FUNDAMENTAL SYSTEMS

In this chapter we shall develop, by the methods and processes of preceding chapters, typical fundamental systems of concomitants of single forms and of sets of forms.

6.1 Simultaneous Systems

In Chapter V, Section 1, II, it has been proved that if a system of forms (A) is both finite and complete, and a second system (B) is also both finite and complete, then the system (S) derived from (A) and (A) by transvection is finite and complete. In view of Gordan's theorem this proves that the simultaneous system of any two binary quantics f, g is finite, and that this simultaneous system may be found from the respective systems of f and g by transvection. Similarly for a set of n quantics.

6.1.1 Linear form and quadratic.

The complete system of two linear forms consists of the two forms themselves and their eliminant. For a linear form $l = l_x$, and a quadratic f, we have

$$(A) = l, (B) = \{f, D\}.$$

Then S consists of the transvectants

$$S = \{(f^\alpha D^\beta, l^\gamma)^\delta\}.$$

Since D is an invariant S is reducible unless $\beta = 0$. Also $\delta \leqq \gamma$, and unless $\delta = \gamma, (f^\alpha, l^\gamma)^\delta$ is reducible by means of the product

$$(f^\alpha, l^\delta)^\delta (1, f^{\gamma-\delta})^0.$$

Hence $\gamma = \delta$. Again, by

$$(f^{\alpha-1}, l^{\delta-2})^{\delta-2}(f, l^2)^2,$$

S is reducible if $\delta > 2$. Hence the fundamental system of f and l is

$$S = \{f, D, l, (f, l), (f, l^2)^2\}.$$

When expressed in terms of the actual coefficients these forms are

$$l = a_0 x_1 + a_1 x_2 = l_x = l'_x = \ldots,$$
$$f = b_0 x_1^2 + 2b_1 x_1 x_2 + b_2 x_2^2 = a_x^2 = b_x^2 = \ldots$$
$$D = 2(b_0 b_2 = b_1^2 = (ab)^2,$$
$$(f, l) = (b_0 a_1 - b_1 a_0)x_1 + (b_1 a_1 - b_2 a_0)x_2 = (al)a_x,$$
$$(f, l^2)^2 = b_0 a_1^2 - 2b_1 a_0 a_1 + b_2 a_0^2 = (al)(al').$$

6.1.2 Linear form and cubic.

If $l = l_x$ and $f = a_x^3 = b_x^3 = \ldots$, then (cf. Table I),

$$(A) = \{l\};\ (B) = \{f, \Delta, Q, R\},$$

and

$$S = (f^\alpha \Delta^\beta Q^\gamma R^\epsilon, l^\delta)^\eta.$$

Since R is an invariant $\epsilon = 0$ for an irreducible transvectant. Also $\eta = \delta$ as in (I). If $\alpha \neq 0$ then, by the product

$$(f, l^3)^3 (f^{\alpha-1} \Delta^\beta Q^\gamma, l^{\delta-3})^{\delta-3}$$

S is reducible unless $\delta \leq 3$, and if $\delta \leq 3$ S is reducible by

$$(f, l^\delta)^\delta (f^{\alpha-1} \Delta^\beta Q^\gamma, 1)^0$$

unless $\beta = \gamma = 0$, $\alpha = 1$. Thus the fundamental system of f and l is

$$\begin{aligned}
S = \ & \{f, \Delta, Q, R, l, (f, l), (f, l^2)^2, (f, l^3)^3, \\
& (\Delta, l), (\Delta, l^2)^2, (Q, l), (Q, l^2)^2, (Q, l^3)^3\}.
\end{aligned}$$

6.1.3 Two quadratics.

Let $f = a_x^2 = a_x'^2;\ g = b_x^2 = b_x'^2 = \ldots.$ Then

$$(A) = \{f, D_1\},\quad (B) = \{g, D_2\},\quad S = (f^\alpha D_1^\beta, g^\gamma D_2^\delta)^\epsilon.$$

Here $\beta = \delta = 0$. Also

$$2\alpha \ \geq \epsilon \geq 2\alpha - 1,$$
$$2\gamma \ \geq \epsilon \geq 2\gamma - 1,$$

and consistent with these we have the fundamental system

$$S = \{f, g, D_1, D_2, (f, g), (f, g)^2\}. \tag{6.1}$$

Written explicitly, these quantities are

$$f = a_0 x_1^2 + 2a_1 x_1 x_2 + a_2^2 x_2^2 = a_x^2 = a_x'^2 = \cdots ,$$
$$g = b_0 x_1^2 + 2b_1 x_1 x_2 + b_2 x_2^2 = b_x^2 = b_x'^2 = \cdots ,$$
$$D_1 = 2(a_0 a_2 - a_1^2) = (aa')^2,$$
$$D_2 = 2(b_0 b_2 - b_1^2) = (bb')^2,$$
$$J = (f, g)$$
$$= (a_0 b_1 - a_1 b_0) x_1^2 + (a_0 b_2 - a_2 b_0) x_1 x_2 + (a_1 b_2 - a_2 b_1) x_2^2 = (ab) a_x b_x,$$
$$h = (f, g)^2 = a_0 b_2 - 2a_1 b_1 + a_2 b_0 = (ab)^2.$$

6.1.4 Quadratic and cubic.

Consider next the simultaneous system of $f = a_x^2 = a_x'^2 = \cdots , g = b_x^3 = b_x'^3 = \cdots$. In this case

$$(A) = \{f, D\}, (B) = \{g, \Delta, Q, R\}, S = (f^\alpha D^\beta, g^a \Delta^b Q^c R^d)^\gamma.$$

In order that S may be irreducible, $\beta = d = 0$. Then in case $\gamma > 2$ and $b \neq 0$, $S = (f^\alpha, g^a \Delta^b Q^c)^\gamma$ is reducible by means of the product

$$(f, \Delta)^2 (f^{\alpha-1}, g^a \Delta^{b-1} Q^c)^{\gamma-2}.$$

Hence only three types of transvectants can be irreducible;

$$(f, \Delta), (f, \Delta)^2, (f^\alpha, g^a Q^c)^\gamma.$$

The first two are, in fact irreducible. Also in the third type if we take $c = 0$, the irreducible transvectants given by $(f^\alpha, g^a)^\gamma$ will be those determined in Chapter IV, Section 3, III, and are

$$f, g, (f, g), (f, g)^2, (f^2, g)^3, (f^3, g^2)^6.$$

If $c > 1$, we may substitute in our transvectant $(f^\alpha, g^a Q^c)^\gamma$ the syzygy

$$Q^2 = -\frac{1}{2}(\Delta^3 + Rg^2);$$

and hence all transvectants with $c > 1$ are reducible. Taking $a = 0, c = 1$ we note that (f, Q) is reducible because it is the Jacobian of a Jacobian. Then the only irreducible cases are

$$(f, Q)^2, (f^2, Q)^3.$$

Finally if $c = 1, a \neq 0$, the only irreducible transvectant is

$$(f^3, gQ)^6.$$

Therefore the fundamental system of a binary cubic and a binary quadratic consists of the fifteen concomitants given in Table III below.

TABLE III

DEGREE	ORDER			
	0	1	2	3
1			f	g
2	D	$(f,g)^2$	Δ	(f,g)
3	$(f,\Delta)^2$	$(f^2,g)^3$	(f,Δ)	Q
4	R	$(f,Q)^2$		
5	$(f^3,g^2)^6$	$(f^2,Q)^3$		
7	$(f^3,gQ)^6$			

6.2 System of the Quintic

The most powerful process known for the discovery of a fundamental system
of a single binary form is the process of Gordan developed in the preceding
chapter. In order to summarize briefly the essential steps in this process let
the form be f. Construct, then, the system A_0 which is finite and complete
modulo $(ab)^2$, i.e. a system of forms which are not expressible in terms of forms
congruent to zero modulo $(ab)^2$. Next construct A_1, the corresponding system
modulo $(ab)^4$, and continue this step by step process until the system which is
finite and complete modulo $(ab)^n$ is reached. In order to construct the system
A_k which is complete modulo $(ab)^{2k+2}$ from A_{k-1}, complete modulo $(ab)^{2k}$, a
subsidiary *system B_{k-1} is introduced. The system B_{k-1} consists of covariants
of $\phi = (ab)^{2k} a_x^{n-2k} b_x^{n-2k}$. If $2n - 4k < n$ then B_{k-1} consists of the fundamental
system of ϕ. If $2n - 4k > n$, B_{k-1} consists of ϕ itself, and if $2n - 4k = n$, B_{k-1}
consists of ϕ and the invariant $(ab)^{\frac{n}{2}}(bc)^{\frac{n}{2}}(ca)^{\frac{n}{2}}$. The system derived from A_{k-1},
B_{k-1} by transvection is the system A_k.

6.2.1   The quintic.

Suppose that $n = 5$; $f = a_x^5 = b_x^5 = \cdots$. Here, the system A_0 is f itself. The
system B_0 consists of the one form $H = (ab)^2 a_x^3 b_x^3$. Hence the system A_1 is the
transvectant system given by

$$(f^\alpha, H^\beta)^\gamma.$$

By the standard method of transvection, if $\gamma > 2$ this transvectant always
contains a term of grade 3 and hence, by the theorem in Chapter IV, it may
be transformed so that it contains a series of terms congruent to zero modulo
$(ab)^4$, and so it contains reducible terms with respect to this modulus. Moreover
$(f, H)^2$ is reducible for forms of all orders as was proved by Gordan's series in
Section 1 of Chapter IV. Thus A_1 consists of $f, H, (f, H) = T$.

Proceeding to construct B_1 we note that $i = (ab)^4 a_x b_x$ is of order < 5.
Hence B_1 consists of its fundamental system:

$$B_1 = \{i, D\},$$

where D is the discriminant of i. Hence A_2 which is here the fundamental system of f is the transvectant system given by

$$\phi = (f^\alpha H^\beta T^\gamma, i^\delta D^\varepsilon)^\eta.$$

The values $\alpha = \beta = \gamma = \delta = \eta = 0, \varepsilon = l$ give D. Since D is an invariant ϕ is reducible if $\eta \neq 0$ and $\varepsilon \neq 0$. Hence $\varepsilon = 0$.

If $\beta > 1$, ϕ is reducible by means of such products as

$$(f^\alpha HT^\gamma, i)(H^{\beta-1}, i^{\delta-1})^{\eta-1}.$$

Hence

$$(i)\beta = 0$$
$$(ii)\alpha = 0, \gamma = 0, \beta = 1.$$

By Chapter IV, Section 4, IV,

$$T^2 = -\frac{1}{2}\{(f,f)^2 h^2 - 2(f,H)^2 fH + (H,H)^2 f^2\}.$$

Hence

$$T^2 \equiv -\frac{1}{2} H^3 (\mathrm{mod}(ab)^4).$$

But if $\gamma > 1$, the substitution of this in ϕ raises β above 1 and hence gives a reducible transvectant. Thus $\gamma = 0$ or 1 (of. Chap. V (158)).

Thus we need to consider in detail the following sets only:

$$(i)\alpha = 1 \text{ or } 2, \beta = 0, \gamma = 0,$$
$$(ii)\alpha = 0, \beta = 0, \gamma = 1,$$
$$(iii)\alpha = 1, \beta = 0, \gamma = 1,$$
$$(iv)\alpha = 0, \beta = 1, \gamma = 0.$$

In (i) we are concerned with $(f^\alpha, i^\delta)^\gamma$. By the method of Section 3, Chapter IV,

$$2\delta - 1 \leqq \gamma \leqq 2\delta,$$
$$5\alpha - 4 \leqq \gamma \leqq 5\alpha,$$

and consistent with this pair of relations we have

$$i, f, (f,i), (f,i)^2, (f,i^2)^3, (f,i^2)^4, (f,i^3)^5,$$
$$(f^2, i^3)^6, (f^2, i^4)^7, (f^2, i^4)^8, (f^2, i^6)^9, (f^2, i^5)^{10}.$$

Of these, $(f^2, i^3)^6$ contains reducible terms from the product

$$(f, i^2)^4 (f, i)^2,$$

and in similar fashion all these transvectants are reducible except the following eight:

$$f, i, (f, i), (f, i)^2, (f, i^2)^3, (f, i^2)^4, (f, i^8)^5, (f^2 i^5)^{10}.$$

In (ii) we have (T^γ, i^δ). But $T = -(ab)^2(bc)a_x^3 b_x^2 c_x^4$, and (T, i) contains the term $t = -(ab)^2(bc)(bi)a_x^3 b_x c_x^4$. Again

$$(bc)(bi)c_x i_x = \frac{1}{2}[(bc)^2 i_x^2 + (bi)^2 c_x^2 - (ci)^2 b_x^2].$$

Hence t involves a term having the factor f. The analysis of the remaining cases proceeds in precisely the same way as in Cases (i), (ii). In Case (ii) the irreducible transvectants prove to be

$$(T, i)^2, (T, i^2)^4, (T, i^3)^6, (T, i^4)^8, (T, i^5)^9.$$

Case (iii) gives but one irreducible case, viz. $(fT, i^7)^{14}$.

In Case (iv) we have

$$(H, i), (H, i)^2, (H, i^2)^3, (H, i^2)^4, (H, i^3)^5, (H, i^3)^6.$$

Table IV contains the complete summary. The fundamental system of f consists of the 23 forms given in this table.

TABLE IV

DEGREE	ORDER							
	0	1	2	3	4	5	6	7
1						f		
2			i				H	
3				$(i, f)^2$		(i, f)		
4	D				$(i, H)^2$		(i, H)	
5		$(i^2, f)^4$		$(i^2, f)^3$				$(i, T)^2$
6			$(i^2, H)^4$		$(i^2, H)^3$			
7		$(i^3, f)^5$				$(i^2, T)^4$		
8	$(i^3, H)^6$		$(i^3, H)^5$					
9				$(i^3, T)^6$				
11		$(i^4, T)^8$						
12	$(i^5, f^2)^{10}$							
13		$(i^5, T)^9$						
18	$(i^7, fT)^{14}$							

6.3   Resultants in Aronhold's Symbols

In order to express the concomitants derived in the preceding section in symbolical form the standard method of transvection may be employed and gives readily any concomitant of that section in explicit symbolical form. We leave

124

details of this kind to be carried out by the reader. However, in this section we give a derivation, due to Clebsch, which gives the symbolical representation of the resultant of two given forms. In view of the importance of resultants in invariant theories, this derivation is of fundamental consequence.

6.3.1 Resultant of a linear form and an n-ic.

The resultant of two binary forms equated to zero is a necessary and sufficient condition for a common factor.

Let
$$f = a_x^n; \quad \phi = \alpha_x = \alpha_1 x_1 = \alpha_2 x_2 = 0.$$
Then $x_1 : x_2 = -\alpha_2 : \alpha_1$. Substitution in f evidently gives the resultant, and in the form

$$R = (a\alpha)^n$$

6.3.2 Resultant of a quadratic and an n-ic.

Let
$$\phi = \alpha_x^2 = p_x q_x.$$
The resultant $R = 0$ is evidently the condition that f have either p_x or q_x as a factor. Hence, by I,
$$R = (ap)^n (bq)^n.$$

Let us express R entirely in terms of $a, b, \cdots$, and $\alpha, \beta, \cdots$ symbols.
We have, since a, b are equivalent symbols,
$$R = \frac{1}{2}\{(ap)^n (bq)^n + (aq)^n (bp)^n\}.$$

Let $(ap)(bq) = \mu$, $(aq)(bp) = \nu$, so that
$$R = \frac{\mu^n + \nu^n}{2}$$

Theorem. *If n is even, $R = \frac{\mu^n + \nu^n}{2}$ is rationally and integrally expressible in terms of $\rho^2 = (\mu - \nu)^2$ and $\sigma = \mu\nu$. If n is odd, $(\mu + \nu)^{-1} R$ is so expressible.*

In proof write
$$S_k = \mu^k + (-1)^{n-k} \nu^k.$$
Then
$$R = \frac{1}{2} S_n.$$
Moreover it follows directly that
$$S_n = (\mu - \nu)S_{n+1} + \mu\nu S_{n-2},$$
$$S_{n-1} = (\mu - \nu)S_{n-2} + \mu\nu S_{n-3},$$
$$\cdots\cdots\cdots\cdots\cdots\cdots\cdots$$
$$S_2 = (\mu - \nu)S_1 + \mu\nu S_0.$$

Also for n even
$$S_1 = \mu - \nu, S_0 = 2,$$

and for n odd
$$S_1 = \mu + \nu, S_0 = 0.$$

Now let

$$\Omega = S_2 + zS_3 + z^2 S_4 + \cdots$$
$$= \rho S_1 + \sigma S_0 + z\rho S_2 + z\sigma S_1 + z^2 \rho S_3 + z^2 \sigma S_2 + \ldots$$

Then we have
$$\Omega = \rho(S_1 + z\Omega) + \sigma(S_0 + zS_1 + z^2\Omega),$$

and
$$\Omega = \frac{(\rho + \sigma z)S_1 + \sigma S_0}{1 - \rho z + \sigma z^2}.$$

Then S_n is the coefficient of x^{n-2} in the expansion of Ω. Now

$$\frac{1}{1 - \rho z - \sigma z^2} = \frac{1}{1 - \rho z} + \frac{\sigma z^2}{(1 - \rho z)^2} + \frac{\sigma^2 z^4}{(1 - \rho z)^3} + \cdots$$
$$= 1 + \rho z + \rho^2 z^2 + \rho^3 z^3 + \cdots$$
$$+ (1 + 2\rho z + 3\rho^2 z^2 + 4\rho^3 z^3 + \cdots)\sigma z^2$$
$$+ (1 + \frac{2\cdot 3}{1\cdot 2}\rho z + \frac{3\cdot 4}{1\cdot 2}\rho^2 z^2 + \frac{4\cdot 5}{1\cdot 2}\rho^3 z^3)\sigma^2 z^4$$
$$+ \ldots\ldots\ldots\ldots\ldots$$
$$= K_0 + K_1 z + K_2 z^2 + K_3 z^3 + \cdots,$$

where

$$
\begin{aligned}
K_0 &= 1, K_2 = \rho^2 + \sigma, K_4 = \rho^4 + 3\rho^2\sigma + \sigma^2, \\
K_1 &= \rho, K_3 = \rho^3 + 2\rho\sigma, K_5 = \rho^5 + 4\rho^3\sigma + 3\rho\sigma^2, \\
&\quad \cdots \\
K_h &= \rho^h + (h-1)\sigma\rho^{h-2} + \frac{(h-2)(h-3)}{1\cdot 2}\sigma^2\rho^{h-4} \\
&\quad + \frac{(h-3)(h-4)(h-5)}{1\cdot 2\cdot 3}\sigma^3\rho^{h-6} + \cdots
\end{aligned}
$$

But
$$\Omega = \{(\rho S_1 + \sigma S_0) + z\sigma S_1\}\{K_0 + K_1 z + K_2 z^2 + \cdots\}.$$

In this, taking the coefficient of z^{n-2},

$$2R = S_n = (\rho S_1 + \sigma S_0)K_{n-2} + \sigma S_1 K_{n-3}.$$

But,
$$\rho K_{n-2} + \sigma K_{n-3} = K_{n-1}.$$

Hence,

$$R + \frac{1}{2}\{S_1 K_{n-1} + \sigma S_0 K_{n-2}\}.$$

Hence according as n is even or odd we have

$$2R \;=\; \rho^n + n\sigma\rho^{n-2} + \frac{n(n-3)}{1\cdot 2}\sigma^2\rho^{n-4} + \frac{n(n-4)(n-5)}{1\cdot 2\cdot 3}\sigma^3\rho^{n-6} + \cdots,$$

$$2R \;=\; (\mu+\nu)\{\rho^{n-1} + (n-2)\sigma\rho^{n-3} + \frac{(n-3)(n-4)}{1\cdot 2}\sigma^2\rho^{n-5} + $$
$$\frac{(n-4)(n-5)(n-6)}{1\cdot 2\cdot 3}\sigma^3\rho^{n-7} + \cdots\},$$

which was to be proved.

Now if we write

$$\phi = p_x q_x = \alpha_x^2 = \beta_x^2 = \cdots,$$

we have

$$p_1 q_1 = \alpha_1^2, \; p_1 q_2 + p_2 q_1 = 2\alpha_1\alpha_2, \; p_2 q_2 = \alpha_2^2.$$

Then

$$\begin{aligned}
\mu + \nu \;&=\; (ap)(bq) + (aq)(bp) \\
&=\; (a_1 p_2 - a_2 p_1)(b_1 q_2 - b_2 q_1) + (a_1 q_2 - a_2 q_1)(b_1 p_2 - b_2 p_1) \\
&=\; 2[a_1 b_1 a_2^2 - a_1 b_2 \alpha_1\alpha_2 - a_2 b_1 \alpha_1\alpha_2 + a_2 b_2 \alpha_1^2] \\
&=\; 2(a\alpha)(b\alpha),
\end{aligned}$$

$$\mu\nu = \sigma = (ap)(aq)(bp)(bq)$$
$$= p_a q_a \cdot p_b q_b = (\alpha a)^2 (ab)^2,$$
$$(\mu - \nu)^2 = \rho^2 = \{(ap)(bq) - (aq)(bp)\}^2 = (ab)^2 (pq)^2$$
$$= -2(ab)^2 (\alpha\beta)^2 = -2(ab)^2 D.$$

Let the symbols of ϕ be $\alpha', \alpha'', \cdots ; \beta', \beta'', \cdots, \gamma, \cdots$. Then we can write for the general term of R,

$$\rho^{n-2k}\sigma^k = (\mu - \nu)^{n-2k}(\mu\nu)^k = (-2)^{\frac{n}{2}-k} D^{\frac{n}{2}-k}(ab)^{n-2k}$$
$$\times (a\alpha')^2 (b\beta')^2 (a\alpha'')^2 (b\beta'')^2 \cdots (a\alpha^{(k)})^2 (b\beta^{(k)})^2$$
$$= (-2)^{\frac{n}{2}-k} D^{\frac{n}{2}-k} A_k.$$

Evidently A_k is itself an invariant. When we substitute this in $2R$ above we write the term for which $k = \frac{1}{2}n$ last. This term factors. For if

$$B = (a\alpha')^2 (a\alpha'')^2 \cdots (a\alpha^{(\frac{n}{2})})^2$$
$$= (b\beta')^2 (b\beta'')^2 \cdots (b\beta^{(\frac{n}{2})})^2,$$

then

$$\sigma^{\frac{n}{2}} = B^2.$$

Thus when n is even,

$$R = (-D)^{\frac{n}{2}} \cdot 2^{\frac{n-2}{2}} A_0 + n(-D)^{\frac{n-2}{2}} 2^{\frac{n-4}{2}} A_1$$
$$+ \frac{n(n-3)}{1\cdot 2}(-D)^{\frac{n-4}{2}} 2^{\frac{n-6}{2}} A_2$$
$$+ \frac{n(n-4)(n-5)}{1\cdot 2\cdot 3}(-D)^{\frac{n-6}{2}} 2^{\frac{n-8}{2}} A_3 \qquad (159)$$
$$+ \cdots - \frac{n^2}{4} D A_{\frac{n}{2}-1} + B^2.$$

We have also,

$$\rho^{n-2k-1}\sigma^k(\mu+\nu) = 2(-2)^{\frac{n-1}{2}} D^{\frac{n-1}{2}-k} A_k,$$

where A_k is the invariant,

$$A_k = (ab)^{n-1-2k}(a\gamma)(b\gamma)\cdot(a\alpha')(a\alpha'')^2\cdots(a\alpha^{(k)})^2\cdot(b\beta')^2(b\beta'')^2\cdots(b\beta^{(k)})^2.$$

In this case,

$$R = (-2D)^{\frac{n-1}{2}} A_0 + (n-2)(-2D)^{\frac{n-3}{2}} A_1$$
$$+ \frac{(n-3)(n-4)}{1\cdot 2}(-2d)^{\frac{n-5}{2}} A_2 \qquad (159_1)$$
$$+ \cdots - \frac{n^2-1}{4} D A_{\frac{n-3}{2}} + A_{\frac{n-1}{2}}.$$

Thus we have the following:

Theorem. *The resultant of a form of second order with another form of even order is always reducible in terms of invariants of lower degree, but in the case of a form of odd order this is not proved owing to the presence of the term* $A_{\frac{n-1}{2}}$.

A few special cases of such resultants will now be given; $(a), (b), (c), (d)$.

$$(a)\, n = 1 : R = A_0, A_0 = (a\alpha)^2$$
$$(b)\, n = 2 : R = -DA_0 + B^2, A_0 = (ab)^2, B = (a\alpha)^2.$$
$$R = -(\alpha\beta)^2(ab)^2 + (a\alpha)^2(b\beta)^2.$$
$$(c)\, n = 3 : R = -2DA_0 + A_1, A_0 = (ab)^2(a\gamma)(b\gamma).$$
$$A_1 = (a\gamma)(b\gamma)(a\alpha)^2(b\beta)^2.$$
$$R = -2(\alpha\beta)^2(ab)^2(a\gamma)(b\gamma) + (a\gamma)(b\gamma)(a\alpha)^2(b\beta)^2.$$
$$(d)\, n = 4 : R = 2D^2 A_0 - 4DA_1 + B^2, A_0 = (ab)^4.$$
$$A_1 = (ab)^2(a\alpha)^2(b\beta)^2.$$
$$B = (a\alpha)^2(a\alpha')^2.$$
$$R = 2(\alpha\beta)^2(\alpha'\beta')^2(ab)^4 - 4(\alpha\beta)^2(ab)^2(a\alpha')^2(b\beta')^2$$
$$+ (a\alpha)^2(a\alpha')^2(b\beta)^2(b\beta')^2.$$

6.4 Fundamental Systems for Special Groups of Transformations

In the last section of Chapter I we have called attention to the fact that if the group of transformations to which a form f is subjected is the special group given by the transformations

$$x_1 = \frac{\sin(\omega - \alpha)}{\sin \omega}x_1' + \frac{\sin(\omega - \beta)}{\sin \omega}x_2'; \quad x_2 = \frac{\sin \alpha}{\sin \omega}x_1' + \frac{\sin \beta}{\sin \omega}x_2',$$

then

$$q = x_1^2 + 2x_1 x_2 \cos \omega + x_2^2$$

is a universal covariant. Boole was the first to discover that a simultaneous concomitant of q and any second binary quantic f is, when regarded as a function of the coefficients and variables of f, a concomitant of the latter form alone under the special group. Indeed the fundamental simultaneous system of q and f taken in the ordinary way is, from the other point of view, evidently a fundamental system of f under the special group. Such a system is called a Boolean system of f. We proceed to give illustrations of this type of fundamental system.

6.4.1 Boolean system of a linear form.

The Boolean system for a linear form,

$$l = a_o x_1 + a_1 x_2,$$

is obtained by particularizing the coefficients of f in Paragraph I, Section 1 above by the substitution

$$\begin{pmatrix} b_0, & b_1, & b_2 \\ 1, & \cos \omega & 1 \end{pmatrix}.$$

Thus this fundamental system is

$$l = a_0 x_1 + a_1 x - 2,$$
$$q = x_1^2 + 2x_1 x_2 \cos \omega + x_2^2,$$
$$a = \sin^2 \omega,$$
$$b = (a_0 \cos \omega - a_1)x_1 + (a_0 - a_1 \cos \omega)x_2,$$
$$c = a_0^2 - 2a_0 a - 1 \cos \omega + a_1^2.$$

6.4.2 Boolean system of a quadratic.

In order to obtain the corresponding system for a quadratic form we make the above particularization of the b coefficients in the simultaneous system of two quadratics (cf. Section 1, III above).

Thus we find that the Boolean system of f is

$$f = a_0 x_1^2 + 2a_1 x_1 x_2 + a_2 x_2^2,$$
$$q = x_1^2 + 2x_1 x_2 \cos \omega + x_2^2,$$
$$D = 2(a_0 a_2 - a_1^2),$$
$$d = \sin^2 \omega,$$
$$e = a_0 + a_2 - 2a_1 \cos \omega,$$
$$F = (a_0 \cos \omega - a_1)x_1^2 + (a_0 - a_1)x_1 x_2 + (a_1 - a_2 \cos \omega)x_2^2.$$

6.4.3 Formal modular system of a linear form.

If the group of transformations is the finite group formed by all transformations T_p whose coefficients are the positive residues of a prime number p then, as was mentioned in Chapter I,

$$L = x_1^p x_2 - x_1 x_2^p$$

is a universal covariant. Also one can prove that all other universal covariants of the group are covariants of L. Hence the simultaneous system of a linear form l and L, taken in the algebraic sense as the simultaneous system of a linear form and a form of order $p + 1$ will give formal modular invariant formations of l. We derive below a fundamental system of such concomitants for the case $p = 3$. Note that some forms of the system are obtained by polarization. Let $f = a_0 x_1 + a_1 x_2$; $p = 3$. The algebraical system of f is f itself. Polarizing this,

$$C = \left(x^3 \frac{\partial}{\partial x}\right) f = a_0 x_1^3 + a_1 x_2^3, \ \left(x^9 \frac{\partial}{\partial x}\right) f = a_0 x_1^9 + a_1 x_2^9 = C',$$

$$D = \left(a^3 \frac{\partial}{\partial a}\right) f = a_0^3 + a_1^3 x_2.$$

The fundamental system of universal covariants of the group T_3 is

$$L = x_1^3 x_2 - x_1 x_2^3, Q = x_1^6 + x_1^4 x_2^2 + x_1^2 x_2^4 + x_2^6 = ((L, L)^2, L).$$

The simultaneous system of f and L is (cf. §1, II)

$$(L, f^r)^r (r = 1, \ldots, 4); \quad (Q, f^s)^s (s = 1, \ldots, 6).$$

Of these some belong to the above polar system and some are reducible; as $(Q, f^2)^2 \equiv fC \pmod 3$. But

$$A = (L, f^4)^4 \equiv a_0^3 a_1 - a_0 a_1^3,$$
$$B = (Q, f^6)^6 \equiv a_0^6 + a_0^4 a_1^2 + a_0^2 a_1^4 + a_1^6,$$
$$E = (Q, f^3)^3 \equiv a_1(a_0^2 - a_1^2)x_1^3 - a_0^3 x_1^2 x_2 + a_1^3 x_1 x_2^2 + a_0(a_0^2 - a_1^2)x_2^3 \pmod 3.$$

The polars

$$\left.\begin{array}{l} \left(x^3 \frac{\partial}{\partial x}\right) D \equiv f^3, \left(x^3 \frac{\partial}{\partial x}\right) E \equiv DL \\ \left(a^3 \frac{\partial}{\partial a}\right) A \equiv 0, \left(a^3 \frac{\partial}{\partial a}\right) B \equiv A^2 \end{array}\right\} \pmod 3,$$

are reducible. The polar C' is also reducible. In fact,

$$C' \equiv CQ - fL^2 \pmod 3.$$

The formal fundamental system of f modulo 3 is

$$A, B, C, D, E, f, L, Q.$$

6.5 Associated Forms

Consider any two covariants ϕ_1, ϕ_2 of a binary form $f(x_1, x_2)$ of order m. Let the first polars of these be

$$\lambda = \phi_{1x}^{n-1}\phi_{1y}, \; \mu = \phi_2^{p-1}x\phi_{2y}$$

or

$$\lambda = \lambda_1 y_1 + \lambda_2 y_2, \; \mu = \mu_1 y_1 + \mu_2 y_2 \tag{159_1}$$

where

$$\lambda_i = \frac{1}{n}\frac{\partial\phi_1}{\partial x_i}, \; \mu_i = \frac{1}{p}\frac{\partial\phi_2}{\partial x_i} \; (i = 1, 2).$$

Let the equations (159_1) be solved for y_1, y_2. Then if J is the Jacobian of the two covariants ϕ_1, ϕ_2, the result of substituting y_1, y_2 for x_1, x_2 in $f(x_1, x_2)$ is

$$f(y_1, y_2) = \frac{1}{J^m}(A_0\lambda^m + A_1\lambda^{m-1}\mu + \ldots + A_m\mu^m)$$

and the forms $A_0, A_1, \cdots, A_n$ are covariants of f, as will be proved below. But the inverse of (159_1) constitutes a linear transformation on the variables y_1, y_2 in which the new variables are λ, μ. Hence if

$$\phi(a_0, a_1, \cdots, a_m; y_1, y_2)$$

is any covariant of f with x_1, x_2 replaced by the cogredient set y_1, y_2, and if $f(y_1, y_2)$ above is taken as the transformed form, the corresponding invariant relation is

$$C'\phi(a_0, a_1, \cdots, a_m; y_1, y_2) = J^k\phi\left(\frac{A_0}{J^m}, \frac{A_1}{J^m}, \cdots, \frac{A_m}{J^m}; \lambda, \mu\right),$$

where C' is a constant. Now let $(y) = (x)$, and this relation becomes, on account of the homogeneity in the coefficients,

$$\phi(a_0, a_1, \cdots, a_m; a_1, x_2) = \frac{C}{J^\tau}\phi(A_0, A_1, \cdots, A_m; \phi_1, \phi_2).$$

Thus every covariant ϕ of f is expressible rationally in terms of the $m + 3$ covariants of the system

$$A_0, A_1, A_2, \cdots, A_m, \phi_1, \phi_2.$$

Such a system of covariants in terms of which all covariants of a form are rationally expressible is called a system of *associated forms* (Hermite). The expression for $f(y_1, y_2)$ above is called a *typical representation* of f.

Now we may select for ϕ_2 in this theory the universal covariant

$$\phi_{2_y} = x_1 y_2 - x_2 y_1,$$

and then the coefficient covariants $A_0, A_1, \cdots$ can be given in explicit symbolical form. First, however, we obtain the typical representation of f as an expansion based upon a formal identity. From

$$\lambda = \lambda_1 y_1 + \lambda_2 y_2, \mu = \mu_1 y_1 + \mu_2 y_2,$$

i.e. $\lambda = \lambda_y, \mu = \mu_y$; and $f = a_y^m$, we have the identity

$$(\lambda\mu) a_y = (a\mu)\lambda - (a\lambda)\mu.$$

If we raise both sides of this identity to the mth power we have at once the symbolical representation of the typical representation of f, in the form

$$(\lambda\mu)^m f(y_1, y_2) = B_0 \lambda_m - m B_1 \lambda^{m-1} \mu + \cdots + (-1)^m B_m \mu^m,$$

where

$$B_0 = (a\mu)^m, B_1 = (a\mu)^{m-1}(a\lambda), B_2 = (a\mu)^{m-2}(a\lambda)^2, \cdots, B_m = (a\lambda)^m.$$

Also

$$(\lambda\mu)^m = J^m.$$

Now with $\mu = (xy)$ we have

$$J = \lambda_1 x_1 + \lambda_2 x_2 = \phi_1,$$

by Euler's theorem. Moreover we now have

$$B_0 = a_x^m = f, B_1 = a_x^{m-1}(a\lambda), B_2 = a_x^{m-2}(a\lambda)^2, \cdots,$$

for the associated forms, and

$$\phi(a_0, a_1, \cdots ; y_1, y_2) = \frac{1}{\phi_1^\tau} \phi(B_0, -B_1, B_2, \cdots ; \lambda, \mu),$$

and

$$\phi(a_0, a_1, \cdots ; x_1, x_2) = \frac{1}{\phi_1^\tau} \phi(f, -B_1, B_2, \cdots ; \phi, 0).$$

Again a further simplification may be had by taking for ϕ the form f itself. Then we have

$$B_0 = f, B_1 = (ab)a_x^{m-1}b_x^{m-1} = 0, B_2 = (ab)(ac)a_x^{m-2}b_x^{m-1}c_x^{m-1}, \cdots$$

and the following theorem:

132

Theorem. *If in the leading coefficient of any covariant ϕ we make the replacements*

$$\begin{pmatrix} a_0, & a_1, & a_2, & a_3, & \cdots, \\ \phi_1(=f), & -B_1(=0), & B_2, & -B_3, & \cdots, \end{pmatrix}$$

and divide by a properly chosen power of $\phi(=f)$ we have an expression for ϕ as a rational function of the set of m associated forms

$$\phi_1(=f), B_1(=0), B_2, B_3, \cdots .$$

For illustration let $m = 3$, f being a binary cubic. Let ϕ be the invariant R. Then since

$$B_2 = (ab)(ac)b_x c_x \cdot a_x b_x c_x = \frac{1}{2}(ab)^2 a_x b_x c_x^3 = \frac{1}{2}\Delta \cdot f, B_3 = fQ,$$

where Δ is the Hessian, and Q the cubic covariant of f, the typical representation of f is

$$f^2 f(y) = \xi^3 + \frac{3}{2}\Delta \xi \eta^2 + Q\eta^3.$$

If one selects for ϕ the invariant

$$-\frac{1}{2}R = (a_0 a_3 - a_1 a_2)^2 - 4(a_0 a_2 - a_1^2)(a_1 a_3 - a_2^2),$$

and substitutes

$$\begin{pmatrix} a_0, & a_1, & a_2, & a_3 \\ f^{-2}, & 0, & \frac{1}{2}\Delta f^{-2}, & -Qf^{-2} \end{pmatrix},$$

there results

$$-\frac{1}{2}R = \left[(f^{-4}Q)^2 + \frac{1}{2}f^{-3}\Delta^3 \right] f^6.$$

That is,

$$-Rf^2 = 2Q^2 + \Delta^3.$$

This is the syzygy connecting the members of the fundamental system of the cubic f (cf. Chap. IV, §4). Thus the expression of R in terms of the associated forms leads to a known syzygy.

Chapter 7

COMBINANTS AND RATIONAL CURVES

7.1 Combinants

In recent years marked advances have been made in that branch of algebraic invariant theory known as the theory of combinants.

7.1.1 Definition.

Let $f, g, h, \cdots$ be a set of m binary forms of order n, and suppose that $m < n$;

$$f = a_0 x_1^n + \cdots, \quad g = b_0 x_1^n + \cdots, \quad h = c_0 x_1^n + \cdots.$$

Let

$$\phi(a_1, a_1, \cdots; \, b_0, \cdots; \, c_0, \cdots; \, x_1, x_2)$$

be a simultaneous concomitant of the set. If ϕ is such a function that when $f, g, h, \cdots$ are replaced by

$$f' = \xi_1 f + \eta_1 g + \zeta_1 h + \cdots, \quad g' = \xi_2 f + \eta_2 g + \zeta_2 h + \cdots,$$
$$h' = \xi_3 f + \eta_3 g + \zeta_3 h + \cdots, \cdots \tag{160}$$

the following relation holds:

$$\phi(a_0', a_1', \cdots; b_0', \cdots; c_0', \cdots; x_1, x_2)$$
$$= (\xi \eta \zeta \cdots)^k \phi(a_0, a_1, \cdots; b_0, \cdots; c_0, \cdots; x_1, x_2); \tag{161}$$

where

$$D \equiv (\xi \eta \zeta \cdots) = \begin{vmatrix} \xi_1, & \eta_1, & \zeta_1, & \cdots \\ \xi_2, & \eta_2, & \zeta_2, & \cdots \\ \xi_3, & \eta_3, & \zeta_3, & \cdots \\ \xi_4, & \eta_4, & \zeta_4, & \cdots \\ \cdot & \cdot & \cdot & \cdot \end{vmatrix},$$

then ϕ is called a combinant of the set (Sylvester).

We have seen that a covariant of f in the ordinary sense is an invariant function under two linear groups of transformations. These are the group given by T and the induced group (23_1) on the coefficients. A combinant is not only invariantive under these two groups but also under a third group given by the relations

$$
\begin{aligned}
a_0' &= \xi_1 a_0 + \eta_1 b_0 + \zeta_1 c_0 + \cdots, \\
a_1' &= \xi_1 a_1 + \eta_1 b_1 + \zeta_1 c_1 + \cdots, \\
&\cdots \\
b_0' &= \xi_2 a_0 + \eta_2 b_0 + \zeta_2 c_0 + \cdots, \\
&\cdots
\end{aligned}
\tag{162}
$$

As an illustration of a class of combinants we may note that all transvectants of odd index of f and g are combinants of these forms. Indeed

$$
\begin{aligned}
(\xi_1 f &+ \eta_1 g, \xi_2 f + \eta_2 g)^{2r+1} \\
&= \xi_1 \xi_2 (f, f)^{2r+1} + (\xi\eta)(f, g)^{2r+1} + \eta_1 \eta_2 (g, g)^{2r+1} \\
&= (\xi\eta)(f, g)^{2r+1},
\end{aligned}
\tag{163}
$$

by (79) and (81). Hence $(f, g)^{2r+1}$ is a combinant. Included in the class (163) is the Jacobian of f and g, and the bilinear invariant of two forms of odd order (Chap. III, V).

7.1.2   Theorem on Aronhold operators.

Theorem. *Every concomitant, ϕ, of the set $f, g, h, \cdots$ which is annihilated by each one of the complete system of Aronhold's polar operators*

$$
\left(a \frac{\partial}{\partial b} \right), \quad \left(a \frac{\partial}{\partial c} \right), \quad \left(b \frac{\partial}{\partial c} \right), \quad \left(b \frac{\partial}{\partial a} \right), \quad \cdots
$$

is a combinant of the set.

Observe first that ϕ is homogeneous, and in consequence

$$
\left(a \frac{\partial}{\partial a} \right) \phi = i_1 \phi, \quad \left(b \frac{\partial}{\partial b} \right) = i_2 \phi, \cdots,
$$

where i_1 is the partial degree of ϕ in the coefficients a of f, i_2 the degree of ϕ in the coefficients of g, and so forth. Since $(a \frac{\partial}{\partial b})\phi = 0$, then $(a' \frac{\partial}{\partial b'})\phi' = 0$. Thus

$$
\begin{aligned}
&+ (\xi_1 a_0 + \eta_1 b_0 + \cdots + \sigma_1 e_0) \frac{\partial \phi'}{\partial(\xi_2 a_0 + \eta_2 b_0 + \cdots + \sigma_2 e_0)} \\
&+ (\xi_1 a_1 + \eta_1 b_1 + \cdots + \sigma_1 e_1) \frac{\partial \phi'}{\partial(\xi_2 a_1 + \eta_2 b_1 + \cdots + \sigma_2 e_1)} \\
&\qquad \cdots \cdots \cdots \cdots \cdots \cdots \cdots \cdots \cdots \cdots \cdots \cdots \\
&+ (\xi_1 a_n + \eta_1 b_n + \cdots + \sigma_1 e_n) \frac{\partial \phi'}{\partial(\xi_2 a_n + \eta_2 b_n + \cdots + \sigma_2 e_n)} = 0.
\end{aligned}
\tag{164}
$$

$$\xi_1 \sum_{i=0}^{n} a_i \frac{\partial \phi'}{\partial(\xi_2 a_i + \cdots + \sigma_2 e_i)} + \cdots + \sigma_1 \sum_{i=0}^{n} e_i \frac{\partial \phi'}{\partial(\xi_2 a_i + \cdots + \sigma_2 e_i)} = 0. \quad (165)$$

$$\xi_1 \sum_{i=0}^{n} \frac{\partial \phi'}{\partial(\xi_2 a_i + \cdots + \sigma_2 e_i)} \frac{\partial(\xi_2 a_i + \cdots + \sigma_2 e_i)}{\partial \xi_2}$$

$$+ \cdots \cdots \cdots \cdots \cdots \cdots \cdots \cdots \cdots$$

$$+ \sigma_1 \sum_{i=0}^{n} \frac{\partial \phi'}{\partial(\xi_2 a_i + \cdots + \sigma_2 e_i)} \frac{\partial(\xi_2 a_i + \cdots + \sigma_2 e_i)}{\partial \sigma_2} = 0. \quad (166)$$

Hence

$$\delta_{12}\phi' \equiv \left(\xi_1 \frac{\partial}{\partial \xi_2} + \eta_1 \frac{\partial}{\partial \eta_2} + \cdots + \sigma_1 \frac{\partial}{\partial \sigma_2} \right) \phi' = 0,$$

and generally,

$$\delta_{st}\phi' \equiv \left(\xi_s \frac{\partial}{\partial \xi_t} + \eta_s \frac{\partial}{\partial \eta_t} + \cdots + \sigma_s \frac{\partial}{\partial \sigma_t} \right) \phi' \left. \right\} \begin{aligned} &= 0 (s \gtrless t) \\ &= i_s \phi' (s = t), \end{aligned} \quad (167)$$

where i is the total degree of ϕ in all of the coefficients. In (167) we have m^2 equations given by $(s, t = 1, \cdots, m)$. We select the following m of these and solve them for the derivatives $\frac{\partial \phi'}{\partial \xi_1}, \cdots$:

$$\xi_1 \frac{\partial \phi'}{\partial \xi_1} + \eta_1 \frac{\partial \phi'}{\partial \eta_1} + \cdots + \sigma_1 \frac{\partial \phi'}{\partial \sigma_1} = i_1 \phi',$$

$$\xi_2 \frac{\partial \phi'}{\partial \xi_1} + \eta_2 \frac{\partial \phi'}{\partial \eta_1} + \cdots + \sigma_2 \frac{\partial \phi'}{\partial \sigma_1} = 0, \quad (168)$$

$$\cdots \cdots \cdots \cdots \cdots \cdots \cdots \cdots \cdots$$

$$\xi_m \frac{\partial \phi'}{\partial \xi_1} + \eta_m \frac{\partial \phi'}{\partial \eta_1} + \cdots + \sigma_m \frac{\partial \phi'}{\partial \sigma_1} = 0.$$

Solution of these linear equations gives

$$\frac{\partial \phi'}{\partial \xi_1} = \frac{\frac{\partial D}{\partial \xi_1}}{(\xi \eta \zeta \cdots)} i_1 \phi', \frac{\partial \phi'}{\partial \eta_1} = \frac{\frac{\partial D}{\partial \eta_1}}{(\xi \eta \zeta \cdots)} i_1 \phi', \cdots, \frac{\partial \phi'}{\partial \sigma_1} = \frac{\frac{\partial D}{\partial \sigma_1}}{(\xi \eta \zeta \cdots)} i_1 \phi'.$$

But we know that

$$d\phi' = \frac{\partial \phi'}{\partial \xi_1} d\xi_1 + \frac{\partial \phi'}{\partial \eta_1} d\eta_1 + \cdots + \frac{\partial \phi'}{\partial \sigma_1} d\sigma_1.$$

Hence

$$d\phi' = \left(\frac{\partial D}{\partial \xi_1} d\xi_1 + \frac{\partial D}{\partial \eta_1} d\eta_1 + \cdots + \frac{\partial D}{\partial \sigma_1} d\sigma_1 \right) \frac{i_1 \phi'}{D}$$

$$= \frac{dD}{D} i_1 \phi'.$$

Hence we can separate the variables and integrate:

$$\frac{d\phi'}{\phi'} = i_1 \frac{dD}{D},$$

$$\phi' = D^{i_1} F(a_0, \ldots), \tag{169}$$

where F is the constant of integration. To determine F, particularize the relations (162) by taking all coefficients $\xi, \eta, \cdots$ zero except

$$\xi_1 = \eta_2 = \cdots = \sigma_m = 1.$$

Then $a_0' = a_0, a_1' = a_1, \cdots, b_i' = b_i$, etc., and (169) becomes

$$\phi \equiv F.$$

Hence

$$\phi' = D^{i_1} \phi,$$

which proves the theorem.

It is to be noted that the set (168) may be chosen so that the differentiations are all taken with respect to $\xi_k, \eta_k, \cdots$ in (168). Then we obtain in like manner

$$\phi' = D^{i_k} \phi.$$

Thus

$$i_1 = i_2 = \cdots = i_m.$$

That is, a combinant is such a simultaneous concomitant that its partial degrees in the coefficients of the several forms are all equal. This may be proved independently as the

7.1.3   Partial degrees.

Theorem. *A combinant is of equal partial degrees in the coefficients of each form of the set.*

We have

$$\left[\left(a\frac{\partial}{\partial b} \right) \left(b\frac{\partial}{\partial a} \right) - \left(b\frac{\partial}{\partial a} \right) \left(a\frac{\partial}{\partial b} \right) \right] \phi = 0.$$

Hence

$$\left[\left(a\frac{\partial}{\partial a} \right) - \left(b\frac{\partial}{\partial b} \right) \right] \phi \equiv (i_1 - i_2)\phi = 0.$$

Thus $i_1 = i_2$. Similarly $i_j = i_k (j, k = 1, 2, \cdots, m)$.

7.1.4 Resultants are combinants.

Theorem. *The resultant of two binary forms of the same order is a combinant.*

Let

$$f = f(x_1, x_2), \; g = g(x_1, x_2).$$

Suppose the roots of f are $(r_1^{(i)}, r_2^{(i)})(i = 1, \cdots, n)$, and of g $(s_1^{(i)}, s_2^{(i)})(i = 1, \cdots, n)$. Then the resultant may be indicated by

$$R = g(r_1^{(1)}, r_2^{(1)})g(r_1^{(2)}, r_2^{(2)}) \cdots g(r_1^{(n)}, r_2^{(n)}),$$

and by

$$R = f(s_1^{(1)}, s_2^{(1)})f(s_1^{(2)}, s_2^{(2)}) \cdots f(s_1^{(n)}, s_2^{(n)}).$$

Hence

$$\left(a\frac{\partial}{\partial b}\right) R = \Sigma f(r_1^{(1)}, r_2^{(1)})g(r_1^{(2)}, r_2^{(2)}) \cdots g(r_1^{(n)}, r_2^{(n)}) = 0,$$

$$\left(b\frac{\partial}{\partial a}\right) R = \Sigma g(s_1^{(1)}, s_2^{(1)})f(s_1^{(2)}, s_2^{(2)}) \cdots f(s_1^{(n)}, s_2^{(n)}) = 0.$$

Thus R is a combinant by Theorem II.

Gordan has shown[1] that there exists a fundamental combinant of a set of forms. A fundamental combinant is one of a set which has the property that its fundamental system of concomitants forms a fundamental system of combinants of the set of forms. The proof of the Theorem II of this section really proves also that every combinant is a homogeneous function of the determinants of order m,

$$\begin{vmatrix} a_{k_1} & b_{k_1} & c_{k_1} & \cdots & l_{k_1} \\ a_{k_2} & b_{k_2} & c_{k_2} & \cdots & l_{k_2} \\ \vdots & \vdots & \vdots & \ddots & \vdots \\ a_{k_m} & b_{k_m} & c_{k_m} & \cdots & l_{k_m} \end{vmatrix},$$

that can be formed from the coefficients of the forms of the set. This also follows from (162). For the combinant is a simultaneous invariant of the linear forms

$$\xi a_k + \eta b_k + \zeta c_k + \cdots + \sigma l_k (k = 0, 1, \cdots, n), \tag{170}$$

and every such invariant is a function of the determinants of sets of m such linear forms. Indeed if we make the substitutions

$$\xi = \xi_1 \xi' + \xi_2 \eta' + \cdots + \xi_m \sigma',$$
$$\eta = \eta_1 \xi' + \eta_2 \eta' + \cdots + \eta_m \sigma',$$
$$\cdots \cdots \cdots \cdots \cdots$$

---

[1] Mathematische Annalen, Vol. 5.

in (170) we obtain

$$a'_k = \xi_1 a_k + \eta_1 b_k + \zeta_1 c_k + \cdots ,$$
$$b'_k = \xi_2 a_k + \eta_2 b_k + \zeta_2 c_k + \cdots ,$$

$$\ldots \ldots \ldots \ldots$$

and these are precisely the equations (162).

For illustration, if the set of n-ics consists of

$$f = a_0 x_1^2 + 2a_1 x_1 x_2 + a_2 x_2^2,$$
$$g = b_0 x_1^2 + 2b_1 x_1 x_2 + b_2 x_2^2,$$

any combinant of the set is a function of the three second order determinants

$$(a_0 b_1 - a_1 b_0), (a_0 b_2 - a_2 b_0), (a_1 b_2 - a_2 b_1).$$

Now the Jacobian of f and g is

$$J = (a_0 b_1 - a_1 b_0) x_1^2 + (a_0 b_2 - a_2 b_0) x_1 x_2 + (a_1 b_2 - a_2 b_1) x_2^2.$$

Hence any combinant is a concomitant of this Jacobian. In other words J is the fundamental combinant for two quadratics. The fundamental system of combinants here consists of J and its discriminant. The latter is also the resultant of f and g.

The fundamental system of combinants of two cubics f, g, is (Gordan)

$$\vartheta = (f,g), \quad \theta = (f,g)^3, \quad \Delta = (\vartheta,\vartheta)^2, \quad (\vartheta,\vartheta)^4, \quad (\Delta,\vartheta), \quad (\Delta,\vartheta)^4.$$

The fundamental combinants are ϑ and θ, the fundamental system consisting of the invariant θ and the system of the quartic ϑ (cf. Table II).

7.1.5 Bezout's form of the resultant.

Let the forms f, g be quartics,

$$f = a_0 x_1^4 + a_1 x_1^3 x_2 + \cdots ,$$
$$g = b_0 x_1^4 + b_1 x_1^3 x_2 + \cdots .$$

From $f = 0$, $g = 0$ we obtain, by division,

$$\frac{a_0}{b_0} = \frac{a_1 x_1^3 + a_2 x_1^2 x_2 + a_3 x_1 x_2^2 + a_4 x_2^3}{b_1 x_1^3 + b_2 x_1^2 x_2 + b_3 x_1 x_2^2 + b_4 x_2^3},$$

$$\frac{a_0 x_1 + a_1 x_2}{b_0 x_1 + b_1 x_2} = \frac{a_2 x_1^2 + a_3 x_1 x_2 + a_4 x_2^2}{b_2 x_1^2 + b_3 x_1 x_2 + b_4 x_4^2},$$

$$\frac{a_0 x_1^2 + a_1 x_1 x_2 + a_2 x_2^2}{b_0 x_1^2 + b_1 x_1 x_2 + b_2 x_2^2} = \frac{a_3 x_1 + a_4 x_2}{b_3 x_1 + b_4 x_2},$$

$$\frac{a_0 x_1^3 + a_1 x_1^2 x_2 + a_2 x_1 x_2^2 + a_3 x_2^3}{b_0 x_1^3 + b_1 x_1^2 x_2 + b_2 x_1 x_2^2 + b_3 x_2^3} = \frac{a_4}{b_4}.$$

Now we clear of fractions in each equation and write

$$\begin{bmatrix} a_i & b_i \\ a_k & b_k \end{bmatrix} = p_{ik}.$$

We then form the eliminant of the resulting four homogeneous cubic forms. This is the resultant, and it takes the form

$$R = \begin{vmatrix} p_{01} & p_{02} & p_{03} & p_{04} \\ p_{02} & p_{08}+p_{12} & p_{04}+p_{13} & p_{14} \\ p_{03} & p_{04}+p_{13} & p_{14}+p_{23} & p_{24} \\ p_{04} & p_{14} & p_{24} & p_{34} \end{vmatrix}$$

Thus the resultant is exhibited as a function of the determinants of the type peculiar to combinants. This result is due to Bezout, and the method to Cauchy.

7.2 Rational Curves

If the coordinates of the points of a plane curve are rational integral functions of a parameter the curve is called a rational curve. We may adopt a homogeneous parameter and write the parametric equations of a plane quartic curve in the form

$$\begin{aligned}
x_1 &= a_{10}\xi_1^4 + a_{11}\xi_1^8\xi_2 + \cdots + a_{14}\xi_2^4 = f_1(\xi_1,\xi_2), \\
x_2 &= a_{20}\xi_1^4 + a_{21}\xi_1^3\xi_2 + \cdots + a_{24}\xi_2^4 = f_2(\xi_1,\xi_2), \\
x_3 &= a_{30}\xi_1^4 + a_{31}\xi_1^3\xi_2 + \cdots + a_{34}\xi_2^4 = f_3(\xi_1,\xi_2).
\end{aligned} \qquad (170_1)$$

We refer to this curve as the R_4, and to the rational plane curve of order n as the R_n.

7.2.1 Meyer's translation principle.

Let us intersect the curve R_4 by two lines

$$\begin{aligned}
u_x &= u_1 x_1 + u_2 x_2 + u_3 x_3 = 0, \\
v_x &= v_1 x_1 + v_2 x_2 + v_3 x_3 = 0.
\end{aligned}$$

The binary forms whose roots give the two tetrads of intersections are

$$\begin{aligned}
u_f ={} & (a_{10}u_1 + a_{20}u_2 + a_{30}u_3)\xi_1^4 + (a_{11}u_1 + a_{21}u_2 + a_{31}u_3)\xi_1^3\xi_2 \\
& + (a_{12}u_1 + a_{22}u_2 + a_{32}u_3)\xi_1^2 u_3)\xi_1^2\xi_2^2 + (a_{18}u_1 + a_{23}u_2 + a_{33}u_3)\xi_1\xi_2^3 \\
& + (a_{14}u_1 + a_{24}u_2 + a_{34}u_3)\xi_2^4,
\end{aligned}$$

and the corresponding quartic v_f. A root $(\xi_1^{(i)}, \xi_2^{(i)})$ of $u_f = 0$ substituted in (170_1) gives one of the intersections $(x_1^{(i)}, x_2^{(i)}, x_3^{(i)})$ of $u_x = 0$ and the R_4.

Now $u_f = 0$, $v_f = 0$ will have a common root if their resultant vanishes. Consider this resultant in the Bezout form R. We then have, by taking

$$a_{iu} = a_{1i}u_1 + a_{2i}u_2 + a_{3i}u_3 \ (i = 0, \cdots, 4),$$

$$p_{ik} = a_{iu}a_{kv} - a_{iv}a_{ku}.$$

Thus

$$p_{ik} = (uv)_1(a_{2i}a_{3k} - a_{2k}a_{3i}) + (uv)_2(a_{3i}a_{1k} - a_{1i}a_{3k})$$
$$+ (uv)_3(a_{1i}a_{2k} - a_{1k}a_{2i}),$$

where $(uv)_1 = u_2v_3 - u_3v_2$, $(uv)_2 = u_3v_1 - u_1v_3$, $(uv)_3 = u_1v_2 - u_2v_1$. Hence

$$p_{ik} = \begin{vmatrix} (uv)_1 & (uv)_2 & (uv)_3 \\ a_{1i} & a_{2i} & a_{3i} \\ a_{1k} & a_{2k} & a_{3k} \end{vmatrix}.$$

But if we solve $u_x = 0$, $v_x = 0$ we obtain

$$x_1 : x_2 : x_3 = (uv)_1 : (uv)_2 : (uv)_3.$$

Therefore

$$p_{ik} = \sigma \begin{vmatrix} x_1 & x_2 & x_3 \\ a_{1i} & a_{2i} & a_{3i} \\ a_{1k} & a_{2k} & a_{3k} \end{vmatrix} (i, k = 0, \cdots, 4),$$

where σ is a constant proportionality factor. We abbreviate

$$p_{ik} = \sigma |xa_i a_k|.$$

Now substitute these forms of p_{ik} in the resultant R. The result is a ternary form in x_1, x_2, x_3 whose coefficients are functions of the coefficients of the R_4. Moreover the vanishing of the resulting ternary form is evidently the condition that $u_x = 0$, $v_x = 0$ intersect on the R_4. That is, this ternary form is the cartesian equation of the rational curve. Similar results hold true for the R_n as an easy extension shows.

Again every combinant of two forms of the same order is a function of the determinants

$$p_{ik} = \begin{vmatrix} a_i & a_k \\ b_i & b_k \end{vmatrix}.$$

Hence the substitution

$$p_{ik} = \sigma |xa_i a_k|,$$

made in any combinant gives a plane curve. This curve is covariantive under ternary collineations, and is called a covariant curve. It is the locus of the intersection of $u_x = 0$, $v_x = 0$ when these two lines move so as to intersect the rational curve in two point ranges having the projective property represented by the vanishing of the combinant in which the substitutions are made.

7.2.2 Covariant curves.

For example two cubics

$$f = a_0 x_1^3 + a_1 x_1^2 x_3 + \cdots, \, g = b + 0 x_1^3 + b_1 x_1^2 x_2 + \cdots,$$

have the combinant

$$K = (a_0 b_3 - a_3 b_0) - \frac{1}{3}(a_1 b_2 - a_2 b_1).$$

When $K = 0$ the cubics are said to be apolar. The rational curve R_3 has, then, the covariant curve

$$K(x) \equiv |x a_0 a_3| - \frac{1}{3}|x a_1 a_2| = 0.$$

This is a straight line. It is the locus of the point (u_x, v_x) when the lines $u_x = 0$, $v_x = 0$ move so as to cut R_3 in apolar point ranges. It is, in fact, the line which contains the three inflections of R_3, and a proof of this theorem is given below. Other theorems on covariant curves may be found in W. Fr. Meyer's Apolarität und Rationale Curven (1883). The process of passing from a binary combinant to a ternary covariant here illustrated is called a *translation principle*. It is easy to demonstrate directly that all curves obtained from combinants by this principle are covariant curves.

Theorem. *The line $K(x) = 0$ passes through all of the inflexions of the rational cubic curve R_3.*

To prove this we first show that if g is the cube of one of the linear factors of $f = \alpha_x^{(1)} x_1 + \alpha_2^{(1)} x_2)^3$,

$$g = (\alpha_1^{(1)} x_1 + \alpha_2^{(1)} x_2)^3,$$

then the combinant K vanishes identically. In fact we then have

$$b_0 = \alpha_1^{(1)3}, b_1 = 3\alpha_1^{(1)2}\alpha_2^{(1)}, \cdots,$$

and

$$a_0 = \alpha_1^{(1)}\alpha_1^{(2)}\alpha_1^{(3)}, a_1 = \sum \alpha_1^{(1)}\alpha_1^{(2)}\alpha_2^{(3)}, \cdots.$$

When these are substituted in K it vanishes identically.

Now assume that u_x is tangent to the R_3 at an inflexion and that v_x passes through this inflexion. Then u_f is the cube of one of the linear factors of v_f, and hence $K(x)$ vanishes, as above. Hence $K(x) = 0$ passes through all inflexions.

The bilinear invariant of two binary forms f, g of odd order $2n + 1 = m$ is

$$K_m = a + 0b_m - ma_1 b_{m-1} + \binom{m}{2}a_2 b_{m-2} + \cdots + ma_{m-1} b_1 - a_m b_0,$$

or

$$K_m = P_{0m} - mp_{1m-1} + \binom{m}{2}p_{2m-2} - \cdots + (-1)^n \binom{m}{n} p_{nn+1},$$

where $f = a_0 x_1^m + m a_1 x_1^{m-1} x_2 + \cdots$.

If two lines $u_x = 0$, $v_x = 0$ cut a rational curve R_m of order $m = 2n+1$ in two ranges given by the respective binary forms

$$u_f, v_f$$

of order m, then in order that these ranges may have the projective property $K_m = 0$ it is necessary and sufficient that the point (u_x, v_x) trace the line

$$K_m(x) \equiv \sum_{i=1}^{n} (-1)^i \frac{|a_i a_{m-i} x|}{\binom{m}{i}} = 0.$$

This line contains all points on the R_m where the tangent has m points in common with the curve at the point of tangency. The proof of this theorem is a direct extension of that above for the case $m = 3$, and is evidently accomplished with the proof of the following:

Theorem. *A binary form, f, of order m is apolar to each one of the m, m-th powers of its own linear factors.*

Let the quantic be

$$f = a_x^m = a_0 x_1^m + \cdots = \prod_{j=1}^{m} (r_2^{(j)} x_1 - r_1^{(j)} x_2).$$

The condition for apolarity of f with any form $g = b_x^m$ is

$$(ab)^m = a_0 b_m - m a_1 b_{m-1} + \cdots + (-1)^m a_m b_0 = (f, g)^m = 0$$

But if g is the perfect m-th power,

$$g = (r_2^{(j)} x_1 - r_1^{(j)} x_2)^m = (xr^{(j)})^m,$$

we have (cf. (88))

$$(f, g)^m = (a_x^m, (xr^{(j)})^m)^m = (-1)^m a_{r(j)}^m,$$

which vanishes because $(r_1^{(j)}, r_2^{(j)})$ is a root of f.

To derive another type of combinant, let f, g be two binary quartics,

$$f = a_0 x_1^4 + 4 a_1 x_1^3 x_2 + \cdots . \qquad g = b_0 x_1^4 + 4 b_1 x_1^3 x_2 + \cdots .$$

Then the quartic $F \equiv f + kg = A_0 x_1^4 + \cdots$, has the coefficient

$$A_i = a_i + k b_i \qquad (i = 0, 1, \cdots, 4).$$

The second degree invariant $i_F = A_0 A_4 - 4 A_1 A_3 + 3 A_2^2$ of F now takes the form

$$i = \delta i \cdot k + \frac{\delta^2 i}{|2} k^2 = i_F,$$

where δ is the Aronhold operator

$$\delta = b_0\frac{\partial}{\partial a_0} + b_1\frac{\partial}{\partial a_1} + b_2\frac{\partial}{\partial a_2} + b_3\frac{\partial}{\partial a_3} + b_4\frac{\partial}{\partial a_4},$$

and

$$i = a_0 a_4 - 4a_1 a_3 + 3a_2^2.$$

The discriminant of i_F, e.g.,

$$G \equiv (\delta i)^2 - 2i(\delta^2 i),$$

is a combinant of the two quartics f, g. Explicitly,

$$G = p_{04}^2 + 16p_{13}^2 - 8p_{03}p_{14} - 8p_{01}p_{34} + 12p_{02}p_{24} - 48p_{12}p_{23}.$$

Applying the translation principle to $G = 0$ we have the covariant curve

$$G(x) = |a_0 a_4 x|^2 + \frac{1}{16}|a_1 a_3 x|^2 - \frac{1}{2}|a_0 a_3 x|\,|a_1 a_4 x| - \frac{1}{2}|a_0 a_1 x|\,|a_3 a_4 x|$$
$$+ \frac{1}{3}|a_0 a_2 x|\,|a_2 a_4 x| - \frac{1}{12}|a_1 a_2 x|\,|a_2 a_3 x| = 0.$$

If $i_F = 0$ the quartic F is said to be self-apolar, and the curve $G(x) = 0$ has the property that any tangent to it cuts the R_4 in a self-apolar range of points.

Chapter 8

SEMINVARIANTS. MODULAR INVARIANTS

8.1 Binary Semivariants

We have already called attention, in Chapter I, Section 1, VIII, to the fact that a complete group of transformations may be built up by combination of several particular types of transformations.

8.1.1 Generators of the group of binary collineations.

The infinite group given by the transformations T is obtainable by combination of the following particular linear transformations:

$$t : x_1 = \lambda x, x_2 = \mu y,$$
$$t_1 : x = x' + \nu y', y = y',$$
$$t_2 : x' = x_1', y' = \sigma x_1' + x_2'.$$

For this succession of three transformations combines into

$$x_1 = \lambda (1 + \sigma \nu) x_1' + \lambda \nu x_2', x_2 = \sigma \mu x_1' + \mu x_2',$$

and evidently the four parameters,

$$\mu_2 = \mu, \lambda_2 = \sigma \mu, \mu_1 = \lambda \nu, \lambda_1 = \lambda (1 + \sigma \nu),$$

are independent. Hence the combination of t, t_1, t_2 is

$$T : x_1 = \lambda_1 x_1' + \mu_1 x_2', x_2 = \lambda_2 x_1' + \mu_2 x_2'.$$

In Section 4 of Chapter VI some attention was given to fundamental systems of invariants and covariants when a form is subjected to special groups of transformations T_p. These are the *formal modular* concomitants. *Booleans* are also of this character. We now develop the theory of invariants of a binary form f subject to the special transformations t_1.

8.1.2 Definition.

Any homogeneous, isobaric function of the coefficients of a binary form f whose coefficients are arbitrary variables, which is left invariant when f is subjected to the transformation t_1 is called a *seminvariant*. Any such function left invariant by t_2 is called an *anti-seminvariant*.

In Section 2 of Chapter I it was proved that a necessary and sufficient condition that a homogeneous function of the coefficients of a form f of order m be an invariant is that it be annihilated by

$$O = ma_1\frac{\partial}{\partial a_0} + (m-1)a_2\frac{\partial}{\partial a_1} + \cdots + a_m\frac{\partial}{\partial a_{m-1}},$$

$$\Omega = a_0\frac{\partial}{\partial a_1} + 2a_1\frac{\partial}{\partial a_2} + \cdots + ma_{m-1}\frac{\partial}{\partial a_m}.$$

We now prove the following:

8.1.3 Theorem on annihilator Ω.

Theorem. *A necessary and sufficient condition in order that a function I, homogeneous and isobaric in the coefficients of $f = a_x^m$, may be a seminvariant of f is that it satisfy the linear partial differential equation $\Omega I = 0$.*

Transformation of $f = a_0 x_1^m + ma_1 x_1^{m-1} x_2 + \cdots$ by t_1 gives $f' = a_0' x_1'^m + ma_1' x_1'^{m-1} x_2' + \cdots$, where

$$a_0' = a_0,$$
$$a_1' = a_1 + a_0 v,$$
$$a_2' = a_2 + 2a_1 v + a_0 v^2,$$

$$\cdots\cdots\cdots$$

$$a_m' = a_m + ma_{m-1}v + \binom{m}{2}a_{m-2}v^2 + \cdots + a_0 v^m.$$

Hence

$$\frac{\partial a_0'}{\partial v} = 0, \; \frac{\partial a_1'}{\partial v} = a_0', \; \frac{\partial a_2'}{\partial v} = 2a_1', \; \frac{\partial a_3'}{\partial v} = 3a_2', \cdots, \; \frac{\partial a_m'}{\partial v} = ma_{m-1}'.$$

Now we have

$$\frac{\partial I(a_0', a_1', \cdots)}{\partial v} = \frac{\partial I}{\partial a_0'}\frac{\partial a_0'}{\partial v} + \frac{\partial I}{\partial a_1'}\frac{\partial a_1'}{\partial v} + \cdots + \frac{\partial I}{\partial a_m'}\frac{\partial a_m'}{\partial v}$$

$$= (a_0'\frac{\partial}{\partial a_1'} + 2a_1'\frac{\partial}{\partial a_2'} + \cdots + ma_{m-1}'\frac{\partial}{\partial a_m'})I = \Omega' I(a_0', \cdots). \tag{172}$$

But $\frac{\partial I(a_0', \cdots)}{\partial v} = 0$ is a necessary and sufficient condition in order that $I(a_0', \cdots, a_m')$ may be free from v, *i.e.* in order that $I(a_0', \cdots)$ may be unaffected when we make $v = 0$. But when $v = 0, a_j' = a_j$ and

$$I(a_0', \cdots, a_m') = I(a_0, \cdots, a_m).$$

Hence $\frac{\partial I}{\partial v} = \Omega'(a'_0, \cdots) = 0$ is the condition that $I(a'_0, \cdots)$ be a seminvariant. Dropping primes, $\Omega I(a_0, \cdots) = 0$ is a necessary and sufficient condition that $I(a_0, \cdots)$ be a seminvariant.

8.1.4 Formation of seminvariants.

We may employ the operator Ω advantageously in order to construct the seminvariants of given degree and weight. For illustration let the degree be 2 and the weight w. If w is even every seminvariant must be of the form

$$I = a_0 a_w + \lambda_1 a_1 a_{w-1} + \lambda_2 a_2 a_{w-2} + \cdots + \lambda_{\frac{1}{2}w} a_{\frac{1}{2}w}^2.$$

Then by the preceding theorem

$$\Omega I = (w + \lambda_1)a_0 a_{w-1} + ((w-1)\lambda_1 + 2\lambda_2)a_1 a_{w-2} + \cdots \equiv 0.$$

Or

$$w + \lambda_1 = 0,\ (w-1)\lambda_1 + 2\lambda_2 = 0,\ (w-2)\lambda_2 + 3\lambda_3 = 0, \cdots,\ \left(\frac{1}{2}w + 1\right)\lambda_{\frac{1}{2}w-1} + w\lambda_{\frac{1}{2}w} = 0.$$

Solution of these linear equations for $\lambda_1, \lambda_2, \cdots$ gives

$$I = a_0 a_w - \binom{w}{1} a_1 a_{w-1} + \binom{w}{2} a_2 a_{w-2} - \cdots$$

$$+ (-1)^{\frac{1}{2}w-1} \binom{w}{\frac{1}{2}w - 1} a_{\frac{1}{2}w-1} a_{\frac{1}{2}w+1} + \frac{1}{2}(-1)^{\frac{1}{2}w} \binom{w}{\frac{1}{2}w} a_{\frac{1}{2}w}^2.$$

Thus there is a single seminvariant of degree 2 for every even weight not exceeding m.

For an odd weight w we would assume

$$I = a_0 a_w + \lambda_1 a_1 a_{w-1} + \cdots + \lambda_{\frac{1}{2}(w-1)} a_{\frac{1}{2}(w-1)} a_{\frac{1}{2}(w+1)}.$$

Then $\Omega I = 0$ gives

$$w + \lambda_1 = 0,\ (w-1)\lambda_1 + 2\lambda_2 = 0, \cdots,\ \frac{1}{2}(w+3)\lambda_{\frac{1}{2}(w-3)} + \frac{1}{2}(w-1)\lambda_{\frac{1}{2}(w-1)} = 0,\ \lambda_{\frac{1}{2}(w-1)} = 0.$$

Hence $\lambda_1 = \lambda_2 = \cdots = \lambda_{\frac{1}{2}(w-1)} = 0$, and no seminvariant exists.

Thus the complete set of seminvariants of the second degree is

$$A_0 = a_0^2,$$
$$A_2 = a_0 a_2 - a_1^2,$$
$$A_4 = a_0 a_4 - 4a_1 a_3 + 3a_2^2,$$
$$A_6 = a_0 a_6 - 6a_1 a_5 + 15a_2 a_4 - 10a_3^2,$$
$$A_8 = a_0 a_8 - 8a_1 a_7 + 28a_2 a_6 - 56a_3 a_5 + 35a_4^2.$$

$$\cdots\cdots\cdots$$

The same method may be employed for the seminvariants of any degree and weight. If the number of linear equations obtained from $\Omega I = 0$ for the determination is just sufficient for the determination of $\lambda_1, \lambda_2, \lambda_3, \cdots$ and if these equations are consistent, then there is just one seminvariant I of the given degree and weight. If the equations are inconsistent, save for $\lambda_0 = \lambda_1 = \lambda_2 = \cdots = 0$, there is no seminvariant. If the number of linear equations is such that one can merely express all λ's in terms of r independent ones, then the result of eliminating all possible λ's from I is an expression

$$I = \lambda_1 I_1 + \lambda_2 I_2 + \cdots + \lambda_r I_r.$$

In this case there are r linearly independent seminvariants of the given degree and weight. These may be chosen as

$$I_1, I_2, \cdots, I_r.$$

8.1.5 Roberts' Theorem.

Theorem. *If C_0 is the leading coefficient of a covariant of $f = a_0 x_1^m + \cdots$ of order ω, and C_ω is its last coefficient, then the covariant may be expressed in the forms*

$$C_0 x_1^\omega + \frac{OC_0}{1!} x_1^{\omega-1} x_2 + \frac{O^2 C_0}{2!} x_1^{\omega-2} x_2^2 + \cdots + \frac{O^\omega C_0}{\omega!} x_2, \qquad (173)$$

$$\frac{\Omega^\omega C_\omega}{\omega!} x_1^\omega + \frac{\Omega^{\omega-1} C_\omega}{(\omega-1)!} x_1^{\omega-1} x_2 + \cdots + \frac{\Omega C_\omega}{1!} x_1 x_2^{\omega-1} + C_\omega x_2^\omega. \qquad (174)$$

Moreover, C_0 is a seminvariant and C_ω an anti-seminvariant.

Let the explicit form of the covariant be

$$K = C_0 x_1^\omega + \binom{\omega}{1} C_1 x_1^{\omega-1} x_2 + \cdots + C_\omega x_2^\omega.$$

Then by Chapter I, Section 2, XII,

$$\left(\Omega - x_2 \frac{\partial}{\partial x_1} \right) K \equiv 0.$$

Or

$$\Omega C_0 x^\omega + \omega(\Omega C_1 - C_0) x_1^{\omega-1} x_2 + \binom{\omega}{2}(\Omega C_2 - 2C_1) x_1^{\omega-2} x_2^2 + \cdots$$

$$+ \omega(\Omega C_{\omega-1} - \omega - 1 C_{\omega-2}) x_1 x_2^{\omega-1} + (\Omega C_\omega - \omega C_{\omega-1}) x_2^\omega \equiv 0.$$

Hence the separate coefficients in the latter equation must vanish, and therefore

$$\Omega C_0 = 0,$$
$$\Omega C_1 = C_0,$$
$$\Omega C_2 = 2C_1,$$

$$\cdots\cdots$$

$$\Omega C_{\omega-1} = (\omega - 1)C_{\omega-2},$$
$$\Omega C_\omega = \omega C_{\omega-1}.$$

The first of these shows that C_0 is a seminvariant. Combining the remaining ones, beginning with the last, we have at once the determination of the coefficients indicated in (174).

In a similar manner

$$\left(O - x_1 \frac{\partial}{\partial x_2}\right) K \equiv 0,$$

and this leads to

$$OC_0 = \omega C_1, \ OC_1 = (\omega - 1)C_2, \cdots, \ OC_{\omega-1} = C_\omega, OC_\omega = 0;$$
$$C_i = \frac{1}{\omega(\omega-1)(\omega-2)\cdots(\omega-i+1)} O^i C_0 (i = 0, \cdots, \omega).$$

This gives (173).

It is evident from this remarkable theorem that a covariant of a form f is completely and uniquely determined by its leading coefficient. Thus in view of a converse theorem in the next paragraph the problem of determining covariants is really reduced to the one of determining its seminvariants, and from certain points of view the latter is a much simpler problem. To give an elementary illustration let f be a cubic. Then

$$0 = 3a_1 \frac{\partial}{\partial a_0} + 2a_2 \frac{\partial}{\partial a_1} + a_3 \frac{\partial}{\partial a_2},$$

and if C_0 is the seminvariant $a_0 a_2 - a_1^2$ we have

$$OC_0 = a_0 a_3 - a_1 a_2, \ O^2 C_0 = 2(a_1 a_3 - a_2^2), \ O^3 C_0 = 0.$$

Then $2K$ is the Hessian of f, and is determined uniquely from C_0.

8.1.6 Symbolical representation of seminvariants.

The symbolical representation of the seminvariant leading coefficient C_0 of any covariant K of f, i.e.

$$K = (ab)^p (ac)^q \cdots a_x^r b_x^s c_x^t \cdots (r + s + t + \cdots = \omega),$$

is easily found. For, this is the coefficient of x_1 in K, and in the expansion of

$$(ab)^p (ac)^q \cdots (a_1 x_1 + a_2 x_2)^r (b_1 x_1 + b_2 x_2)^s \cdots$$

the coefficient of x_1^ω is evidently the same as the whole expression K except that a_1 replaces a_x, b_1 replaces b_x, and so forth. Hence the seminvariant leader of K is

$$C_0 = (ab)^p(ac)^q \cdots a_1^r b_1^s c_1^t \cdots$$
$$(r + s + t + \cdots \text{a positive number}).$$

$$(175)$$

In any particular case this may be easily computed in terms of the actual coefficients of f (cf. Chap. III, §2, I).

Theorem. *Every rational integral seminvariant of f may be represented as a polynomial in expressions of the type C_0, with constant coefficients.*

For let ϕ be the seminvariant and

$$\phi(a_0', \cdots) = \phi(a_0, \cdots)$$

the seminvariant relation. The transformed of

$$f = (\alpha_1 x_1 + \alpha_2 x_2)^m$$

by

$$t_1 : x_1 = x_1' + \nu x_2', x_2 = x_2',$$

is

$$f' = [\alpha_1 x_1' + (\alpha_1 \nu + \alpha_2)x_2']^m.$$

If the $a_0, a_1, \cdots$ in $\phi(a_0, \cdots)$ are replaced by their symbolical equivalents it becomes a polynomial in $\alpha_1, \alpha_2, \beta_1, \beta_2, \cdots$ say $F(\alpha_1, \alpha_2, \beta_1, \beta_2, \ldots)$. Then

$$\begin{aligned}
\phi(a_0', \cdots) &= F(\alpha_1, \alpha_1\nu + \alpha_2, \beta_1, \beta_1\nu + \beta_2, \cdots) \\
&= F(\alpha_1, \alpha_2, \beta_1, \beta_2, \cdots).
\end{aligned}$$

Expansion by Taylor's theorem gives

$$\nu\left(\alpha_1\frac{\partial}{\partial\alpha_2} + \beta_1\frac{\partial}{\partial\beta_2} + \gamma_1\frac{\partial}{\partial\gamma_2} + \cdots\right) F(\alpha_1, \alpha_2, \beta_1, \beta_2, \cdots) = 0.$$

Now a necessary and sufficient condition that F should satisfy the linear partial differential relation

$$\delta F = \left(\alpha_1\frac{\partial}{\partial\alpha_2} + \beta_1\frac{\partial}{\partial\beta_2} + \cdots\right) F = 0,$$

is that F should involve the letters $\alpha_2, \beta_2, \ldots$ only in the combinations

$$(\alpha\beta), (\alpha\gamma), (\beta\gamma), \cdots.$$

In fact, treating $\delta F = 0$ as a linear equation with constant coefficients ($\alpha_1, \beta_1, \cdots$ being unaltered under t_1) we have the auxiliary equations

$$\frac{d\alpha_2}{\alpha_1} = \frac{d\beta_2}{\beta 1} = \frac{d\gamma_2}{\gamma_1} = \cdots = \frac{dF}{0}.$$

152

Hence F is a function of $(\alpha\beta), (\alpha\gamma), \cdots$ with constant coefficients which may involve the constants $\alpha_1, \beta_1, \cdots$. In other words, since $\phi(a_0) = F(a_1, \cdots)$ is rational and integral in the a's F is a polynomial in these combinations with coefficients which are algebraical rational expressions in the $\alpha_1, \beta_1, \cdots$. Also every term of such an expression is invariant under t_1, i.e. under

$$\alpha_1' = \alpha_1, \alpha_2' = \alpha_1\nu + \alpha_2, \cdots,$$

and is of the form

$$\Gamma_0 = (\alpha\beta)^{p_1} (\alpha\gamma)^{p_2} \cdots \alpha_1^{\sigma} \beta_1^{\sigma} \cdots,$$

required by the theorem.

We may also prove as follows: Assume that F is a function of $(\alpha\beta)$, $(\alpha\gamma)$, $(\alpha\delta)$, $\cdots$ and of any other arbitrary quantity s. Then

$$\alpha_1 \frac{\partial F}{\partial \alpha_2} = \alpha_1 \frac{\partial F}{\partial(\alpha\beta)} \frac{\partial(\alpha\beta)}{\partial \alpha_2} + \alpha_1 \frac{\partial F}{\partial(\alpha\gamma)} \frac{\partial(\alpha\gamma)}{\partial \alpha_2} + \cdots + \alpha_1 \frac{\partial F}{\partial s} \frac{\partial s}{\partial \alpha_2},$$

$$\beta_1 \frac{\partial F}{\partial beta_2} = \beta_1 \frac{\partial F}{\partial(\alpha\beta)} \frac{\partial(\alpha\beta)}{\partial \beta_2} + \beta_1 \frac{\partial F}{\partial(\alpha\gamma)} \frac{\partial(\alpha\gamma)}{\partial \beta_2} + \cdots + \beta_1 \frac{\partial F}{\partial s} \frac{\partial s}{\partial \beta_2},$$

etc. But

$$\alpha_1 \frac{\partial F}{\partial(\alpha\beta)} \frac{\partial(\alpha\beta)}{\partial \alpha_2} = -\alpha_1 \beta_1 \frac{\partial F}{\partial(\alpha\beta)},$$

$$\beta_1 \frac{\partial F}{\partial(\alpha\beta)} \frac{\partial(\alpha\beta)}{\partial \beta_2} = +\alpha_1 \beta_1 \frac{\partial F}{\partial(\alpha\beta)},$$

$$\cdots$$

Hence by summing the above equations we have

$$\delta F = \frac{\partial F}{\partial s} \left(\alpha_1 \frac{\partial s}{\partial \alpha_2} + \beta_1 \frac{\partial s}{\partial \beta_2} + \cdots \right) = \frac{\partial F}{\partial s} \delta s = 0.$$

Since s is entirely arbitrary we can select it so that $\delta s \neq 0$. Then $\frac{\partial F}{\partial s} = 0$, and F, being free from s, is a function of the required combinations only.

Theorem. *Every seminvariant of f of the rational integral type is the leading coefficient of a covariant of f.*

It is only required to prove that for the terms Γ_0 above $w = \rho + \sigma + \cdots$ is constant, and each index

$$\rho, \sigma, \cdots$$

is always a positive integer or zero. For if this be true the substitution of $\alpha_x, \beta_x, \cdots$ for $\alpha_1, \beta_1, \cdots$ respectively in the factors $\alpha_1^{\rho} \beta_1^{\sigma} \cdots$ of Γ_0 and the other terms of F, gives a covariant of order ω whose leading coefficient is $\phi(a_0, \cdots)$. We have

$$\sum \Gamma_0 = \sum (\alpha\beta)^{p_1} (\alpha\gamma)^{p_2} \cdots \alpha_1^{\rho} \beta_1^{\sigma} \cdots = \phi(a_0, \cdots).$$

If the degree of ϕ is i, the number of symbols involved in Γ_0 is i and its degree in these symbols im. The number of determinant factors $(\alpha\beta)\cdots$ is, in general,

$$w = p_1 + p_2 + \cdots + p_{\frac{1}{2}i(i-1)},$$

and this is the weight of ϕ. The degree in the symbols contributed to Γ_0 by the factors $(\alpha\beta)\cdots$ is evidently $2w$, and we have $\rho, \sigma, \cdots$ all positive and

$$im \geqq 2w,$$

that is,

$$\omega = im - 2w \geqq 0.$$

For a more comprehensive proof let

$$d = \alpha_2 \frac{\partial}{\partial \alpha_1} + \beta_2 \frac{\partial}{\partial \beta_1} + \cdots .$$

Then

$$\delta d - d\delta = \alpha_1 \frac{\partial}{\partial \alpha_1} + \beta_1 \frac{\partial}{\partial \beta_1} + \cdots - \alpha_2 \frac{\partial}{\partial \alpha_2} - \beta_2 \frac{\partial}{\partial \beta_2} + \cdots .$$

Hence, since Γ_0 is homogeneous in the symbols we have by Euler's theorem,

$$
\begin{aligned}
(\delta d - d\delta)\Gamma_0 &= (w + \omega - w)\Gamma_0 = \omega\Gamma_0, \\
(\delta d^2 - d^2\delta)\Gamma_0 &= (\delta d - d\delta)d\Gamma_0 + d(\delta d - d\delta)\Gamma_0 = 2(\omega - 1)d\Gamma_0, \\
&\quad\vdots \qquad\qquad \vdots \\
(\delta d^k - d^k\delta)\Gamma_0 &= k \quad (\omega - k + 1)d^{k-1}\Gamma_0 (k = 1, 2, \ldots), \\
&\quad\cdots \qquad\qquad \cdots
\end{aligned}
$$

But

$$\delta\Gamma_0 = 0, \text{ hence } \delta d^k\Gamma_0 = k(\omega - k + 1)d^{k-1}\Gamma_0.$$

Also

$$
\begin{aligned}
da_i &= da_1^{m-i}a_2^i = (m - i)a_{i-1} = Oa_i \quad (i = 0, 1, \ldots, m - 1), \\
d\phi &= \frac{\partial\phi}{\partial a_0}da_0 + \frac{\partial\phi}{\partial a_1}da_1 + \cdots + \frac{\partial\phi}{\partial a_{m-1}}da_{m-1} = O\phi.
\end{aligned}
$$

Hence $d^k\Gamma_0$ is of weight $w + k$. Then

$$d^{im-w+1}\Gamma_0 = 0.$$

For this is of weight $im+1$ whereas the greatest possible weight of an expression of degree i is im, the weight of a_m^i.

Now assume ω to be negative. Then $d^{im-w}\Gamma_0 = 0$ because

$$\delta d^{im-w+1}\Gamma_0 = (im - w + 1)[\omega - (im - w + 1) + 1]d^{im-w}\Gamma_0 = 0.$$

Next $d^{im-w-1}\Gamma_0 = 0$ because

$$\delta d^{im-w}\Gamma_0 = (im - w)[\omega - (im - w) + 1]d^{im-w-1}\Gamma_0 = 0.$$

Proceeding in this way we obtain $\Gamma_0 = 0$, contrary to hypothesis. Hence the theorem is proved.

8.1.7 Finite systems of binary seminvariants.

If the binary form $f = a_0 x_1^m + m a_1 x_1^{m-1} + \cdots$ be transformed by

$$x_1 = x_1' + \nu x_2', \quad x_2 = x_2',$$

there will result,

$$f' = C_0 x_1'^m + m C_1 x_1'^{m-1} x_2' + \binom{m}{2} C_2 x_1'^{m-2} x_2'^2 + \cdots + C_m x_2'^m,$$

in which

$$C_i = a_0 \nu^i + i a_1 \nu^{i-1} + \binom{i}{2} a_2 \nu^{i-2} + \cdots + i a_{i-1} \nu + a_i. \tag{176}$$

Since $\Omega C_0 = \Omega a_0 = 0$, C_0 is a seminvariant. Under what circumstances will all of the coefficients $C_i (i = 0, \cdots, m)$ be seminvariants? If C_1 is a seminvariant

$$\Omega C_1 = \Omega(a_0 \nu + a_1) = a_0 \Omega \nu + a_0 = 0.$$

That is, $\Omega \nu = -1$. We proceed to show that if this condition is satisfied $\Omega C_i = 0$ for all values of i.

Assume $\Omega \nu = -1$ and operate upon C_i by Ω. The result is capable of simplification by

$$\Omega \nu^s = s \nu^{s-1} \Omega \nu = -s \nu^{s-1},$$

and is

$$\begin{aligned}
\Omega C_i \;=\; & -i a_0 \nu^{i-1} - \binom{i}{1}(i-1) a_1 \nu^{i-2} - \cdots - \binom{i}{r}(i-r) a_r \nu^{i-r-1} - \cdots \\
& -i a_{i-1} + \binom{i}{1} a_0 \nu^{i-1} + 2\binom{i}{2} a_1 \nu^{i-2} + \cdots \\
& +\binom{i}{r+1}(r+1) a_r \nu^{i-r-1} + \cdots + i a_{i-1}.
\end{aligned}$$

But

$$\binom{i}{r+1}(r+1) = \frac{i(i-1)\cdots(i-r+1)(i-r)}{r!} = \binom{i}{r}(i-r).$$

Hence $\Omega C_i = 0$.

Now one value of ν for which $\Omega \nu = -1$ is $\nu = -\frac{a_1}{a_0}$. If f be transformed by

$$x_1 = x_1' - \frac{a_1}{a_0} x_2', \quad x_2 = x_2',$$

then $C_1 \equiv 0$, and all of the remaining coefficients C_i are seminvariants. Moreover, in the result of the transformation,

$$
\begin{aligned}
\Gamma_i \equiv a_0^{i-1}C_i \;=\;& a_0^{i-1}a_i - \binom{i}{1}a_0^{i-2}a_{i-1}a_1 + \binom{i}{2}a_0^{i-3}a_{i-2}a_1^2 - \cdots \\
+\;& (-1)^{i-2}\binom{i}{2}a_0a_2a_1^{i-2} + (-1)^{i-1}(i-1)a_1^i \\
=\;& \sum_{r=2}^{i-2}(-1)^r\binom{i}{r}a_0^{i-r-1}a_{i-r}a_1^r + (-1)^{i-1}(i-1)a_1^i.
\end{aligned}
$$

This gives the explicit form of the seminvariants. The transformed form itself may now be written

$$
f' = \Gamma_0 x_1'^m + \binom{m}{2}\frac{\Gamma_2}{\Gamma_0}x_1'^{m-2}x_2'^2 + \binom{m}{3}\frac{\Gamma_3}{\Gamma_0^2}x_1'^{m-3}x_2'^3 + \cdots + \frac{\Gamma_m}{\Gamma_0^{m-1}}x_2'^m.
$$

Theorem. *Every seminvariant of f is expressible rationally in terms of Γ_0, Γ_2, Γ_3, $\cdots$, Γ_m. One obtains this expression by replacing a_1 by 0, a_0 by Γ_0, and $a_i(i \neq 0, 1)$ by*
$\frac{\Gamma_i}{\Gamma_0^{i-1}}$ *in the original form of the seminvariant. Except for a power of $\Gamma_0 =$*
a_0 *in the denominator the seminvariant is rational and integral in the $\Gamma_i(i = 0, 2, \cdots, m)$ (Cayley).*

In order to prove this theorem we need only note that f' is the transformed form of f under a transformation of determinant unity and that the seminvariant, as S, is invariantive under this transformation. Hence

$$
S\left(\Gamma_0, 0, \frac{\Gamma_2}{\Gamma_0}, \frac{\Gamma_3}{\Gamma_0^2}, \cdots, \frac{\Gamma_m}{\Gamma_0^{m-1}}\right) = S(a_0, a_1, a_2, \cdots, a_m), \tag{177}
$$

which proves the theorem.

For illustration consider the seminvariant

$$
S = a_0 a_4 - 4a_1 a_3 + 3a_2^2.
$$

This becomes

$$
S = \frac{1}{\Gamma_0^2}(3\Gamma_2^2 + \Gamma_4),
$$

or

$$
\begin{aligned}
S \;=\;& a_0 a_4 - 4a_1 a_3 + 3a_2^2 \\
=\;& \frac{1}{a_0^2}[3(a_0 a_2 - a_1^2)^2 + (a_0^3 a_4 - 4a_0^2 a_1 a_3 + 6a_0 a_1^2 a_2 - 3a_1^4)].
\end{aligned}
$$

This is an identity. If the coefficients appertain to the binary quartic the equation becomes (cf. (125))

$$
\frac{1}{2}a_0^2 i = 3\Gamma_2^2 + \Gamma_4.
$$

Again if we take for S the cubic invariant J of the quartic we obtain

$$\frac{1}{6}J = \begin{vmatrix} a_0 & 0 & \frac{1}{a_0}\Gamma_2 \\ 0 & \frac{1}{a_0}\Gamma_2 & \frac{1}{a_0^2}\Gamma_3 \\ \frac{1}{a_0}\Gamma_2 & \frac{1}{a_0^2}\Gamma_3 & \frac{1}{a_0^3}\Gamma_4 \end{vmatrix},$$

or

$$\frac{1}{6}a_0^3 J = \Gamma_2\Gamma_4 - \Gamma_2^3 - \Gamma_3^2.$$

Combining the two results for i and J we have

$$\Gamma_2\Gamma_4 = \frac{1}{2}a_0^2 i\Gamma_2 - 3\Gamma_2^3 = \frac{1}{6}a_0^3 J + \Gamma_2^3 + \Gamma_3^2.$$

Now $2\Gamma_2$ is the seminvariant leading coefficient of the Hessian H of the quartic f, and Γ_3 is the leader of the covariant T. In view of Roberts' theorem we may expect the several covariants of f to satisfy the same identity as their seminvariant leaders. Substituting $\frac{1}{2}H$ for Γ_2, T for Γ_3, and f for a_0, the last equation gives

$$H^3 + \frac{1}{3}f^3 J + 2T^2 - \frac{1}{2}if^2 H = 0,$$

which is the known syzygy (cf. (140)).

8.2 Ternary Seminvariants

We treat next the seminvariants of ternary forms, Let the ternary quantic of order m be

$$f = \sum_{m_i} \frac{m!}{m_1! m_2! m_3!} a_{m_1 m_2 m_3} x_1^{m_1} x_2^{m_2} x_3^{m_3}, \ (m_1 + m_2 + m_3 = m).$$

When this is transformed by ternary collineations,

$$V: \ \begin{aligned} x_1 &= \lambda_1 x_1' + \mu_1 x_2' + \nu_1 x_3', \\ x_2 &= \lambda_2 x_1' + \mu_2 x_2' + \nu_2 x_3', \\ x_3 &= \lambda_3 x_1' + \mu_3 x_1' + \nu_3 x_3', \ \ (\lambda\mu\nu) \neq 0 \end{aligned}$$

it becomes f', where the new coefficients a' are of order m in the λ's, μ's, and ν's. This form f may be represented symbolically by

$$f = a_x^m = (a_1 x_1 + a_2 x_2 + a_3 x_3)^m$$

The transformed form is then (cf. (76))

$$f' = (a_\lambda x_1' + a_\mu x_2' + a_\nu x_3')^m \tag{178}$$

$$= \sum_{m_i} \frac{m!}{m_1! m_2! m_3!} a_\lambda^{m_1} a_\mu^{m_2} a_\mu^{m_3} x_1^{m_1} x_2^{m_2} x_3^{m_3} \ \ (m_1 + m_2 + m_3 = m).$$

Then we have

$$a'_{m_1 m_2 m_3} = a_\lambda^{m_1} a_\mu^{m_2} a_\nu^{m_3}$$

Now let

$$\left(\mu \frac{\partial}{\partial \lambda}\right) = \mu_1 \frac{\partial}{\partial \lambda_1} + \mu_2 \frac{\partial}{\partial \lambda_2} + \mu_3 \frac{\partial}{\partial \lambda_3},$$
$$\left(\nu \frac{\partial}{\partial \lambda}\right) = \nu_1 \frac{\partial}{\partial \lambda_1} + \nu_2 \frac{\partial}{\partial \lambda_2} + \nu_3 \frac{\partial}{\partial \lambda_3} \quad \text{(cf. (58))}.$$

Then, evidently (cf. (75) and (23$_1$))

$$\frac{m!}{(m - m_2 - m_3)!} a'_{m_1 m_2 m_3} = \left(\mu \frac{\partial}{\partial \lambda}\right)^{m_2} \left(\nu \frac{\partial}{\partial \lambda}\right)^{m_3} a_\lambda^m \qquad (m_1 + m_2 + m_3 = m).$$

$$(179)$$

This shows that the leading coefficient of the transformed form is a_λ^m, *i.e.* the form f itself with (x) replaced by (λ), and that the general coefficient results from the double ternary polarization of a_λ^m as indicated by (179).

Definition.

Let ϕ be a rational, integral, homogeneous function of the coefficients of f, and ϕ' the same function of the coefficients of f'. Then if for any operator $\left(\mu \frac{\partial}{\partial \lambda}\right)$, $\left(\lambda \frac{\partial}{\partial \nu}\right)$, $\cdots$, say for $\left(\lambda \frac{\partial}{\partial \mu}\right)$, the relation

$$\left(\lambda \frac{\partial}{\partial \mu}\right) \phi' = 0$$

is true, ϕ is called a seminvariant of f.

The reader should compare this definition with the analytical definition of an invariant, of Chapter I, Section 2, XI.

8.2.1 Annihilators

. A consequence of this definition is that a seminvariant satisfies a linear partial differential equation, or annihilator, analogous to Ω in the binary theory.

For,

$$\left(\lambda \frac{\partial}{\partial \mu}\right) \phi' = \frac{\partial \phi'}{\partial a'_{m00}} \left(\lambda \frac{\partial a'_{m00}}{\partial \mu}\right) + \cdots + \frac{\partial \phi'}{\partial a'_{m_1 m_2 m_3}} \left(\lambda \frac{\partial a'_{m_1 m_2 m_3}}{\partial \mu}\right) + \cdots$$
$$+ \frac{\partial \phi'}{\partial a'_{00m}} \left(\lambda \frac{\partial a'_{00m}}{\partial \mu}\right),$$

and

$$\lambda \frac{\partial a'_{m_1 m_2 m_3}}{\partial \mu} = \left(\lambda \frac{\partial}{\partial \mu}\right) a_\lambda^{m_1} a_\mu^{m_2} a_\nu^{m_3} = m_2 a_\lambda^{m_1+1} a_\mu^{m_2-1} a_\nu^{m_3} = m_2 a'_{m_1+1\, m_2-1\, m_3}.$$

158

Hence

$$\left(\lambda\frac{\partial}{\partial\mu}\right)\phi' = \sum_{m_i} m_2 a'_{m_1+1\,m_2-1\,m_3}\frac{\partial\phi'}{\partial a'_{m_1 m_2 m_3}} = 0\,(m_1 + m_2 + m_3 = m).$$

$$(180)$$

Now since the operator

$$\sum_{m_i} m_2 a'_{m_1+1\,m_2-1\,m_3}\frac{\partial}{\partial a'_{m_1 m_2 m_3}}$$

annihilates ϕ' then the following operator, which is ordinarily indicated by $\Omega_{x_2 x_1}$, is an annihilator of ϕ.

$$\Omega_{x_2 x_1} = \sum_{m_i} m_2 a_{m_1+1\,m_2-1\,m_3}\frac{\partial}{\partial a_{m_1 m_2 m_3}}\quad(m_1 + m_2 + m_3 = m)\qquad(181)$$

The explicit form of a ternary cubic is

$$f = a_{300}x_1^3 + 3a_{210}x_1^2 x_2 + 3a_{120}x_1 x_2^2 + a_{030}x_2^3 + 3a_{201}x_1^2 x_3$$
$$+ 6a_{111}x_1 x_2 x_3 + 3a_{021}x_2^2 x_3 + 3a_{102}x_1 x_3^2 + 3a_{012}x_2 x_3^2 + a_{003}x_3^3.$$

In this particular case

$$\Omega_{x_2 x_1} = a_{300}\frac{\partial}{\partial a_{210}} + 2a_{210}\frac{\partial}{\partial a_{120}} + 3a_{120}\frac{\partial}{\partial a_{080}} + a_{201}\frac{\partial}{\partial a^{111}}$$
$$+ 2a_{111}\frac{\partial}{\partial a_0 21} + a_{102}\frac{\partial}{\partial a_{012}}.\qquad(182)$$

This operator is the one which is analogous to Ω in the binary theory. From $\left(\mu\frac{\partial}{\partial\lambda}\right)\phi'$ by like processes, one obtains the analogue of O, e.g. $\Omega_{x_1 x_2}$. Similarly $\Omega_{x_1 x_3}, \Omega x_3 x_1, \Omega x_2 x_3, \Omega x_3 x_2$ may all be derived. An independent set of these six operators characterize full invariants in the ternary theory, in the same sense that Ω, O characterize binary invariants. For such we may choose the cyclic set $\Omega_{x_1 x_2}, \Omega_{x_2 x_3}, \Omega_{x_3} x_1$.

Now let the ternary m-ic form

$$\begin{aligned}
f \;=\;& a_{m00}x_1^m + ma_{m-110}x_1^{m-1}x_2 + \cdots + a_{0m0}x_2^m \\
+\;& m(a_{m-101}x_1^{m-1} + (m-1)a_{m-211}x_1^{m-2}x_2 + \cdots + a_{0m-11}x_2^{m-1})x_3 \\
+\;& \cdots\cdots\cdots\cdots\cdots
\end{aligned}$$

be transformed by the following substitutions of determinant unity:

$$x_1 = x_1' - \frac{a_{m-110}}{a_{m00}}x_2' - \frac{a_{m-101}}{a_{m00}}x_3',$$
$$x_2 = x_2',$$
$$x_3 = x_3'.\qquad(183)$$

Then the transformed form f' lacks the terms $x_1'^{m-1}x_2'$, $x_1'^{m-1}x_3'$. The coefficients of the remaining terms are seminvariants. We shall illustrate this merely. Let $m = 2$,

$$f = a_{200}x_1^2 + 2a_{110}x_1x_2 + a_{020}x_2^2 + 2a_{101}x_1x_3 + 2a_{011}x_2x_3 + a_{002}x_3^2.$$

Then

$$a_{200}f' = a_{200}^2x_1'^2 + (a_{020}a_{200} - a_{110}^2)x_2'^2 + 2(a_{011}a_{200} - a_{101}a_{110})x_2'x_3'$$
$$+(a_{002}a_{200} - a_{101}^2)x_3'^2.$$

It is easy to show that all coefficients of f' are annihilated by $\Omega_{x_2x_1}$.

Likewise if the ternary cubic be transformed by

$$x_1 = x_1' - \frac{a_{210}}{a_{300}}x_2' - \frac{a_{201}}{a_{300}}x_3',$$
$$x_2 = x_2', \quad x_3 = x_3',$$

and the result indicated by $a_{300}^2 f' = A_{300}x_1'^3 + 3A_{210}x_1'^2x_2' + \ldots$, we have

$$A_{300} = a_{300}^3, \tag{184}$$
$$A_{210} = 0,$$
$$A_{120} = a_{300}\left(a_{300}a_{120} - a_{210}^2\right),$$
$$A_{030} = 2a_{210}^3 - 3a_{210}a_{120}a_{300} + a_{030}a_{300}^2,$$
$$A_{201} = 0,$$
$$A_{111} = a_{300}\left(a_{300}a_{111} - a_{210}a_{201}\right),$$
$$A_{021} = a_{300}^2a_{021} - a_{300}a_{201}a_{120} - 2a_{210}a_{111}a_{300} + 2a_{210}^2a_{201},$$
$$A_{102} = a_{300}\left(a_{300}a_{102} - a_{201}^2\right),$$
$$A_{012} = a_{300}^2a_{012} - a_{300}a_{102}a_{210} - 2a_{300}a_{201}a_{111} + 2a_{201}^2a_{210},$$
$$A_{003} = 2a_{201}^3 - 3a_{300}a_{201}a_{102} + a_{003}a_{300}^2.$$

These are all seminvariants of the cubic. It will be noted that the vanishing of a complete set of seminvariants of this type gives a (redundant) set of sufficient conditions that the form be a perfect mth power. All seminvariants of f are expressible rationally in terms of the A's, since f' is the transformed of f by a transformation of determinant unity.

8.2.2 Symmetric functions of groups of letters.

If we multiply together the three linear factors of

$$f = \left(\alpha_1^{(1)}x_1 + \alpha_2^{(1)}x_2 + \alpha_3^{(1)}x_3\right)\left(\alpha_1^{(2)}x_1 + \alpha_2^{(2)}x_2 + \alpha_3^{(2)}x_3\right)\left(\alpha_1^{(3)}x_1 + \alpha_2^{(3)}x_2 + \alpha_3^{(3)}x_3\right)$$

the result is a ternary cubic form (a 3-line), $f = a_{300}x_1^3 + \ldots$. The coefficients of this quantic are

$$a_{300} = \sum \alpha_1^{(1)}\alpha_1^{(2)}\alpha_1^{(3)} = \alpha_1^{(1)}\alpha_1^{(2)}\alpha_1^{(3)},$$

$$a_{210} = \sum \alpha_1^{(1)}\alpha_1^{(2)}\alpha_2^{(3)} = \alpha_1^{(1)}\alpha_1^{(2)}\alpha_2^{(3)} + \alpha_1^{(1)}\alpha_2^{(2)}\alpha_1^{(3)} + \alpha_2^{(1)}\alpha_1^{(2)}\alpha_1^{(3)},$$

$$a_{120} = \sum \alpha_1^{(1)}\alpha_2^{(2)}\alpha_2^{(3)} = \alpha_1^{(1)}\alpha_2^{(2)}\alpha_2^{(3)} + \alpha_2^{(1)}\alpha_1^{(2)}\alpha_2^{(3)} + \alpha_2^{(1)}\alpha_2^{(2)}\alpha_1^{(3)},$$

$$a_{030} = \sum \alpha_2^{(1)}\alpha_2^{(2)}\alpha_2^{(3)} = \alpha_2^{(1)}\alpha_2^{(2)}\alpha_2^{(3)},$$

$$a_{201} = \sum \alpha_1^{(1)}\alpha_1^{(2)}\alpha_3^{(3)} = \alpha_1^{(1)}\alpha_1^{(2)}\alpha_3^{(3)} + \alpha_1^{(1)}\alpha_3^{(2)}\alpha_1^{(3)} + \alpha_3^{(1)}\alpha_1^{(2)}\alpha_1^{(3)},$$

$$a_{111} = \sum \alpha_1^{(1)}\alpha_2^{(2)}\alpha_3^{(3)} = \alpha_1^{(1)}\alpha_2^{(2)}\alpha_3^{(3)} + \alpha_1^{(1)}\alpha_3^{(2)}\alpha_2^{(3)} + \alpha_2^{(1)}\alpha_1^{(2)}\alpha_3^{(3)}$$
$$+ \alpha_2^{(1)}\alpha_3^{(2)}\alpha_1^{(3)} + \alpha_3^{(1)}\alpha_1^{(2)}\alpha_2^{(3)} + \alpha_3^{(1)}\alpha_2^{(2)}\alpha_1^{(3)},$$

$$a_021 = \sigma\alpha_2^{(1)}\alpha_2^{(2)}\alpha_3^{(3)} = \alpha_1^{(1)}\alpha_3^{(2)}\alpha_3^{(3)} + \alpha_2^{(1)}\alpha_3^{(2)}\alpha_2^{(3)} + \alpha_3^{(1)}\alpha_2^{(2)}\alpha_2^{(3)},$$

$$a_102 = \sigma\alpha_1^{(1)}\alpha_3^{(2)}\alpha_3^{(3)} = \alpha_1^{(1)}\alpha_3^{(2)}\alpha_3^{(3)} + \alpha_3^{(1)}\alpha_1^{(2)}\alpha_3^{(3)} + \alpha_3^{(1)}\alpha_3^{(2)}\alpha_1^{(3)},$$

$$a_012 = \sigma\alpha_2^{(1)}\alpha_3^{(2)}\alpha_3^{(3)} = \alpha_2^{(1)}\alpha_3^{(2)}\alpha_3^{(3)} + \alpha_3^{(1)}\alpha_2^{(2)}\alpha_3^{(3)} + \alpha_3^{(1)}\alpha_3^{(2)}\alpha_2^{(3)},$$

$$a_003 = \sigma\alpha_3^{(1)}\alpha_3^{(2)}\alpha_3^{(3)} = \alpha_3^{(1)}\alpha_3^{(2)}\alpha_3^{(3)}.$$

These functions σ are all unaltered by those interchanges of letters which have the effect of permuting the linear factors of f among themselves. Any function of the $\alpha_i^{(j)}$ having this property is called a symmetric function of the three groups of three homogeneous letters,

$$\left(\alpha_1^{(1)}, \alpha_2^{(1)}, \alpha_3^{(1)}\right),$$
$$\left(\alpha_1^{(2)}, \alpha_2^{(2)}, \alpha_3^{(2)}\right),$$
$$\left(\alpha_1^{(3)}, \alpha_2^{(3)}, \alpha_3^{(3)}\right),$$

In general, a symmetric function of m groups of three homogeneous letters, $\alpha_1, \alpha_2, \alpha_3$, $i.e.$ of the groups

$$\gamma_1\left(\alpha_1^{(1)}, \alpha_2^{(1)}, \alpha_3^{(1)}\right),$$
$$\gamma_2\left(\alpha_1^{(2)}, \alpha_2^{(2)}, \alpha_3^{(2)}\right),$$
$$\ldots$$
$$\gamma_m\left(\alpha_1^{(m)}, \alpha_2^{(m)}, \alpha_3^{(m)}\right),$$

is such a function as is left unaltered by all of the permutations of the letters α which have the effect of permuting the groups $\gamma_1\gamma_2, \ldots, \gamma_m$ among themselves: at least by such permutations. This is evidently such a function as is left unchanged by all permutations of the superscripts of the α's. A symmetric function of m groups of the three letters $\alpha_1, \alpha_2, \alpha_3$, every term of which involves as a factor one each of the symbols $\alpha^{(1)}, \alpha^{(2)}, \ldots, \alpha^{(m)}$ is called an elementary symmetric function. Thus the set of functions $a_3 10, a_2 10, \ldots$ above is the complete set of elementary symmetric functions of three groups of three homogeneous variables. The non-homogeneous elementary symmetric functions are obtained from these by replacing the symbols $\alpha_3^{(1)} \alpha_3^{(2)} \alpha_3^{(3)}$ each by unity.

The number N of elementary symmetric functions of m groups of two non-homogeneous variables $a_{m,0,0}, a m_i - 1, 1, 0 \cdots$ is, by the analogy with the coefficients of a linearly factorable ternary form of order m,

$$N = m + m + (m - l) + (m - 2) + \cdots + 2 + l = \frac{1}{2} m(m + 3).$$

The N equations $a_{ijk} = \Sigma$, regarded as equations in the $2m$ unknowns $a_1^{(r)}, a_2^{(s)} (r, s = 1, \cdots, m)$, can, theoretically, be combined so as to eliminate these $2m$ unknowns. The result of this elimination will be a set of

$$\frac{1}{2} m(m + 3) - 2m = \frac{1}{2} m(m - 1)$$

equations of condition connecting the quantities $a_{m00}, a_{m-110}, \cdots$ only. If these a's are considered to be coefficients of the general ternary form f of order m, whose leading coefficient a_{003} is unity, the $\frac{1}{2} m(m - 1)$ equations of condition constitute a set of necessary and sufficient conditions in order that f may be linearly factorable.

Analogously to the circumstances in the binary case, it is true as a theorem that any symmetric function of m groups of two non-homogeneous variables is rationally and integrally expressible in terms of the elementary symmetric functions. Tables giving these expressions for all functions of weights 1 to 6 inclusive were published by Junker[1] in 1897.

8.2.3   Semi-discriminants

We shall now derive a class of seminvariants whose vanishing gives a set of conditions in order that the ternary form f of order m may be the product of m linear forms.

The present method leads to a set of conditional relations containing the exact minimum number $\frac{1}{2} m(m-1)$; that is, it leads to a set of $\frac{1}{2} m(m-1)$ independent seminvariants of the form, whose simultaneous vanishing gives necessary and sufficient conditions for the factorability. We shall call these seminvariants *semi-discriminants* of the form. They are all of the same degree $2m - 1$; and are readily formed for any order m as simultaneous invariants of a certain set of *binary* quantics related to the original ternary form.

If a polynomial, f_{3m}, of order m, and homogeneous in three variables (x_1, x_2, x_3) is factorable into linear factors, its terms in (x_1, x_2) must furnish the (x_1, x_2) terms of those factors. Call these terms collectively a_{0x}^m, and the

---

[1] Wiener Denkschriften for 1897.

terms linear in x_3 collectively $x_3 a_{1x}^{m-1}$. Then if the factors of the former were known, and were distinct, say

$$a_{0x}^m = a_{00} \Pi_{i=1}^m (r_2^{(i)} x_1 - r_1^{(i)} x_2) \div \Pi_{i=1}^m (r_2^{(i)}),$$

the second would give by rational means the terms in x_3 required to complete the several factors. For we could find rationally the numerators of the partial fractions in the decomposition of a_{1x}^{m-1}/a_{0x}^m, viz.

$$\frac{a_{1x}^{m-1}}{a_{0x}^m} \equiv \frac{\Pi_{i=1}^m r_2^{(i)}}{a_{00}} \sum_{i=1}^m \frac{a_i}{r_2^{(i)} x_1 - r_1^{(i)} x_2},$$

and the factors of the complete form will be, of course,

$$r_2^{(i)} x_1 - r_1^{(i)} x_2 + \alpha_i x_3 (i = 1, 2, \cdots, m).$$

Further, the coefficients of all other terms in f_{3m} are rational integral functions of the $r^{(i)}$ on the.one hand, and of the α_i on the other, symmetrical in the sets $(r_2^{(i)}, -r_1^{(i)}, \alpha_i)$. We shall show in general that all these coefficients in the case of any linearly factorable form are *rationally* expressible in terms of those occurring in a_{0x}^m, a_{1x}^{m-1}. Hence will follow the important theorem,

Theorem. *If a ternary form f_{3m} is decomposable into linear factors, all its coefficients, after certain $2m$, are expressible rationally in terms of those $2m$ coefficients. That is, in the space whose coördinates are all the coefficients of ternary forms of order m, the forms composed of linear factors fill a rational spread of $2m$ dimensions.*

We shall thus obtain the explicit form of the general ternary quantic which is factorable into linear factors. Moreover, in case f_{3m} is not factorable a similar development will give the theorem,

Theorem. *Every ternary form f_{3m}, for which the discriminant D of a_{0x}^m does not vanish, can be expressed as the sum of the product of m distinct linear forms, plus the square of an arbitrarily chosen linear form, multiplied by a "satellite" form of order $m - 2$ whose coefficients are, except for the factor D^{-1}, integral rational seminvariants of the original form f_{3m}.*

A class of ternary seminvariants

Let us write the general ternary quantic in homogeneous variables as follows:

$$f_{3m} = a_{0x}^m + a_{1x}^{m-1} x_3 + a_{2x}^{m-2} x_3^2 + \cdots + a_{m0} x_x^m,$$

where

$$a_{ix}^{m-i} \equiv a_{i0} x_1^{m-i} + a_{i1} x_1^{m-i-1} x_2 + a_{i2} x_1^{m-i-2} x_2^2 + \cdots + a_{im-i} x_1^{m-i} (i = 0, 1, 2, \cdots, m).$$

Then write

$$\frac{a_{1x}^{m-1}}{a_{0x}^m} = \frac{a_{1x}^{m-1}}{\prod_{k=1}^m (r_2^{(k)} x_1 - r_1^{(k)} x_2)} = \sum_{k=1}^m \frac{a^k}{r_2^{(k)} x_1 - r_1^{(k)} x_2} \,(a_{00} = r_2^{(1)} r_2^{(2)} \cdots r_2^{(m)});$$

and we have in consequence, assuming that $D \neq 0$, and writing

$$a_{0r(k)}^{\prime m} = \left[\frac{\partial a_{0x}^m}{\partial x_1}\right]_{x_1 = r_1^{(k)}, x_2 = r_2^{(k)}}, a_{0r(k)}^{\prime\prime m} = \left[\frac{\partial a_{0x}^m}{\partial x_2}\right]_{x_1 = r_1^{(k)}, x_2 = r_2^{(k)}},$$

the results

$$a_k = r_2^{(k)} a_{1r(k)}^{m-1} / a_{0r(k)}^{\prime m} = -r_1^{(k)} a_{1r(k)}^{m-1} / a_{0r(k)}^{\prime\prime m}. \tag{185}$$

Hence also

$$a_{0r(k)}^{\prime\prime m} = -\frac{r_1^{(k)}}{r_2^{(k)}} a_{0r(k)}^{\prime m}. \tag{186}$$

The discriminant of a_{0x}^m can be expressed in the following form:

$$D = \prod_{j=1}^m a_{0r(j)}^{\prime m} / a_{00} (-1)^{\frac{1}{2} m(m-1)}, \tag{187}$$

and therefore

$$a_k = \frac{r_2^{(k)} a_{1r(k)}^{m-1} a_{0r(1)}^{\prime m} a_{0r(2)}^{\prime m} \cdots a_{0r(k-1)}^{\prime m} a_{0r(k+1)}^{\prime m} \cdots a_{0r(m)}^{\prime m}}{a_{00} (-1)^{\frac{1}{2} m(m-1)} D}, \tag{188}$$

and in like manner we get

$$\prod_{k=1}^m a_k = a_{1r(1)}^{m-1} a_{1r(2)}^{m-1} \cdots a_{1r(m)}^{m-1} / (-1)^{\frac{1}{2} m(m-1)} D. \tag{189}$$

The numerator of the right-hand member of this last equality is evidently the resultant (say R_m) of a_{0x}^m and a_{1x}^{m-1}.

Consider next the two differential operators

$$\Delta_1 = m a_{00} \frac{\partial}{\partial a_{10}} + (m-1) a_{01} \frac{\partial}{\partial a_{11}} + \cdots + a_{0m-1} \frac{\partial}{\partial a_{1m-1}},$$

$$\Delta_2 = m a_{0m} \frac{\partial}{\partial a_{1m-1}} + (m-1) a_{0m-1} \frac{\partial}{\partial a_{1m-2}} + \cdots + a_{01} \frac{\partial}{\partial a_{10}};$$

and particularly their effect when applied to a_{1x}^{m-1}. We get (cf. (186))

$$\Delta_1 a_{1r(k)}^{m-1} = a_{0r(k)}^{\prime m}, \Delta_2 a_{1r(k)}^{m-1} = a_{0r(k)}^{\prime\prime m} = -\frac{r_1^{(k)}}{r_2^{(k)}} a_{0r(k)}^{\prime m}, \tag{190}$$

and from these relations we deduce the following:

$$\Delta_1 \prod_{k=1}^{m} a_k, = \frac{\Delta_1 R_m}{(-1)^{\frac{1}{2}m(m-1)}1!D} = a_{00} \sum \frac{a_{1r(1)}^{m-1} a_{1r(2)}^{m-1} \cdots a_{1r(m-1)}^{m-1}}{a_{0r(1)}^{\prime m} a_{0r(2)}^{\prime m} \cdots a_{0r(m-1)}^{\prime m}}, \qquad (191)$$

or, from (185)

$$\frac{\Delta_1 R_m}{(-1)^{\frac{1}{2}m(m-1)}1!D} = \sum \alpha_1 \alpha_2 \cdots \alpha_{m-1} r_2^{(m)}. \qquad (192)$$

In (191) the symmetric function $\sum$ is to be read with reference to the r's, the superscripts of the r's replacing the subscripts usual in a symmetric function. Let us now operate with Δ_2 on both members of (191). This gives

$$\frac{\Delta_1 \Delta_2 R_m}{(-1)^{\frac{1}{2}m(m-1)}1!D} = a_{00} \sum \frac{a_{1r(1)}^{m-1} a_{1r(2)}^{m-1} \cdots a_{1r(m-2)}^{m-1}}{a_{0r(1)}^{\prime m} a_{0r(2)}^{\prime m} \cdots a_{0r(m-2)}^{\prime m}} \left(-\frac{r_1^{(m-1)}}{r_2^{(m-1)}} - \frac{r_1^{(m)}}{r_2^{(m)}} \right).$$

Let Σ_h represent an elementary symmetric function of the two groups of homogeneous variables r_1, r_2 which involves h distinct letters of each group, viz. $r_i^{(m-l+l)}(j = 1, 2, \cdots, h)$. Then we have

$$\frac{\Delta_1 \Delta_2 R_m}{(-1)^{\frac{1}{2}m(m-1)}1!1!D} = \Sigma \left[(-1)\alpha_1 \alpha_2 \cdots \alpha_{m-2} \Sigma_2 r_1^{(m-1)} r_2^{(m)} \right]. \qquad (193)$$

We are now in position to prove by induction the following fundamental formula:

$$\frac{\Delta_1^{m-s-t} \Delta_2^t R_m}{(-1)^{\frac{1}{2}m(m-1)}(m-s-t)!t!D} \qquad (194)$$

$$= \Sigma \left[(-1)^t \alpha_1 \alpha_2 \cdots \alpha_s \Sigma_{m-s} r_1^{(s+1)} r_1^{(s+2)} \cdots r_1^{(s+t)} r^{(s+2)} \cdots r_1^{(s+t)} r_2^{(s+t+1)} \cdots r_2^{(m)} \right]$$

$$(s = 0, 1, \cdots, m; \ t = 0, 1, \cdots, m - s),$$

where the outer summation covers all subscripts from 1 to m, superscripts of the r's counting as subscripts in the symmetric function. Representing by $J_{m-s-t,t}$ the left-hand member of this equality we have from (190)

$$\Delta_2 J_{m-s-t,t} = \Sigma((-1)^{t+1} \frac{a_{1r(1)}^{m-1} a_{1r(2)}^{m-1} \cdots a_{1r(s-1)}^{m-1}}{a_{0r(1)}^{lm} a_{0r(2)}^{lm} \cdots a_{0r(s-1)}^{lm}}$$

$$\times r_2^{(1)} r_2^{(2)} \cdots r_2^{(s)} \frac{r_1^{(s)}}{r_2^{(s)}} \Sigma_{m-s} r_1^{(s+1)} \cdots r_1^{(s+t)} r_2^{(s+t+1)} \cdots r_2^{(m)}).$$

This equals

$$\Sigma(-1)^{t+1} \alpha_1 \alpha_2 \cdots \alpha_{s-1} S,$$

where S is a symmetric function each term of which involves $t + 1$ letters r_1 and $m - s - t$ letters r_2. The number of terms in an elementary symmetric function of any number of groups of homogeneous variables equals the number of permutations of the letters occurring in any one term when the subscripts (here superscripts) are removed. Hence the number of terms in Σ_{m-s} is

$$\frac{(m-s)!}{(m-s-t)!\,t!},$$

and the number of terms in S is

$$(m-s+1)(m-s)!/t!(m-s-t)!.$$

But the number of terms in

$$\Sigma_{m-s+1}\left(r_1^{(s)}r_1^{(s+1)}\cdots r_1^{(s+t)}r_2^{(s+t+1)}\cdots r_2^{(m)}\right)$$

is

$$(m-s+1)!/(m-s-t)!(t+1)!.$$

Hence

$$S=(t+1)\Sigma_{m-s+1},$$

and so

$$\frac{\Delta_2 J_{m-s-t,t}}{t+1}=\sum\left[(-1)^{t+1}\alpha_2\alpha_2\cdots\alpha_{s-1}\Sigma_{m-s+1}\right].$$

This result, with (193), completes the inductive proof of formula (194).

Now the functions $J_{m-s-t,t}$ are evidently simultaneous invariants of the binary forms a_{0x}^m, $a_{0x}'^m$, $a_{0x}''^m$, a_{1x}^{m-1}. We shall show in the next paragraph that the expressions

$$I_{m-s-t,t}\equiv Da_{st}-DJ_{m-s-t,t}(s=2,3,\cdots,m;t=0,1,\cdots,m-s)$$

are, in reality, seminvariants of the form f_{3m} as a whole.

STRUCTURE OF A TERNARY FORM

The structure of the right-hand member of the equality (194) shows at once that the general (factorable or non-factorable) quantic $f_{3m}(D\neq 0)$ can be reduced to the following form:

$$f_{3m}=\prod_{k=1}^{m}\left(r_2^{(k)}x_1-r_1^{(k)}x_2+\alpha_k\right)+\sum_{s=2}^{m}\sum_{t=0}^{m-s}(a_{st}-J_{m-s-t,t})x_1^{m-s-t}x_2^t. \quad (195)$$

This gives explicitly the "satellite" form of f_{3m}, with coefficients expressed rationally in terms of the coefficients of f_{3m}. It may be written

$$D\mu_{m-2}=\sum_{s=2}^{m}\sum_{t=0}^{m-s}\left(Da_{st}-\frac{\Delta_1^{m-s-t}\Delta_2^t R_m}{(-1)^{\frac{1}{2}m(m-1)}(m-s-t)!\,t!}\right)x_1^{m-s-t}x_2^t$$

$$=\sum_{s=2}^{m}\sum_{t=0}^{m-s}I_{m-s-t,t}x_1^{m-s-t}x_2^t. \quad (196)$$

Now the coefficients $I_{m-s-t,t}$ are seminvariants of f_{3m}. To fix ideas let $m = 3$ and write the usual set of ternary operators,

$$\Omega_{x_1 x_2} = \alpha_{01}\frac{\partial}{\partial a_{00}} + 2\alpha_{02}\frac{\partial}{\partial a_{01}} + 3\alpha_{03}\frac{\partial}{\partial a_{02}} + \alpha_{11}\frac{\partial}{\partial a_{10}} + 2\alpha_{12}\frac{\partial}{\partial a_{11}} + 3\alpha_{13}\frac{\partial}{\partial a_{20}},$$

$$\Omega_{x_2 x_1} = 3\alpha_{00}\frac{\partial}{\partial a_{01}} + 2\alpha_{01}\frac{\partial}{\partial a_{02}} + \alpha_{02}\frac{\partial}{\partial a_{03}} + 2\alpha_{10}\frac{\partial}{\partial a_{11}} + \alpha_{11}\frac{\partial}{\partial a_{12}} + \alpha_{20}\frac{\partial}{\partial a_{21}},$$

$$\Omega_{x_3 x_1} = \alpha_{20}\frac{\partial}{\partial a_{30}} + 2\alpha_{10}\frac{\partial}{\partial a_{20}} + 3\alpha_{00}\frac{\partial}{\partial a_{10}} + \alpha_{11}\frac{\partial}{\partial a_{21}} + 2\alpha_{01}\frac{\partial}{\partial a_{11}} + \alpha_{02}\frac{\partial}{\partial a_{12}},$$

etc.

Then I_{10} is annihilated by $\Omega_{x_2 x_1}$, but not by $\Omega_{x_1 x_2}$, I_{01} is annihilated by $\Omega_{x_1 x_2}$ but not by $\Omega_{x_2 x_1}$, and I_{00}, is annihilated by $\Omega_{x_1 x_2}$, but not by $\Omega_{x_3 x_1}$. In general $I_{m-s-t,t}$ fails of annihilation when operated upon by a general operator $\Omega_{x_i x_j}$ which contains a partial derivative with respect to a_{st}. We have now proved the second theorem.

8.2.4 The semi-discriminants

A necessary and sufficient condition that f_{3m} should degenerate into the product of m distinct linear factors is that μ_{m-2} should vanish identically. Hence, since the number of coefficients in μ_{m-2} is $\frac{1}{2}m(m-1)$, these equated to zero give a minimum set of conditions in order that f_{3m} should be factorable in the manner stated. As previously indicated we refer to these seminvariants as a set of semi-discriminants of the form f_{3m}. They are

$$I_{m-s-t,t} = Da_{st} - \frac{\Delta_1^{m-s-t}\Delta_2^t R_m}{(-1)^{\frac{1}{2}m(m-1)}t!(m-s-t)!}\left(\begin{array}{l} s = 2, 3, \ldots, m; \\ t = 0, 1, \ldots, m-s \end{array}\right) \quad (197)$$

They are obviously independent since each one contains a coefficient (a_{st}) not contained in any other. They are free from adventitious factors, and each one is of degree $2m - 1$.

In the case where $m = 2$ we have

$$I_{00} = -a_{20}\begin{vmatrix} 2a_{00} & a_{01} \\ a_{01} & 2a_{02} \end{vmatrix} + \begin{vmatrix} a_{00} & a_{01} & a_{02} \\ a_{10} & a_{11} & 0 \\ 0 & a_{10} & a_{11} \end{vmatrix}.$$

This is also the *ordinary* discriminant of the ternary quadratic.

The three semi-discriminants of the ternary cubic are given in Table V. In this table we have adopted the following simpler notation for the coefficients of f:

$$\begin{aligned} f = \ & a_0 x_1^3 + a_1 x_1^2 x_2 + a_2 x_1 x_2^2 + a_3 x_2^3 \\ + \ & b_0 x_1^2 x_3 + b_1 x_1 x_2 x_3 + b_2 x_2^2 x_3 \\ + \ & c_0 x_1 x_3^2 + c_1 x_2 x_3^2 \\ + \ & d_0 x_3^3. \end{aligned}$$

TABLE V

I_{10}	$-I_{01}$	$-I_{00}$
$4a_1a_2a_3b_0^2$	$a_2^2a_3b_0^2$	$a_3^2b_0^2$
$-a_2^3b_0^2$	$-3a_1a_3^2b_0^2$	$+a_1a_3b_0b_1^2$
$-9a_3^2b_0^2$	$+a_1^2a_3b_1^2$	$+a_1^2b_0b_2^2$
$+3a_1a_3b_1^2$	$-3a_2a_3b_1^2$	$-2a_2b_0b_2^2$
$-a_2^2b_1^2$	$+a_1^3b_2^2$	$-a_2a_3n_0^2b_1$
$+3a_2b_2^2$	$-4a_1a_2b_2^2$	$+a_2^2b_0^2b_2$
$+6a_1a_3b_0b_2$	$+9a_3b_2^2$	$-2a_1a_3b_0^2b_2$
$-2a_2^2b_0b_2$	$-a_1a_2a_3b_0b_1$	$-a_1a_2b_0b_1b_2$
$+a_1a_2^2b_0b_1$	$+2a_1^2a_3b_0b_2$	$-a_2b_1^3$
$+3a_2a_3b_0b_1$	$-6a_2a_3b_0b_2$	$-a_1b_1b_2^2$
$-4a_1^2a_3b_0b_1$	$+4a_2^2b_1b_2$	$+a_2b_1^2b_2$
$+a_1a_2b_1b_2$	$-3a_1a_3b_1b_2$	$+b_2^3$
$-9a_3b_1b_2$	$-a_1^2a_2b_1b_2$	$+a_1^2a_2^2d_0$
$-a_1^2a_2^2c_0$	$+a_1^2a_2^2c_1$	$+18a_1a_2a_3d_0$
$-18a_1a_2a_3c_0$	$+18a_1a_2a_3c_1$	$-4a_2^3d_0$
$+4a_2^3c_0$	$-4a_2^3c_1$	$-4a_1^3a_3d_0$
$+4a_1^3a_3c_0$	$-4a_1^3a_3c_1$	$-27a_3^2d_0$
$+27a_3^2c_0$	$-27a_3^2c_1$	

In the notation of (197) the seminvariants in this table are

$$
\begin{aligned}
I_{00} &= Da_{30} + R_3, \\
I_{10} &= Da_{20} + \Delta_1 R_3, \\
I_{01} &= Da_{21} + \Delta_2 R_3,
\end{aligned}
$$

where D is the discriminant of

$$\alpha \equiv a_{00}x_1^3 + a_{01}x_1^2x_2 + \cdots + a_{03}x_2^3,$$

and R_3 the resultant of α and

$$\beta = a_{10}x_1^2 + a_{11}x_1x_2 + a_{12}x_2^2.$$

Corresponding results for the case $m = 4$ are the following:

$$I_{00} = \frac{1}{27}a_{40}(4i_1^3 - J_1^2) - R_4,$$

where

$$
\begin{aligned}
i_1 &= a_{02}^2 - 3a_{01}a_{03} + 12a_{00}a_{04}, \\
J_1 &= 27a_{01}^2a_{04} + 27a_{00}a_{03}^2 + 2a_{02}^3 - 72a_{00}a_{02}a_{04} - 9a_{01}a_{02}a_{03},
\end{aligned}
$$

$$
R_4 \;=\;
\begin{vmatrix}
a_{10} & a_{11} & a_{12} & a_{13} & 0 & 0 \\
0 & a_{10} & a_{11} & a_{12} & a_{13} & 0 \\
0 & 0 & a_{10} & a_{11} & a_{12} & a_{13} \\
a_{01}a_{10} - a_{00}a_{11} & a_{02}a_{10} - a_{00}a_{12} & a_{03}a_{10} - a_{00}a_{13} & a_{04}a_{10} & 0 & 0 \\
a_{00} & a_{01} & a_{02} & a_{03} & a_{04} & 0 \\
0 & a_{00} & a_{01} & a_{02} & a_{03} & a_{04}
\end{vmatrix},
$$

the other members of the set being obtained by operating upon R_4 with powers of Δ_1, Δ_2:

$$
\Delta_1 \;=\; 4a_{00}\frac{\partial}{\partial a_{10}} + 3a_{01}\frac{\partial}{\partial a_{11}} + 2a_{02}\frac{\partial}{\partial a_{12}} + a_{03}\frac{\partial}{\partial a_{13}},
$$

$$
\Delta_2 \;=\; 4a_{04}\frac{\partial}{\partial a_{13}} + 3a_{03}\frac{\partial}{\partial a_{12}} + 2a_{02}\frac{\partial}{\partial a_{11}} + a_{01}\frac{\partial}{\partial a_{10}},
$$

according to the formula

$$
I_{4-s-t,t} = a_{st}D - \frac{\Delta_1^{4-s-t}\Delta_2^{t}R_4}{(4-s-t)!\,t!}\;(s = 2,3,4; t = 0,1,...,4-s).
$$

8.2.5 Invariants of m-lines.

The factors of a_{0x}^{m} being assumed distinct we can always solve $I_{m-s-t,t} = 0$ for a_{st}, the result being obviously rational in the coefficients occurring in a_{0x}^{m}, a_{1x}^{m-1}. This proves the first theorem of III as far as the case $D \neq 0$ is concerned. Moreover by carrying the resulting values of $a_{st}(s = 2,3,\ldots,m; t = 0,1,\ldots,m-s)$ back into f_{3m} we get the general form of a ternary quantic which is factorable into linear forms. In the result a_{0x}^{m}, a_{1x}^{m-1} are perfectly general (the former, however, subject to the negative condition $D \neq 0$), whereas

$$
(-1)^{\frac{1}{2}m(m-1)}Da_{jx}^{m-j} \;\equiv\; \frac{\Delta_1^{m-j}R_m}{(m-j)!}x_1^{m-j} + \frac{\Delta_1^{m-j-1}\Delta_2 R_m}{(m-j-1)!1!}x_1^{m-j-1}x_2 + \cdots
$$

$$
+\; \frac{\Delta_2^{m-j}R_m}{(m-j)!}x_2^{m-j} \quad (j = 2,3,\ldots,m).
$$

Thus the ternary form representing a group of m straight lines in the plane, or in other words the form representing an m-line is, explicitly,

$$
f = a_{0x}^{m} + x_3 a_{1x}^{m-1}
$$

$$
+\, D^{-1}(-1)^{\frac{1}{2}m(m-1)} \sum_{j=2}^{m} x_3^{j} \sum_{i=0}^{m-j} \frac{\Delta_1^{m-i-j}\Delta_2^{i}R_m}{(m-i-j)!i!}x_1^{m-i-j}x_2^{i}. \tag{198}
$$

This form, regarded as a linearly factorable form, possesses an invariant theory, closely analogous to the theory of binary invariants in terms of the roots.

If we write $a_{0x}^{3} = x_2^{3}l_{0x_1/x_2}, a_{1x}^{2} = x_2^{2}l_{1x_1/x_2}$ $(a_{00} = 1)$, and assume that the roots of $l_{0\xi} = 0$ are $-r_1, -r_2, -r_3$, then the factored form of the three-line will be, by the partial fraction method of III (185),

$$f = \prod_{i=1}^{3}(x_1 + r_i x_2 - l_{1-r_i}/l'_{0-r_i}).$$

Hence the invariant representing the condition that the 3-line f should be a pencil of lines is

$$Q = \begin{vmatrix} 1 & r_1 & l_{1-r_1}/l'_{0-r_1} \\ 1 & r_2 & l_{1-r_2}/l'_{0-r_2} \\ 1 & r_3 & l_{1-r_3}/l'_{0-r_3} \end{vmatrix}.$$

This will be symmetric in the quantities r_1, r_2, r_3 after it is divided by $\sqrt{R}$, where $R = (r_l - r_2)^2(r_2 - r_3)^2(r_3 - r_1)^2$ is the discriminant of the binary cubic a_{0x}^3. Expressing the symmetric function $Q_1 = Q/\sqrt{R}$, in terms of the coefficients of a_{0x}^3, we have

$$Q_1 = 2a_{01}^2 a_{12} - a_{01}a_{02}a_{11} + 9a_{00}a_{03}a_{11} - 6a_{01}a_{03}a_{10} + 2a_{02}^2 a_{10} - 6a_{00}a_{02}a_{12}.$$

This is the simplest full invariant of an m-line f.

8.3   Modular Invariants and Covariants

Heretofore, in connection with illustrations of invariants and covariants under the finite modular linear group represented by T_p, we have assumed that the coefficients of the forms were arbitrary variables. We may, however, in connection with the formal modular concomitants of the linear form given in Chapter VI, or of any form f taken simultaneously with L and Q, regard the coefficients of f to be themselves parameters which represent positive residues of the prime number p. Let f be such a modular form, and quadratic,

$$f = a_0 x_1^2 + 2a_1 x_1 x_2 + a_2 x_2^2.$$

Let $p = 3$. In a fundamental system of formal invariants and covariants modulo 3 of f we may now reduce all exponents of the coefficients below 3 by Fermat's theorem,

$$a_i^3 \equiv a_i(\bmod 3)(i = 0, 1, 2).$$

The number of individuals in a fundamental system of f is, on account of these reductions, less than the number in the case where the a's are arbitrary variables. We call the invariants and covariants of f, where the a's are integral, *modular* concomitants (Dickson). The theory of modular invariants and covariants has been extensively developed. In particular the finiteness of the totality of this type of concomitants for any form or system of forms has been proved. The proof that the concomitants of a quantic, of the formal modular type, constitute a finite, complete system has, on the contrary, not been accomplished up to the present (December, 1914).   The most advantageous method for evolving fundamental systems of modular invariants is one discovered by Dickson depending essentially upon the separation of the totality of forms f with particular integral coefficients modulo p into classes such that all forms in a class are permuted among themselves by the transformations of the modular group given by $T_p{}^2$. The presentation of the elements of this modern theory is beyond the scope of this book. We shall, however, derive by the transvection process the fundamental system of modular concomitants of the quadratic form f, modulo 3. We have by transvection the following results (cf. Appendix, 48, p. 241):

8.3.1 Fundamental system of modular quadratic form, modulo 3.

TABLE VI

Notation	Transvectant	Concomitant (Mod 3)
Δ	$(f,f)^2$	$a_1^2 - a_0 a_2$
q	$(f^3,Q)^6$	$a_0^2 a_2 + a_0 a_2^2 + a_0 a_1^2 + a_1^2 a_2 - a_0^3 - a_2^3$
L		$x_1^3 x_2 - x_1 x_2^3$
Q	$((L,L)^2 L)$	$x_1^6 + x_1^4 x_2^2 + x_1^2 x_2^4 + x_2^6$
f		$a_0 x_1^2 + 2 a_1 x_1 x_1 + a_2 x_2^2$
f_4	$(f,Q)^2$	$a_0 x_1^4 + a_1 x_1^3 x_2 + a_1 x_1 x_2^3 + a_2 x_2^4$
C_1	$(f^3,Q)^5$	$(a_0^2 a_1 - a_1^3)x_1^2 + (a_0 - a_2)(a_1^2 + a_0 a_2)x_1 x_2 + (a_1^3 - a_1 a_2^2)x_2^2$
C_2	$(f^2,Q)^4$	$(a_0^2 + a_1^2 - a_0 a_2)x_1^2 + a_1(a_0 + a_2)x_1 x_2 + (a_1^2 + a_2^2 - a_0 a_2)x_2^2$

Also in q and C_1 we may make the reductions $a \equiv a_i (\bmod\ 3)(i = 0,1,2)$. We now give a proof due to Dickson, that these eight forms constitute a fundamental system of modular invariants and covariants of f.

Much use will be made, in this proof, of the reducible invariant

$$I = (a_0^2 - 1)(a_1^2 - 1)(a_2^2 - 1) \equiv q^2 + \Delta^2 - 1 \quad (\bmod\ 3).$$

In fact the linearly independent invariants of f are

$$1, \Delta, I, q, \Delta^2. \tag{i}$$

Proceeding to the proposed proof, we require the seminvariants of f. These are the invariants under

$$x_1 \equiv x_1' + x_2', x_2 \equiv x_2' \quad (\bmod\ 3).$$

These transformations replace f by f', where

$$a_0' \equiv a_0, a_1' \equiv a_0 + a_1, a_2' \equiv a_0 - a_1 + a_2 \quad (\bmod\ 3). \tag{t}$$

Hence, as may be verified easily, the following functions are all seminvariants:

$$a_0, a_0^2, a_0\Delta, a_0\Delta^2, a_0^2\Delta, B = (a_0^2 - 1)a_1. \tag{s}$$

---

[2]Transactions American Math. Society, Vol. 10 (1909), p. 123.

171

Theorem. *Any modular seminvariant is a linear homogeneous function of the eleven linearly independent seminvariants* $(i), (s)$.

For, after subtracting constant multiples of these eleven, it remains only to consider a seminvariant

$$S = \alpha_1 a_1 a_2^2 + \alpha_2 a_1 a_2 + \alpha_3 a_1 + \alpha_4 a_1^2 a_2^2 + \alpha_5 a_1^2 a_2 + \alpha_6 a_1^2 + \beta a_2^2 + \gamma a_2,$$

in which α_1, α_2 are linear expressions in $a_0^2, a_0, 1$; and $\alpha_3, \ldots, \alpha_6$ are linear expressions in $a_0, 1$; while the coefficients of these linear functions and β, γ are constants independent of $\alpha_0, \alpha_1, \alpha_2$. In the increment to S under the above induced transformations (t) on the a's the coefficient of $a_1 a_2^2$ is $-a_0\alpha_4$, whence $\alpha_4 = 0$. Then that of $a_1^2 a_2$ is $\alpha_1 \equiv 0$; then that of $a_1 a_2$ is $\beta - a_0\alpha_5$, whence $\beta \equiv \alpha_5 \equiv 0$; then that of a_1^2 is $-\alpha_2 \equiv 0$; then that of a_1 is $-\gamma - a_0\alpha_6$, whence $\gamma \equiv \alpha_6 \equiv 0$. Now $S = \alpha_3 a_1$, whose increment is $\alpha_3 a_0$, whence $\alpha_3 \equiv 0$ Hence the theorem is proved.

Any polynomial in Δ, I, q, a_0, B is congruent to a linear function of the eleven seminvariants $(i), (s)$ by means of the relations

$$
\text{(A)} \quad
\left.
\begin{aligned}
&I^2 \equiv -I, q^2 \equiv I - \Delta^2 + 1, \\
&I\Delta \equiv Iq \equiv Ia_0 \equiv IB \equiv q\Delta \equiv qB \equiv a_0 B \equiv 0, \\
&\Delta B \equiv B, a_0^2\Delta^2 \equiv \Delta^2 + a_0^2\Delta - \Delta, \\
&a_0 q \equiv a_0^2\Delta^2 - a_0^2, B^2 \equiv \Delta(1 - a_0^2)
\end{aligned}
\right\} \quad (\text{mod } 3),
$$

together with $a_0^3 \equiv a_0, \Delta^3 \equiv \Delta \pmod 3$.

Now we may readily show that any covariant, K, of order $6t$ is of the form $P + LC$, where C is a covariant of order $6t - 4$ and P is a polynomial in the eight concomitants in the above table omitting f_4. For the leading coefficient of a modular covariant is a modular seminvariant. And if t is odd the covariants

$$i f^{3t}, i Q^t, C_1^{3t}, C_2^{3t}, (i \text{ an invariant})$$

have as coefficients of x_1^{6t}

$$a_0 i, i, B, \Delta + a_0^2,$$

respectively. The linear combinations of the latter give all of the seminvariants $(i), (s)$. Hence if we subtract from K the properly chosen linear combination the term in x_1^{6t} cancels and the result has the factor x_2. But the only covariants having x_2 as a factor are multiples of L. Next let t be even. Then

$$f^{3t}, \Delta f^{3t}, iQf^{3t-3}, QC_1^{3t-3}, i_1 Q^t, \left(\begin{aligned} &i = 1, \Delta, \Delta^2. \\ &i_1 = I, \Delta, \Delta^2, q. \end{aligned} \right)$$

have as coefficients of x_1^{6t}

$$a_0^2, a_0^2\Delta, a_0 i, B, i_1.$$

Lemma 6. *If the order ω of a covariant C of a binary quadratic form modulo 3 is not divisible by 3, its leading coefficient S is a linear homogeneous function of the seminvariants $(i), (s)$, other than $1, I, q$.*

In proof of this lemma we have under the transformation $x_1 \equiv x_1{}'+x_2{}'$, $x_2 \equiv x_2{}'$,

$$C = Sx_1^{\omega} + S_1 x_1^{\omega-1} x_2 + \ldots \equiv Sx_1'^{\omega} + (S_1 + \omega S)x_1'^{\omega-1} x_2' + \ldots .$$

For a covariant C the final sum equals

$$Sx_1'^{\omega} + S_1' x_1'^{\omega-1} x_2' + \ldots, \; S_1' = S_1(a_0', a_1', a_2'),$$

where $a_0', \ldots$ are given by the above induced transformation on the a's. Hence

$$S_1' - S_1 \equiv \omega S \,(\mathrm{mod}\ 3).$$

Now write

$$S_1 = ka_0^2 a_1^2 a_2^2 + t \;(t \text{ of degree} < 6),$$

and apply the induced transformations. We have

$$S_1' = ka_0^2(a_0 + a_1)^2(a_0 - a_1 + a_2)^2 + t' \equiv ka_0^2(a_0 r + a_1^2 + a_1 a_2 + a_1^2 a_2^2) + t',$$

where r is of degree 3 and t' of degree < 6. Hence

$$\omega S \equiv k(a_o r + a_0^2 a_1^2 + a_0^2 a_1 a_2) + t' - t \;(\mathrm{mod}\ 3).$$

Since ω is prime to 3, S is of degree < 6. Hence S does not contain the term $a_0^2 a_1^2 a_2^2$, which occurs in I but not in any other seminvariant (i), (s). Next if $S = 1 + \sigma$, where σ is a function of a_0, a_1, a_2, without a constant term, IC is a covariant C' with $S' = I$. Finally let $S = q + \alpha_1 + \alpha_2\Delta + \alpha_3\Delta^2 + tB$ where t is a constant and the α_i are functions of a_0. Then by (A)

$$qS = I - \Delta^2 + 1 + \alpha_1 q,$$

which has the term $a_0^2 a_1^2 a_2^2$ (from I). The lemma is now completely proved.

Now consider covariants C of order $\omega = 6t + 2$. For t odd, the covariants

$$f^{3t+1}, Q^t f, C_2^{3t+1}, f^{3t}C_2, C_1^{3t}C_2,$$

have as coefficients of x_1^{ω}

$$a_0^2, a_0, \Delta^2 - a_0^2\Delta + a_0^2, a_0\Delta + a_0, B,$$

respectively. Linear combinations of products of these by invariants give the seminvariants (s) and Δ, Δ^2. Hence, by the lemma, $c \equiv P + LC'$, where P is a polynomial in the covariants of the table omitting f_4. For t even the covariants

$$fQ^t, f^4 Q^{t-1}, C_2 Q^t, C_1 Q^t$$

have $a_0, a_0^2, Delta + a_0^2, B$ as coefficients of x_1^{ω}.

Taking up next covariants C of order $\omega = 6t + 4$ coefficients of x_1^{ω} in

$$f_4 Q^t, f^2 Q^t, C_1 C_2 Q^t, C_1^2 Q^t$$

are, respectively, $a_0, a_0^2, B, \Delta - a_0^2\Delta$. Linear combinations of their products by invariants give all seminvariants not containing $1, I, q$. Hence the eight concomitants of the table form a fundamental system of modular concomitants of f (modulo 3). They are connected by the following syzygies:

$$\left. \begin{array}{l} fC_1 \equiv 2(\Delta^2 + \Delta)L, \; fC_2 \equiv (1+\Delta)f_4 \\ C_2^2 - C_1^2 \equiv (\Delta+1)^2 f^2, \; C_2^3 - ff^4 \equiv \Delta Q \end{array} \right\} \quad (\mathrm{mod}\ 3).$$

No one of these eight concomitants is a rational integral function of the remaining seven. To prove this we find their expressions for five special sets of values of a_0, a_1, a_2 (in fact, those giving the non-equivalent fs under the group of transformations of determinant unity modulo 3):

	f	Δ	q	C_1	C_2	f_4
(1)	0	0	0	0	0	0
(2)	x_1^2	0	-1	0	x_1^2	x_1^4
(3)	$-x_1^2$	0	1	0	x_1^2	$-x_1^4$
(4)	$x_1^2 + x_2^2$	-1	0	0	0	$x_1^4 + x_2^4$
(5)	$2x_1x_2$	1	0	$-x_1^2 + x_2^2$	$x_1^2 + x_2^2$	$x_1^3 x_2 + x_1 x_2^3$

To show that L and Q are not functions of the remaining concomitants we use case (1). For f_4, use case (4). No linear relation holds between f, C_1, C_2 in which C_1 is present, since C_1 is of index 1, while f, C_2 are absolute covariants. Now $f \neq kC_2$ by case (4); $C_2 \neq kf$ by case (5). Next $q \neq F(\Delta)$ by (2) and (3); $\Delta \neq F(q)$ by (4) and (5).

Chapter 9

INVARIANTS OF TERNARY FORMS

In this chapter we shall discuss the invariant theory of the general ternary form

$$f = a_x^m = b_x^m = \cdots .$$

Contrary to what is a leading characteristic of binary forms, the ternary f is not linearly factorable, unless indeed it is the quantic (198) of the preceding chapter. Thus f represents a plane curve and not a collection of linear forms. This fact adds both richness and complexity to the invariant theory of f. The symbolical theory is in some ways less adequate for the ternary case. Nevertheless this method has enabled investigators to develop an extensive theory of plane curves with remarkable freedom from formal difficulties.[1]

9.1 Symbolical Theory

As in Section 2 of Chapter VIII, let

$$f(x) = a_x^m = (a_1 x_1 + a_2 x_2 + a_3 x_3)^m = b_x^m = \cdots .$$

Then the transformed of f under the collineations V (Chap. VIII) is

$$f' = (a_\lambda x_1' + a_\mu x_2' + a_\nu x_3')^m. \tag{199}$$

9.1.1 Polars and transvectants.

If (y_1, y_2, y_3) is a set cogredient to the set (x_1, x_2, x_3), then the (y) polars of f are (cf. (61))

$$f_{y^k} = a_x^{m-k} a_y^k (k = 0, 0, \cdots , m). \tag{200}$$

---

[1] Clebsch, Lindemann, Vorlesungen über Geometrie.

If the point (y) is on the curve $f = 0$, the equation of the tangent at (y) is

$$a_x a_y^{m-1} = 0. \tag{201}$$

The expression

$$\frac{(m-1)!(n-1)!(p-1)!}{m!n!p!} \left. \begin{bmatrix} \frac{\partial}{\partial x_1} & \frac{\partial}{\partial x_2} & \frac{\partial}{\partial x_3} \\ \frac{\partial}{\partial y_1} & \frac{\partial}{\partial y_2} & \frac{\partial}{\partial y_3} \\ \frac{\partial}{\partial z_1} & \frac{\partial}{\partial z_2} & \frac{\partial}{\partial z_3} \end{bmatrix} f(0)\phi(y)\psi(z) \right\}_{y=z=x} \tag{202}$$

is sometimes called the first transvectant of $f(x)$, $\phi(x)$, $\psi(x)$, and is abbreviated (f, ϕ, ψ). If

$$f(x) = a_x^m = a_x'^{fm} = \cdots , \phi(x) = b_x^n = b_x'^{fn} = \cdots , \psi(x) = c_x^p = c_x'^p = \cdots$$

then, as is easily verified,

$$(f, \phi, \psi)^r = (abc)a_x^{m-1}b_x^{n-1}c_x^{p-1}.$$

This is the Jacobian of the three forms. The rth transvectant is

$$(f, \phi, \psi)^r = (abc)^r a_x^{m-r}b_x^{n-r}c_x^{p-r}\,(r = 0, 1, \cdots). \tag{203}$$

For $r = 2$ and $f = \phi = \psi$ this is called the Hessian curve. Thus

$$(f, f, f)^2 = (abc)^2 a_x^{m-2}b_x^{n-2}c_x^{p-2} = 0$$

is the equation of the Hessian. It was proved in Chapter I that Jacobians are concomitants. A repetition of that proof under the present notation shows that transvectants are likewise concomitants. In fact the determinant Δ in (202) is itself an invariant operator, and

$$\Delta' = (\lambda\mu\nu)\Delta.$$

Illustration.

As an example of the brevity of proof which the symbolical notation affords for some theorems we may prove that the Hessian curve of $f = 0$ is the locus of all points whose polar conics are degenerate into two straight lines.

If $g = \alpha_x^2 = \beta_x^2 = \cdots = a_{200}x_1^2 + \cdots$ is a conic, its second transvectant is its discriminant, and equals

$$(\alpha\beta\gamma)^2 = \left(\sum \pm \alpha_1\beta_2\gamma_3\right)^2 = 6 \begin{vmatrix} a_{200} & a_{110} & a_{101} \\ a_{110} & a_{020} & a_{011} \\ a_{101} & a_{011} & a_{002} \end{vmatrix},$$

since $\alpha_1^2 = \beta_1^2 = \cdots = a_{200}$ etc. If $(\alpha\beta\gamma)^2 = 0$ the conic is a 2-line.

Now the polar conic of f is

$$P = a_x^2 a_y^{m-2} = a_x'^2 a_y'^{m-2} = \cdots,$$

and the second transvectant of this is

$$(P, P, P)^2 = (aa'a'')^2 a_y^{m-2} a_y'^{m-2} a_y''^{m-2}, \qquad (204)$$

But this is the Hessian of f in (y) variables. Hence if (y) is on the Hessian the polar conic degenerates, and conversely.

Every symbolical monomial expression ϕ consisting of factors of the two types (abc), a_x is a concomitant. In fact if

$$\phi = (abc)^p (abd)^q \cdots a_x^r b_x^s \cdots,$$

then

$$\phi' = \begin{vmatrix} a_\lambda & b_\lambda & c_\lambda \\ a_\mu & b_\mu & c_\mu \\ a_\nu & b_\nu & c_\nu \end{vmatrix}^p \begin{vmatrix} a_\lambda & b_\lambda & d_\lambda \\ a_\mu & b_\mu & d_\mu \\ a_\nu & b_\nu & d_\nu \end{vmatrix}^q \cdots a_x^r b_x^s \cdots,$$

since, by virtue of the equations of transformation $a_x' = a_x, \cdots$. Hence by the formula for the product of two determinants, or by (14), we have at once

$$\phi' = (\lambda\mu\nu)^{p+q+\cdots} (abc)^p (abd)^q \cdots a_x^r b_x^s \cdots = (\lambda\mu\nu)^{p+q+\cdots} \phi.$$

The ternary polar of the product of two ternary forms is given by the same formula as that for the polar of a product in the binary case. That is, formula (77) holds when the forms and operators are ternary.

Thus, the formula for the rth transvectant of three quantics, $e.g.$

$$T = (f, \phi, \psi)^r = (abc)^r a_x^{m-r} b_x^{n-r} c_x^{p-r},$$

may be obtained by polarization: That is, by a process analogous to that employed in the standard method of transvection in the binary case. Let

$$(bc)_1 = b_2 c_3 - b_3 c_2, (bc)_2 = b_3 c_1 - b_1 c_3, (bc)_3 = b_1 c_2 - b_2 c_1. \qquad (205)$$

Then

$$a_{(bc)} = (abc). \qquad (206)$$

Hence T may be obtained by polarizing a_x^m r times, changing y_i into $(bc)_i$ and multiplying the result by $b_x^{n-r} c_x^{p-r}$. Thus

$$(a_x^2 b_x, c_x^3, x_x^3) = \frac{1}{3} \left[\binom{2}{1}\binom{1}{1} a_x a_y b_y + \binom{2}{2}\binom{1}{0} a_y^2 b_x \right]_{y=(cd)} c_x$$

$$= \frac{2}{3} (acd)(bcd) a_x c_x + \frac{1}{3} (acd)^2 b_x c_x.$$

Before proceeding to further illustrations we need to show that there exists for all ternary collineations a *universal covariant*. It will follow from this that a complete fundamental system for a single ternary form is in reality a simultaneous system of the form itself and a definite universal covariant. We introduce these facts in the next paragraph.

9.1.2 Contragrediency.

Two sets of variables (x_1, x_2, x_3), (u_1, u_2, u_3) are said to be contragredient when they are subject to the following schemes of transformation respectively:

$$V : \begin{aligned} x_1 &= \lambda_1 x_1' + \mu_1 x_2' + \nu_1 x_3' \\ x_2 &= \lambda x_1' + \mu_2 x_2' + \nu_2 x_3' \\ x_3 &= \lambda_3 x_1' + \mu_3 x_2' + \nu_3 x_3' \end{aligned}$$

$$\Lambda : \begin{aligned} u_1' &= \lambda_1 u_1 + \lambda_2 u_2 + \lambda_3 u_3 \\ u_2' &= \mu_1 u_1 + \mu_2 u_2 + \mu_3 u_3 \\ u_3' &= \nu_1 u_1 + \nu_2 u_2 + \nu_3 u_3. \end{aligned}$$

Theorem. *A necessary and sufficient condition in order that (x) may be contragredient to (u) is that*

$$u_x \equiv u_1 x_1 + u_2 x_2 + u_3 x_3$$

should be a universal covariant.

If we transform u_x by V and use Λ this theorem is at once evident.

It follows, as stated above, that the fundamental system of a form f under V, Λ is a simultaneous system of f and u_x (cf. Chap. VI, §4).

The reason that $u_x = u_1 x_1 + u_2 x_2$ does not figure in the corresponding way in the binary theory is that cogrediency is equivalent to contragrediency in the binary case and u_x is equivalent to $(xy) = x_1 y_2 - x_2 y_1$ which does figure very prominently in the binary theory. To show that cogrediency and contragrediency are here equivalent we may solve

$$\begin{aligned} u_1' &= \lambda_1 u_1 + \lambda_2 u_2 \\ u_2' &= \mu_1 u_1 + \mu_2 u_2, \end{aligned}$$

we find

$$\begin{aligned} -(\lambda\mu)u_1 &= \lambda_2 u_2' + \mu_2(-u_1'), \\ (\lambda\mu)u_2 &= \lambda_1 u_2' + \mu_1(-u_1'), \end{aligned}$$

which proves that $y_1 = +u_2$, $y_2 = -u_1$ are cogredient to x_1, x_2. Then u_x becomes (yx) (cf. Chap. 1, §3, V).

We now prove the principal theorem of the symbolic theory which shows that the present symbolical notation is sufficient to represent completely the totality of ternary concomitants.

9.1.3 Fundamental theorem of symbolical theory.

Theorem. *Every invariant formation of the ordinary rational integral type, of a ternary quantic*

$$f = a_x^m = \cdots = \sum_{mj} \frac{m!}{m_1! m_2! m_3!} a_{m_1 m_2 m_3} x_1^{m_1} x_2^{m_2} x_3^{m_3} \left(\sum m_j = m \right),$$

can be represented symbolically by three types of factors, viz.

$$(abc), (abu), a_x,$$

together with the universal covariant u_x.

We first prove two lemmas.

Lemma 7. *The following formula is true:*

$$\Delta^n D^n \equiv \begin{vmatrix} \dfrac{\partial}{\partial\lambda_1} & \dfrac{\partial}{\partial\lambda_2} & \dfrac{\partial}{\partial\lambda_3} \\[4pt] \dfrac{\partial}{\partial\mu_1} & \dfrac{\partial}{\partial\mu_2} & \dfrac{\partial}{\partial\mu_3} \\[4pt] \dfrac{\partial}{\partial\nu_1} & \dfrac{\partial}{\partial\nu_2} & \dfrac{\partial}{\partial\nu_3} \end{vmatrix}^n \begin{vmatrix} \lambda_1 & \lambda_2 & \lambda_3 \\ \mu_1 & \mu_2 & \mu_3 \\ \nu_1 & \nu_2 & \nu_3 \end{vmatrix}^n = C, \tag{207}$$

where $C \neq 0$ is a numerical constant.

In proof of this we note that D^n, expanded by the multinomial theorem, gives

$$D^n = \sum_{ij} \frac{n!}{i_1! i_2! i_3!} \lambda_1^{i_1} \lambda_2^{i_2} \lambda_3^{i_3} (\mu_2\nu_3 - \mu_3\nu_2)^{i_1} (\mu_3\nu_1 - \mu_1\nu_3)^{i_2} (\mu_1\nu_2 - \mu_2\nu_1)^{i_3} \cdot \left(\sum i_j = n\right).$$

Also the expansion of Δ^n is given by the same formula where now $(\lambda_r \mu_s \nu_t)$ is replaced by $\left(\frac{\partial}{\partial\lambda_r} \frac{\partial}{\partial\mu_s} \frac{\partial}{\partial\nu_t}\right)$. We may call the term given by a definite set i_1, i_2, i_3 of the exponents in D^n, the *correspondent* of the term given by the same set of exponents in Δ^n. Then, in $\Delta^n D^n$, the only term of D^n which gives a non-zero result when operated upon by a definite term of Δ^n is the correspondent of that definite term. But D^n may be written

$$D^n = \sum_{ij} \frac{n!}{i_1! i_2! i_3!} \lambda_1^{i_1} \lambda_2^{i_2} \lambda_3^{i_3} (\mu\nu)_1^{i_1} (\mu\nu)_2^{i_2} (\mu\nu)_3^{i_3}.$$

An easy differentiation gives

$$\left(\frac{\partial}{\partial\mu} \frac{\partial}{\partial\nu}\right)_3 (\mu\nu)_1^{i_1} (\mu\nu)_2^{i_2} (\mu\nu)_3^{i_3} = i_3(i_1 + i_2 + i_3 + 1)(\mu\nu)_1^{i_1} (\mu\nu)_2^{i_2} (\mu\nu)_3^{i_3 - 1},$$

and two corresponding formulas may be written from symmetry. These formulas hold true for zero exponents. Employing them as recursion formulas we have immediately for $\Delta^n D^n$,

$$\begin{aligned}
\Delta_n D^n &= \sum_{i_j=0}^{n} \left(\frac{n!}{i_1! i_2! i_3!}\right)^2 (i_1! i_2! i_3!)^2 (i_1 + i_2 + i_3 + 1)! \\
&= \sum_{i_j=0}^{n} (n!)^2 (n+1)! = \frac{1}{2}(n!)^3 (n+1)^2 (n+2). \tag{208}
\end{aligned}$$

This is evidently a numerical constant $C \neq 0$, which was to be proved (cf. (91)).

Lemma 8. *If P is a product of m factors of type α_λ, n of type β_μ, and p of type γ_ν, then $\Delta^k P$ is a sum of a number of monomials, each monomial of which contains k factors of type $(\alpha\beta\gamma)$, $m-k$ factors of type α_λ, $n-k$ of type β_μ, and $p-k$ of type γ_ν.*

This is easily proved. Let $P = ABC$, where

$$
\begin{aligned}
A &= \alpha_\lambda^{(1)}\alpha_\lambda^{(2)}\cdots\alpha_\lambda^{(m)}, \\
B &= \beta_\mu^{(1)}\beta_\mu^{(2)}\cdots\beta_\mu^{(n)}, \\
C &= \gamma_\nu^{(1)}\gamma_\nu^{(2)}\cdots\gamma_\nu^{(p)}.
\end{aligned}
$$

Then

$$
\frac{\delta^3 P}{\delta\gamma_1\delta\mu_2\delta\nu_3} = \sum_{r,i,t}\alpha_1^{(r)}\beta_2^{(s)}\gamma_3^{(t)}\frac{ABC}{\alpha_\lambda^{(r)}\beta_\mu^{(s)}\gamma_\nu^{(t)}}\left(\begin{array}{l} r = 1,\cdots,m \\ s = 1,\cdots,n \\ t = 1,\cdots,p \end{array}\right).
$$

Writing down the six such terms from ΔP and taking the sum we have

$$
\Delta P = \sum_{r,s,t}\left(\alpha^{(r)}\beta^{(s)}\gamma^{(t)}\right)\frac{ABC}{\alpha_\gamma^{(r)}\beta_\mu^{(s)}\gamma_\nu^{(t)}}, \tag{209}
$$

which proves the lemma for $k = 1$, inasmuch as $\dfrac{A}{\alpha_\lambda^{(r)}}$ has $m-1$ factors; and so forth. The result for $\Delta^k P$ now follows by induction, by operating on both members of equation (209) by Δ, and noting that $\left(\alpha^{(r)}\beta^{(s)}\gamma^{(t)}\right)$ is a constant as far as operations by Δ are concerned.

Let us now represent a concomitant of f by $\phi(a, x)$, and suppose that it does not contain the variables (u), and that the corresponding invariant relation is

$$
\phi(a', x', \cdots) = (\lambda\mu\nu)^\omega \phi(a, x, \cdots). \tag{210}
$$

The inverse of the transformation V is

$$
x_1' = (\lambda\mu\nu)^{-1}[(\mu\nu)_1 x_1 + (\mu\nu)_2 x_2 + (\mu\nu)_3 x_3]
$$

etc. Or, if we consider (x) to be the point of intersection of two lines

$$
\begin{aligned}
v_x &= v_1 x_1 + v_2 x_2 + v_3 x_3, \\
w_x &= w_1 x_1 + w_2 x_2 + w_3 x_3,
\end{aligned}
$$

we have

$$
x_1 : x_2 : x_3 = (vw)_1 : (vw)_2 : (vw)_3.
$$

Substitution with these in $x_1', \cdots$ and rearrangement of the terms gives for the inverse of V

$$
V^{-1} : \begin{cases} x_1' = \dfrac{v_\mu w_\nu - v_\gamma w_\mu}{(\lambda\mu\nu)}, \\[2mm] x_2' = \dfrac{v_\nu w_\lambda - v_\lambda w_\nu}{(\lambda\mu\nu)}, \\[2mm] x_3' = \dfrac{v_\lambda w_\mu - v_\mu w_\lambda}{(\lambda\mu\nu)}. \end{cases}
$$

We now proceed as if we were verifying the invariancy of ϕ, substituting from V^{-1} for x_1', x_3', x_3' on the left-hand side of (210), and replacing $a'_{m_1 m_2 m_3}$ by its symbolical equivalent $a_\lambda^{m_1} a_\mu^{m_2} a_\nu^{m_3}$ (cf. (199)). Suppose that the order of ϕ is ω. Then after performing these substitutions and multiplying both sides of (210) by $(\lambda \mu \nu)^\omega$ we have

$$\phi(a_\lambda^{m_1} a_\mu^{m_2} a_\nu^{m_3}, v_\lambda w_\mu - v_\mu w_\lambda, \cdots) = (\lambda \mu \nu)^{w+\omega} \phi(a, x, \cdots),$$

and every term of the left-hand member of this must contain $w + \omega$ factors with each suffix, since the terms of the right-hand member do. Now operate on both sides by Δ. Each term of the result on the left contains one determinant factor by lemma 2, and in addition $w + \omega - 1$ factors with each suffix. There will be three types of these determinant factors $e.g.$

$$(abc), (avw) = a_x, (abv).$$

The first two of these are of the form required by the theorem. The determinant (abv) must have resulted by operating Δ upon a term containing a_λ, b_μ, v_ν and evidently such a term will also contain the factor w_μ or else w_λ. Let the term in question be

$$R a_\lambda b_\mu v_\nu w_\mu.$$

Then the left-hand side of the equation must also contain the term

$$-R a_\lambda b_\mu v_\mu w_\nu,$$

and operation of Δ upon this gives

$$-R(abw)v_\mu,$$

and upon the sum gives

$$R\left[(abv)w_\mu - (abw)v_\mu\right].$$

Now the first identity of (212) gives

$$(abv)w_\mu - (abw)v_\mu = (bvw)a_\mu - (avw)b_\mu = b_x a_\mu - b_\mu a_x.$$

Hence the sum of the two terms under consideration is

$$R(b_x a_\mu - b_\mu a_x),$$

and this contains in addition to factors with a suffix μ only factors of the required type a_x. Thus only the two required types of symbolical factors occur in the result of operating by Δ.

Suppose now that we operate by $\Delta^{w+\omega}$ upon both members of the invariant equation. The result upon the right-hand side is a constant times the concomitant $\phi(a, x)$ by lemma 1. On the left there will be no terms with λ, μ, ν suffixes, since there are none on the right. Hence by dividing through by a constant we have $\phi(a, x)$ expressed as a sum of terms each of which consists of symbolical factors of only two types viz.

$$(abc), a_x,$$

which was to be proved. Also evidently there are precisely ω factors a_x in each term, and w of type (abc), and $\omega = 0$ if ϕ is an invariant.

The complete theorem now follows from the fact that any invariant formation of f is a simultaneous concomitant of f and u_x. That is, the only new type of factor which can be introduced by adjoining u_x is the third required type (abu).

9.1.4   Reduction identities.

We now give a set of identities which may be used in performing reductions. These may all be derived from

$$\begin{vmatrix} a_x & b_x & c_x \\ a_y & b_y & c_y \\ a_z & b_z & c_z \end{vmatrix} = (abc)(xyz), \tag{211}$$

as a fundamental identity (cf. Chap. III, §3, II). We let u_1, u_2, u_3 be the coördinates of the line joining the points $(x) = (x_1, x_2, x_3), (y) = (y_1, y_2, y_3)$. Then

$$u_1 : u_2 : u_3 = (xy)_1 : (xy)_2 : (xy)_3.$$

Elementary changes in (211) give

$$(bcd)a_x - (cda)b_x + (dab)c_x - (abc)d_x = 0,$$

$$(bcu)a_x - (cua)b_x + (uab)c_x - (abc)u_x = 0, \tag{212}$$

$$(abc)(def) - (dab)(cef) + (cda)(bef) - (bcd)(aef) = 0.$$

Also we have

$$a_x b_y - a_y b_x = (abu), \tag{213}$$
$$v_a w_b - v_b w_a = (abx).$$

In the latter case (x) is the intersection of the lines v, w.

To illustrate the use of these we can show that if $f = a_x^2 = \cdots$ is a quadratic, and D its discriminant, then

$$(abc)(abd)c_x d_x = \frac{1}{3} D f.$$

In fact, by squaring the first identity of (212) and interchanging the symbols, which are now all equivalent, this result follows immediately since $(abc)^2 = D$.

9.2 Transvectant Systems

9.2.1 Transvectants from polars.

We now develop a standard transvection process for ternary forms.

Theorem. *Every monomial ternary concomitant of $f = a_x^m = \cdots$,*

$$\phi = (abc)^p (abd)^q \cdots (bcd)^r \cdots (abu)^s (bcu)^t \cdots a^\sigma \cdots ,$$

is a term of a generalized transvectant obtained by polarization from a concomitant ϕ_1 of lower degree than ϕ.

Let us delete from ϕ the factor a_x^σ, and in the result change a into v, where v is cogredient to u. This result will contain factors of the three types (bcv), (bcd), (buv), together with factors of type b_x. But (uv) is cogredient to x. Hence the operation of changing (uv) into x is invariantive and (buv) becomes b_x. Next change v into u. Then we have a product ϕ_1 of three and only three types, *i.e.*

$$(bcu), (bcd), b_x,$$

$$\phi_1 = (bcd)^\alpha \cdots (bcu)^\beta \cdots b_x^\gamma c_x^\delta \cdots .$$

Now ϕ_1 does not contain the symbol a. Hence it is of lower degree than ϕ. Let the order of ϕ be ω, and its class μ. Suppose that in ϕ there are i determinant factors containing both a and u, and k which contain a but not u. Then

$$\sigma + i + k = m.$$

Also the order of ϕ_1 is

$$\omega_1 = \omega + 2i + k - m,$$

and its class

$$\mu_1 = \mu - i + k.$$

We now polarize ϕ_1, by operating $(v\frac{\partial}{\partial u})^k (y\frac{\partial}{\partial x})^i$ upon it and dividing out the appropriate constants. If in the resulting polar we substitute $v = a$, $y = (au)$ and multiply by a_x^{m-i-k} we obtain the transvectant (generalized)

$$\tau = (\phi_1, a_x^m, u_x^i)^{k,i}. \tag{214}$$

The concomitant ϕ is a term of τ.

For the transvectant τ thus defined $k + i$ is called the *index*. In any ternary concomitant of order ω and class μ the number $\omega + \mu$ is called the *grade*.

DEFINITION.

The mechanical rule by which one obtains from a concomitant

$$C = Aa_{1x}a_{2x}\cdots a_{rx}\alpha_{1u}\alpha_{2u}\cdots\alpha_{su},$$

any one of the three types of concomitants

$$C_1 = A(a_1a_2a_3)a_{4x}\cdots a_{rx}\alpha_{1u}\alpha_{2u}\cdots\alpha_{su},$$
$$C_2 = Aa_{1\alpha_1}a_{2x}\cdots a_{rx}\alpha_{2u}\alpha_{3u}\cdots\alpha_{su},$$
$$C_3 = A(\alpha_1\alpha_2\alpha_3)a_{1x}\cdots a_{rx}\alpha_{4u}\cdots\alpha_{su},$$

is called *convolution*. In this $a_{1\alpha_1}$ indicates the expression

$$a_{11}\alpha_{11} + a_{12}\alpha_{12} + a_{13}\alpha_{13}.$$

Note the possibility that one α might be x, or one a might be u.

9.2.2   The difference between two terms of a transvectant.

Theorem. . *The difference between any two terms of a transvectant τ equals reducible terms whose factors are concomitants of lower grade than τ, plus a sum of terms each term of which is a term of a transvectant $\bar{\tau}$ of index $\leqq k+i$,*

$$\bar{\tau} = (\bar{\phi}_1, a_x^m, u_x^i)^{k,i}.$$

In this $\bar{\phi}_1$ is of lower grade than ϕ_1 and is obtainable from the latter by convolution.

Let ϕ_1 be the concomitant C above, where A involves neither u nor x. Then, with λ numerical, we have the polar

$$P = \lambda\left(v\frac{\partial}{\partial u}\right)^k\left(y\frac{\partial}{\partial x}\right)^i \phi_1$$

$$= A\sum a_{1y}a_{2y}\cdots a_{iy}a_{i+1x}\cdots a_{rx}\alpha_{1v}\cdots\alpha_{kv}\alpha_{k+1u}\cdots\alpha_{su}. \tag{215}$$

Now in the ith polar of a *simple* product like

$$p = \gamma_{1x}\gamma_{2x}\cdots\gamma_{tx},$$

two terms are said to be *adjacent* when they differ only in that one has a factor of type $\gamma_{hy}\gamma_{jx}$ whereas in the other this factor is replaced by $\gamma_{hx}\gamma_{jy}$. Consider two terms, t_1, t_2 of P. Suppose that these differ only in that $\alpha_{nv}\alpha_{ku}a_{hy}a_{jx}$ in t_1 is replaced in t_2 by $\alpha_{\eta u}\alpha_{\kappa v}a_{hx}a_{jy}$. Then $t_1 - t_2$ is of the form

$$t_1 - t_2 = B(\alpha_{\eta v}\alpha_{\kappa u}a_{hy}a_{jx} - \alpha_{\eta u}\alpha_{\kappa v}a_{hx}a_{jy}).$$

We now add and subtract a term and obtain

$$t_1 - t_2 = B[\alpha_{\eta v}\alpha_{\kappa u}(a_{hy}a_{jx} - a_{hx}a_{jy}) + a_{hx}a_{jy}(\alpha_{\eta v}\alpha_{\kappa u} - \alpha_{\eta u}\alpha_{\kappa v})]. \tag{216}$$

Each parenthesis in (216) represents the difference between two adjacent terms of a polar of a simple product, and we have by (213)

$$t_1 - t_2 = B(yx(a_h a_j))\alpha_{\eta v}\alpha_{\kappa u} + B(\alpha_\kappa \alpha_\eta (uv))\alpha_{hx}\alpha_{jy}. \tag{217}$$

The corresponding terms in τ are obtained by the replacements $v = a$, $y = (au)$. They are the terms of

$$S = -B'((au)(a_h a_j)x)a_{\alpha\eta}\alpha_{\kappa u} - B'((au)\alpha_\kappa \alpha_\eta)(a_j au)a_{hx},$$

or, since

$$((au)(a_h a_j)x) = (aa_h a_j)u_x - (a_h a_j u)a_x,$$

of

$$S = B'(a_h a_j u)\alpha_{\eta a}\alpha_{\kappa u}a_x - B'(a_h a_j a)\alpha_{\eta a}\alpha_{\kappa u}u_x$$
$$+ B'(\alpha_\eta \alpha_\kappa (au))(a_j au)a_{hx},$$

where B becomes B' under the replacements $v = a$, $y = (au)$. The middle term of this form of S is evidently reducible, and each factor is of lower grade than τ. By the method given under Theorem I the first and last terms of S are respectively terms of the transvectants

$$\bar{\tau}_1 = (B_1(a_h a_j u)\alpha_{\eta u}\alpha_{\kappa u}, a_x^m, u_x^{i-1})^{k,i-1},$$
$$\bar{\tau}_2 = (B_1(\alpha\alpha_\eta x)a_{jx}a_{hx}, a_x^m, u_x^{i+1})^{k-1,i+1}.$$

The middle term is a term of

$$\bar{\tau}_3 = (-B_1(a_h a_j u)\alpha_{\eta u}\alpha_{\kappa u}, a_x^m, u_x^{i-1})^{k-1,i+1} \cdot u_x.$$

In each of these B_l is what B becomes when $v = u, y = x$; and the first form in each transvectant is evidently obtained from $u_x \phi_1 \equiv C u_x$ by convolution. Also each is of lower grade than ϕ_1.

Again if the terms in the parentheses in form (216) of any difference $t_1 - t_2$ are not adjacent, we can by adding and subtracting terms reduce these parentheses each to the form [2]

$$[(\tau_1 - \tau_2) + (\tau_2 - \tau_3) + \cdots (\tau_{l-1} - \tau_l)], \tag{218}$$

---

[2] Isserlis. On the ordering of terms of polars etc. *Proc. London Math. Society, ser.* 2, Vol. 6 (1908).

where every difference is a difference between adjacent terms, of a *simple* polar. Applying the results above to these differences $\tau_i - \tau_{i+1}$ the complete theorem follows.

As a corollary it follows that the difference between the whole transvectant τ and any one of its terms equals a sum of terms each of which is a term of a transvectant of a_x^m with a form $\bar{\phi}_1$ of lower grade than ϕ_1 obtained by convolution from the latter. For if

$$\tau = \nu_1 \tau_1 + \nu_2 \tau_2 + \cdots + \nu_r \tau_r + \cdots$$

where the ν's are numerical, then τ_r is a term of τ. Also since our transvectant τ is obtained by polarization, $\sum \nu_i = 1$. Hence

$$\tau - \tau_r = \nu_1(\tau_1 - \tau_r) + \nu_2(\tau_2 - \tau_r) + \cdots ,$$

and each parenthesis is a difference between two terms of τ. The corollary is therefore proved.

Since the power of u_x entering τ is determinate from the indices k, i we may write τ in the shorter form

$$\tau = (\phi_1, a_x^m)^{k,i}.$$

The theorem and corollary just proved furnish a method of deriving the fundamental system of invariant formations of a single form $f = a_x^m$ by passing from the full set of a given degree $i - 1$, assumed known, to all those of the fundamental system, of degree i. For suppose that all of those members of the fundamental system of degrees $\leq i - 1$ have been previously determined. Then by forming products of their powers we can build all invariant formations of degree $i - 1$. Let the latter be arranged in an ordered succession

$$\phi', \phi'', \phi''', \cdots$$

in order of ascending grade. Form the transvectants of these with $a^m, \tau_j = (\phi^{(j)}, a_x^m)^{k,i}$. If τ_j contains a single term which is reducible in terms of forms of lower degree or in terms of transvectants $\tau_{j'}, j' < j$, then τ_j may, by the theorem and corollary, be neglected in constructing the members of the fundamental system of degree i. That is, in this construction we need only retain one term from each transvectant which contains no reducible terms. This process of constructing a fundamental system by passing from degree to degree is tedious for all systems excepting that for a single ternary quadratic form. A method which is equivalent but makes no use of the transvectant operation above described, and the resulting simplifications, has been applied by Gordan in the derivation of the fundamental system of a ternary cubic form. The method of Gordan was also successfully applied by Baker to the system of two and of three conics. We give below a derivation of the system for a single conic and a summary of Gordan's system for a ternary cubic (Table VII).

9.2.3 Fundamental systems for ternary quadratic and cubic.

Let $f = a_x^2 = b_x^2 = \cdots$. The only form of degree one is f itself. It leads to the transvectants

$$(a_x^2, b_x^2)^{0,1} = (abu)a_x b_x = 0, \quad (a_x^2, b_x^2)^{0,2} = (abu)^2 = L.$$

Thus the only irreducible formation of degree 2 is L. The totality of degree 2 is, in ascending order as to grade,

$$(abu)^2, \quad a_x^2 b_x^2.$$

All terms of $(f^2, f)^{k,i}$ are evidently reducible, *i.e.* contain terms reducible by means of powers of f and L. Also

$$((abu)^2, c_x^2)^{1,0} = (abc)(abu)c_x$$

$$= \frac{1}{3}(abc)\left[(abu)c_x + (bcu)a_x + (cau)b_x\right] = \frac{1}{3}(abc)^2 u_x,$$

$$((abu)^2, c_x^2)^{2,0} = (abc)^2 = D.$$

Hence the only irreducible formation of the third degree is D. Passing to degree four, we need only consider transvectants of fL with f. Moreover the only possibility for an irreducible case is evidently

$$(fL, f)^{1,1} = (abd)(abu)(cdu)c_x$$

$$= \frac{1}{4}(abu)(cdu)\left[(abd)c_x + (bcd)a_x + (dca)b_x + (acb)d_x\right] \equiv 0.$$

All transvectants of degree ≥ 4 are therefore of the form

$$(f^h L^j, f)^{k,i}(i+k < 3),$$

and hence reducible. Thus the fundamental system of f is

$$u_x, f, L, D.$$

The explicit form of D was given in section 1. A symmetrical form of L in terms of the actual coefficients of the conic is the bordered discriminant

$$L : \begin{vmatrix} a_2 00 & a_1 10 & a_1 01 & u_1 \\ a_1 10 & a_0 20 & a_0 11 & u_2 \\ a_1 01 & a_0 11 & a_0 02 & u_3 \\ u_1 & u_2 & u_3 & 0 \end{vmatrix}.$$

To verify that L equals this determinant we may expand $(abu)^2$ and express the symbols in terms of the coefficients.

We next give a table showing Gordan's fundamental system for the ternary cubic. There are thirty-four individuals in this system. In the table, i indicates the degrees.

The reader will find it instructive to derive by the methods just shown in the case of the quadratic, the forms in this table of the first three or four degrees.

TABLE VII

i	INVARIANT FORMATION
0	u_x
1	a_x^3
2	$(abu)^2 a_x b_x$
3	$(abu)^2 (bcu) a_x c_x^2,\ a_x^3 = (abc)^2 a_x b_x c_x,\ s_u^3 = (abc)(abu)(acu)(bcu)$
4	$(a\alpha u) a_x^2 \alpha_x^2,\ a_s s_u^2 a_x^2,\ S = a_s^3,\ p_u^6 = (abu)^2 (cdu)^2 (bcu)(adu)$
5	$a_s s_u^2 (abu) a_x b_x^2,\ a_s b_s s_u a_x^2 b_x^2,\ a_s (abu)^2 s_u^2 b_x,\ t_u^3 = a_s b_s s_u (abu)^2$
6	$a_s b_s s_u (bcu) a_x^2 b_x c_x^2,\ a_s s_u^2 (abu)^2 (bcu) c_x^2,\ a_t t_u^2 a_x^2,\ T = a_t^3$
7	$s_u^2 p_u^5 (spx),\ a_t t_u^2 (abu) a_x b_x^2,\ a_t b_t t_u a_x^2 b_x^2,\ a_t t_u^2 (abu)^2 b_x$
8	$a_t b_t t_u (bcu) a_x^2 b_x c_x^2,\ q_x^6 = a_t b_t c_t a_x^2 b_x^2 c_x^2,\ a_t t_u^2 (abu)^2 (bcu) c_x^2,\ s_u^2 t_u^2 (stx)$
9	$(aqu) a_x^2 q_x^5,\ p_u^5 t_u^2 (ptx),\ a_t s_u^2 t_u a_x^2 (stx)$
10	$a_t b_t s_u^2 a_x^2 b_x^2 (stx),\ a_t s_u^2 t_u (abu)^2 b_x (stx)$
11	$(\alpha qu) a_x^2 q_x^5$
12	$(a\alpha q) a_x^2 \alpha_x^2 q_x^5,\ p_u^5 s_u^2 t_u^2 (pst)$

9.2.4 Fundamental system of two ternary quadrics.

We shall next define a ternary transvectant operation which will include as special cases all of the operations of transvection which have been employed in this chapter. It will have been observed that a large class of the invariant formations of ternary quantics, namely the mixed concomitants, involve both the (x) and the (u) variables. We now assume, quite arbitrarily, two forms involving both sets of variables $e.g.$

$$
\begin{aligned}
\phi &= A a_{1x} a_{2x} \cdots a_{rx} \alpha_{1u} \alpha_{2u} \cdots \alpha_{su}, \\
\psi &= B b_{1x} b_{2x} \cdots b_{\rho x} \beta_{1u} \beta_{2u} \cdots \beta_{\sigma u},
\end{aligned}
$$

in which A, B are free from (x) and (u). A transvectant of ϕ, and ψ of four indices, the most general possible, may be defined as follows: Polarize ϕ by the following operator,

$$
\sum \left(y_1^{(1)} \frac{\partial}{\partial x} \right)^{\epsilon_1} \left(y_2^{(1)} \frac{\partial}{\partial x} \right)^{\epsilon_2} \cdots \left(y_\rho^{(1)} \frac{\partial}{\partial x} \right)^{\epsilon_\rho} \left(y_1^{(2)} \frac{\partial}{\partial x} \right)^{\iota_1} \left(y_2^{(2)} \frac{\partial}{\partial x} \right)^{\iota_2} \cdots \left(y_\rho^{(2)} \frac{\partial}{\partial x} \right)^{\iota_\rho}
$$

$$
\times \left(v_1^{(1)} \frac{\partial}{\partial u} \right)^{\sigma_1} \left(v_2^{(1)} \frac{\partial}{\partial u} \right)^{\sigma_2} \cdots \left(v_\sigma^{(1)} \frac{\partial}{\partial u} \right)^{\sigma_\sigma} \left(v_1^{(2)} \frac{\partial}{\partial u} \right)^{\nu_1} \left(v_2^{(2)} \frac{\partial}{\partial u} \right)^{\nu_2} \cdots \left(v_\sigma^{(2)} \frac{\partial}{\partial u} \right)^{\nu_\sigma}
$$

wherein $\epsilon_i, \iota_i, \sigma_i, \nu_i = 0$ or 1, and

$$
\sum \epsilon = i, \sum \iota = j, \sum \sigma = k, \sum \nu = l;\ i + j \leq r,\ k + l \leq s.
$$

188

Substitute in the resulting polar

$$
\begin{aligned}
&(a) \quad y_p^{(1)} = \beta_p && (p = 1, 2, \ldots, i),\\
&(b) \quad y_p^{(2)} = (b_p u) && (p = 1, 2, \ldots, j),\\
&(c) \quad v_p^{(1)} = b_p && (p = 1, 2, \ldots, k),\\
&(d) \quad v_p^{(2)} = (\beta_p x) && (p = 1, 2, \ldots, l),
\end{aligned}
$$

and multiply each term of the result by the b_x, β_u factors not affected in it. The resulting concomitant τ we call the transvectant of ϕ and ψ of index $\begin{pmatrix} i, & j \\ k, & l \end{pmatrix}$, and write

$$
\tau = (\phi, \psi)_{k,l}^{i,j}.
$$

An example is

$$
\begin{aligned}
(a_{1x} a_{2x} \alpha_u, b_{1x} b_{2x} \beta_u)_{1,0}^{1,1} = \; & a_{1\beta} \alpha_{b_2} (a_2 b_1 u) + a_{1\beta} \alpha_{b_1} (a_2 b_2 u) \\
+ \; & a_{2\beta} \alpha_{b_2} (a_1 b_1 u) + a_{2\beta} \alpha_{b_1} (a_1 b_2 u).
\end{aligned}
$$

If, now, we introduce in place of ϕ successively products of forms of the fundamental system of a conic, *i.e.* of

$$
f = a_x^2, \; L = \alpha_u^2 = (a'a''u)^2, \; D = (aa'a'')^2,
$$

and for ψ products of forms of the fundamental system of a second conic,

$$
g = b_x^2, \; L' = \beta_u^2 = (b'b''u)^2, \; D' = (bb'b'')^2,
$$

we will obtain all concomitants of f and g. The fundamental simultaneous system of f, g will be included in the set of transvectants which contain no reducible terms, and these we may readily select by inspection. They are 17 in number and are as follows:

$$
\begin{aligned}
\Phi &= (a_x^2, b_x^2)_{0,0}^{0,2} = (abu)^2, \\
C_1 &= (a_x^2, b_x^2)_{0,0}^{0,1} = (abu) a_x b_x, \\
A_{122} &= (a_x^2, \beta_u^2)_{0,0}^{2,0} = a_\beta^2, \\
C_2 &= (a_x^2, \beta_u^2)_{0,0}^{1,0} = a_\beta a_x \beta_u, \\
C_3 &= (a_u^2, b_x^2)_{1,0}^{0,0} = \alpha_b \alpha_u b_x, \\
A_{112} &= (\alpha_u^2, b_x^2)_{2,0}^{0,0} = \alpha_b^2, \\
C_4 &= (\alpha_u^2, \beta_u^2)_{0,1}^{0,0} = (\alpha\beta x) \alpha_u \beta_u, \\
F &= (\alpha_u^2, \beta_u^2)_{0,2}^{0,0} = (\alpha\beta x)^2, \\
C_5 &= (\alpha_u^2, b_x^2 \beta_u^2)_{1,1}^{0,0} = \alpha_b (\alpha\beta x) b_x \beta_u, \\
C_6 &= (a_x^2, b_x^2 \beta_u^2)_{0,0}^{1,1} = a_\beta (abu) b_x \beta_u,
\end{aligned}
$$

$$
\begin{aligned}
C_7 &= (a_x^2 a_u^2, b_x^2)_{1,0}^{0,1} = a_b(abu)a_x\alpha_u, \\
C_8 &= (a_x^2 a_u^2, \beta_u^2)_{0,1}^{1,0} = a_\beta(\alpha\beta x)a_x\alpha_u, \\
G &= (fL, gL')_{1,1}^{1,0} = a_\beta\alpha_b(\alpha\beta x)a_x b_x, \\
\Gamma &= (fL, gL')_{1,0}^{1,1} = a_\beta\alpha_b(abu)\alpha_u\beta_u, \\
K_1 &= (fL, gL')_{0,1}^{1,1} = a_\beta(abu)\alpha_u(\alpha\beta x)b_x, \\
K_2 &= (fL, gL')_{1,1}^{0,1} = a_b(abu)\beta_u(\alpha\beta x)a_x, \\
K_3 &= (fL, gL')_{1,1}^{1,1} = a_\beta\alpha_b(abu)(\alpha\beta x).
\end{aligned}
$$

The last three of these are evidently reducible by the simple identity

$$
(abu)(\alpha\beta x) = \begin{vmatrix} a_a & b_a & \alpha_u \\ a_\beta & b_\beta & \beta_u \\ a_x & b_x & u_x \end{vmatrix}.
$$

The remaining 14 are irreducible. Thus the fundamental system for two ternary quadrics consists of 20 forms. They are, four invariants D, D', A_{112}, A_{122}; four covariants f, g, F, G; four contravariants L, L', Φ, Γ; eight mixed concomitants C_i, $(i = 1, \ldots, 8)$.

9.3   Clebsch's Translation Principle

Suppose that (y), (z) are any two points on an arbitrary line which intersects the curve $f = a_x^m = 0$. Then

$$
u_1 : u_2 : u_3 = (yz)_1 : (yz)_2 : (yz)_3
$$

are contragredient to the x's. If (x) is an arbitrary point on the line we may write

$$
x_1 = \eta_1 y_1 + \eta_2 z_1, \quad x_2 = \eta_1 y_2 + \eta_2 z_2, \quad x_3 = \eta_1 y_3 + \eta_2 z_3,
$$

and then (η_1, η_2) may be regarded as the coordinates of a representative point (x) on the line with (y), (z) as the two reference points. Then a_x becomes

$$
a_x = a_1 x_1 + a_2 x_2 + a_3 x_3 = \eta_1 a_y + \eta_2 a_z,
$$

and the (η) coordinates of the m points in which the line intersects the curve $f = 0$ are the m roots of

$$
g = g_\eta^m = (a_y \eta_1 + a_z \eta_2)^m = (b_y \eta_1 + b_z \eta_2)^m = \cdots .
$$

Now this is a binary form in symbolical notation, and the notation differs from the notation of a binary form $h = a_x^m = (a_1 x_1 + a_2 x_2)^m = \ldots$ only in this, that a_1, a_2 are replaced by a_y, a_z, respectively. Any invariant,

$$
I_1 = \sum k(ab)^p (ac)^q \cdots ,
$$

of h has corresponding to it an invariant I of g,

$$I = \sum k(a_y b_z - a_z b_y)^p (a_y c_z - a_z c_y)^q \cdots .$$

If $I = 0$ then the line cuts the curve $f = a_x^m = 0$ in m points which have the protective property given by $I_1 = 0$. But (cf. (213)),

$$(a_y b_z - a_z b_y) = (abu).$$

Hence,

Theorem. *If in any invariant.* $I_1 = \sum k(ap)^p(ac)^q \cdots$ *of a binary form* $h = a_x^m = (a_1 x_1 + a_2 x_2)^m = \cdots$ *we replace each second order determinant* (ab) *by the third order determinant* (abu), *and so on, the resulting line equation represents the envelope of the line* u_x *when it moves so as to intersect the curve* $f = a_x^m = (a_1 x_1 + a_2 x_2 + a_3 x_3)^m = 0$ *in* m *points having the protective property* $I_1 = 0$.

By making the corresponding changes in the symbolical form of a simultaneous invariant I of any number of binary forms we obtain the envelope of u_x when the latter moves so as to cut the corresponding number of curves in a point range which constantly possesses the projective property $I = 0$. Also this translation principle is applicable in the same way to covariants of the binary forms.

For illustration the discriminant of a binary quadratic $h = a_x^2 = b_x^2 = \cdots$ is $D = (ab)^2$. Hence the line equation of the conic $f = a_x^2 = (a_1 x_1 + a_2 x_2 + a_3 x_3)^2 = \cdots = 0$ is

$$L = (abu)^2 = 0.$$

For this is the envelope of u_x when the latter moves so as to touch $f = 0$, *i.e.* so that $D = 0$ for the range in which u_x cuts $f = 0$.

The discriminant of the binary cubic $h = (a_1 x_1 + a_2 x_2)^3 = b_x^3 = \cdots$ is

$$R = (ab)^2 (ac)(bd)(cd)^2.$$

Hence the line equation of the general cubic curve $f = a_x^3 = \cdots$ is (cf. Table VII)

$$p_u^6 = L = (abu)^2 (acu)(bdu)(cdu)^2 = 0.$$

We have shown in Chapter I that the degree i of the discriminant of a binary form of order m is $2(m-1)$. Hence its index, and so the number of symbolical determinants of type (ab) in each term of its symbolical representation, is

$$k = \frac{1}{2}im = m(m-1).$$

It follows immediately that the degree of the line equation, i.e. the *class* of a plane curve of order m is, in general, $m(m-1)$.

Two binary forms $h_1 = a_x^m = a_x'^m = \ldots$, $h_2 = b_x^m = \ldots$, of the same order have the bilinear invariant

$$I = (ab)^m$$

If $I = 0$ the forms are said to be apolar (cf. Chap. III, (71)); in the case $m = 2$, harmonic. Hence $(abu)^m = 0$ is the envelope of $u_x = 0$ when the latter moves so as to intersect two curves $f = a_x^m = 0, g = b_x^m = 0$, in apolar point ranges.

APPENDIX

EXERCISES AND THEOREMS

1. Verify that $I = a_0 a_4 - 4 a_1 a_3 + 3 a_2^2$ is an invariant of the binary quartic

$$f = a_0 x_1^4 + 4 a_1 x_1^3 x_2 + 6 a_2 x_1^2 x_2^2 + 4 a_3 x_1 x_2^3, + a_4 x_2^4$$

for which

$$I' = (\lambda \mu)^4 I.$$

2. Show the invariancy of

$$\alpha_1 (a_0 x_1 + a_1 x_2) - \alpha_0 (a_1 x_1 + a_2 x_2),$$

for the simultaneous transformation of the forms

$$f = \alpha_0 x_1 + \alpha_1 x_2,$$
$$g = a_0 x_1^2 + 2 a_1 x_1 x_2 + a_2 x_2^2.$$

Give also a verification for the covariant C of Chap. I, §1, V, and for $J_{\phi, \Delta}$ of Chap. II, §3.

3. Compute the Hessian of the binary quintic form

$$f = a_0 x_1^5 + 5 a_1 x_1^4 x_2 + \ldots .$$

The result is

$$\frac{1}{2} H = (a_0 a_2 - a_1^2) x_1^6 + 3(a_0 a_3 - a_1 a_2) x_1^5 x_2 + 3(a_0 a_4 + a_1 a_3 - 2 a_2^2) x_1^4 x_2^3$$
$$+ (a_0 a_5 + 7 a_1 a_4 - 8 a_2 a_3) x_1^3 x_2^3 + 3(a_1 a_5 + a_2 a_4 - 2 a_3^2) x_1^2 x_2^4$$
$$+ 3(a_2 a_5 - a_3 a_4) x_1 x_2^5 + (a_3 a_5 - a_4^2) x_2^6.$$

4. Prove that the infinitesimal transformation of 3-space which leaves the differential element,

$$\sigma = dx^2 + dy^2 + dz^2$$

invariant, is an infinitesimal twist or screw motion around a determinate invariant line in space. (A solution of this problem is given in Lie's Geometrie der Berührungstransformationen §3, p. 206.)

5. The function

$$q = a_0^2 a_2 + a_0 a_2^2 + a_0 a_1^2 + a_1^2 a_2 - a_0^3 - a_2^3,$$

is a formal invariant modulo 3 of the binary quadratic

$$f = a_0 x_1^2 + 2 a_1 x_1 x_2 + a_2 x_2^2 \qquad \text{(Dickson)}$$

6. The function $a_0 a_3 + a_1 a_2$ is a formal invariant modulo 2 of the binary cubic form.

7. Prove that a necessary and sufficient condition in order that a binary
form f of order m may be the mth power of a linear form is that the Hessian
covariant of f should vanish identically.

8. Show that the set of conditions obtained by equating to zero the $2m - 3$
coefficients of the Hessian of exercise 7 is redundant, and that only $m - 1$ of
these conditions are independent.

9. Prove that the discriminant of the product of two binary forms equals
the product of their discriminants times the square of their resultant.

10. Assuming (y) not cogredient to (x), show that the bilinear form

$$f = \sum a_{ik}x_iy_k = a_{11}x_1y_1 + a_{12}x_1y_2 + a_{21}x_2y_1 + a_{22}x_2y_2,$$

has an invariant under the transformations

$$\tau : \begin{aligned} x_1 &= \alpha_1\xi_1 + \beta_1\xi_2, \; x_2 = \gamma_1\xi_1 + \delta_1\xi_2, \\ y_1 &= \alpha_2\eta_1 + \beta_2\eta_2, \; y_2 = \gamma_2\eta_1 + \delta_2\eta_2, \end{aligned}$$

in the extended sense indicated by the invariant relation

$$\begin{bmatrix} a'_{11} & a'_{21} \\ a'_{12} & a'_{22} \end{bmatrix} = \begin{bmatrix} \alpha_1 & \beta_1 \\ \gamma_1 & \delta_1 \end{bmatrix} \begin{bmatrix} \alpha_2 & \beta_2 \\ \gamma_2 & \delta_2 \end{bmatrix} \begin{bmatrix} a_{11} & a_{21} \\ a_{12} & a_{22} \end{bmatrix}.$$

11. Verify the invariancy of the bilinear expression

$$H_{fg} = a_{11}b_{22} + a_{22}b_{11} - a_{12}b_{21} - a_{21}b_{12},$$

for the transformation by τ of the two bilinear forms

$$f = \sum a_{ik}x_iy_k, g = \sum b_{ik}x_iy_k.$$

12. As the most general empirical definition of a concomitant of a single
binary form f we may enunciate the following: Any rational, integral function
ϕ of the coefficients and variables of f which needs, at most, to be multiplied
by a function ψ of the coefficients in the transformations T, in order to be
made equal to the same function of the coefficients and variables of f', is a
concomitant of f.

Show in the case where ϕ is homogeneous that ψ must reduce to a power of
the modulus, and hence the above definition is equivalent to the one of Chap.
I, Section 2. (A proof of this theorem is given in Grace and Young, Algebra of
Invariants, Chapter II.)

13. Prove by means of a particular case of the general linear transformation
on p variables that any p-ary form of order m, whose term in x_1^m is lacking, can
always have this term restored by a suitably chosen linear transformation.

14. An invariant ϕ of a set of binary quantics

$$f_1 = a_0x_1^m + \cdots , f_2 = b_0x_1^n + \cdots , f_3 = c_0x_1^p + \cdots ,$$

satisfies the differential equations

$$\sum \Omega \phi \;=\; \left(a_0 \frac{\partial}{\partial a_1} + 2a_1 \frac{\partial}{\partial a_2} + \cdots + m a_{m-1}\frac{\partial}{\partial a_m} + b_0 \frac{\partial}{\partial b_1} + 2b_1 \frac{\partial}{\partial b_2}\right.$$

$$+ \quad \cdots + c_0 \frac{\partial}{\partial c_1} + \cdots \Big)\phi = 0$$

$$\sum O \phi \;=\; \left(m a_1 \frac{\partial}{\partial a_0} + (m-1)a_2 \frac{\partial}{\partial a_1} + \cdots + a_m \frac{\partial}{\partial a_{m-1}} + n b_1 \frac{\partial}{\partial b_0}\right.$$

$$+ \quad (n-1)b_2 \frac{\partial}{\partial b_1} + \cdots + p c_1 \frac{\partial}{\partial c_0} + \cdots \Big)\phi = 0$$

The covariants of the set satisfy

$$\left(\sum \Omega - x_2 \frac{\partial}{\partial x_1}\right)\phi \;=\; 0,$$

$$\left(\sum O - x_1 \frac{\partial}{\partial x_2}\right)\phi \;=\; 0.$$

15. Verify the fact of annihilation of the invariant

$$J = 6 \begin{vmatrix} a_0 & a_1 & a_2 \\ a_1 & a_2 & a_3 \\ a_2 & a_3 & a_4 \end{vmatrix}$$

of the binary quartic, by the operators Ω and O.

16. Prove by the annihilators that every invariant of degree 3 of the binary quartic is a constant times J.

(SUGGESTION. Assume the invariant with literal coefficients and operate by Ω and O.)

17. Show that the covariant $J_{\phi,\Delta}$ of Chap. II, Section 3 is annihilated by the operators

$$\sum \Omega - x_2 \frac{\partial}{\partial x_1}, \quad \sum O - x_1 \frac{\partial}{\partial x_2}.$$

18. Find an invariant of respective partial degrees 1 and 2, in the coefficients of a binary quadratic and a binary cubic.

The result is

$$I = a_0(b_1 b_3 - b_2^2) - a_1(b_0 b_3 - b_1 b_2) + a_2(b_6 b_2 - b_1^2).$$

19. Determine the index of I in the preceding exercise. State the circumstances concerning the symmetry of a simultaneous invariant.

20. No covariant of degree 2 has a leading coefficient of odd weight.

21. Find the third polar of the product $f \cdot g$, where f is a binary quadratic and g is a cubic.

The result is

$$(fg)_{y^3} = \frac{1}{10}(f g_{y^3} + 6 f_y g_{y^2} + 3 f_{y^2} g_y).$$

22. Compute the fourth transvectant of the binary quintic f with itself.
The result is

$$(f, f)^4 = 2(a_0a_4 - 4a_1a_3 + 3a_2^2)x_1^2 + 2(a_0a_6 - 3a_1a_4 + 2a_2a_3)a_1a_2 + 2(a_1a_5 - 4a_2a_4 + 3a_3^2)x_2^2.$$

23. If $F = a_x^3 b_x^2 c_x$, prove

$$F_{y^3} = \frac{1}{\binom{6}{3}} \left\{ \binom{1}{0}\binom{2}{0}\binom{3}{3} a_y^3 b_x^2 c_x + \binom{1}{0}\binom{2}{1}\binom{3}{2} a_y^2 a_x b_y b_x c_z \right.$$

$$+ \binom{1}{0}\binom{2}{2}\binom{3}{1} a_y a_x^2 b_y^2 c_x + \binom{1}{1}\binom{2}{1}\binom{3}{1} a_y a_x^2 b_y b_x c_y$$

$$\left. + \binom{1}{1}\binom{2}{2}\binom{3}{0} a_x^3 b_y^2 c_y \right\}.$$

24. Express the covariant

$$Q = (ab)^2 (cb) c_x^2 a_x$$

of the binary cubic in terms of the coefficients of the cubic by expanding the symbolical Q and expressing the symbol combinations in terms of the actual coefficients. (Cf. Table I.)

25. Express the covariant $+j = ((f, f)^4, f)^2$ of a binary quintic in terms of the symbols.
The result is

$$-j = (ab)^2 (bc)^2 (ca)^2 a_x b_x c_x = -(ab)^4 (ac)(bc) c_x^3.$$

26. Let ϕ be any symbolical concomitant of a single form f, of degree i in the coefficients and therefore involving i equivalent symbols. To fix ideas, let ϕ be a monomial. Suppose that the i symbols are temporarily assumed non-equivalent. Then ϕ, when expressed in terms of the coefficients, will become a simultaneous concomitant ϕ_1 of i forms of the same degree as f, e.g.

$$f = a_0 x_1^m + m a_1 x_1^{m-1} x_2 + \cdots ,$$

$$f_1 = b_0 x_1^m + m b_1 x_1^{m-1} x_2 + \cdots ,$$

$$\cdots\cdots\cdots\cdots$$

$$f_{i-1} = l_0 x_1^m + m l_1 x_1^{m-1} x_2 + \cdots .$$

Also ϕ_1 will be linear in the coefficients of each f, and will reduce to ϕ again when we set $b_i = \cdots = l_1 = a_1$, that is, when the symbols are again made equivalent. Let us consider the result of operating with

$$\delta = p_0 \frac{\partial}{\partial a_0} + p_1 \frac{\partial}{\partial a_1} + \cdots + p_m \frac{\partial}{\partial a_m} = \left(p \frac{\partial}{\partial a} \right),$$

upon ϕ. This will equal the result of operating upon ϕ_1, the equivalent of δ, and then making the changes

$$b_j = \cdots = l_j = a_j \, (j = 0, \cdots , m).$$

Now owing to the law for differentiating a product the result of operating $\frac{\partial}{\partial a_j}$ upon ϕ is the same as operating

$$\frac{\partial}{\partial a_j} + \frac{\partial}{\partial b_j} + \cdots + \frac{\partial}{\partial l_j}$$

upon ϕ_1 and then making the changes $b = \cdots = l = a$. Hence the operator which is equivalent to δ in the above sense is

$$\delta_1 = \left(p\frac{\partial}{\partial a} \right) + \left(p\frac{\partial}{\partial b} \right) + \cdots + \left(p\frac{\partial}{\partial l} \right).$$

When δ_1 is operated upon ϕ_1 it produces i concomitants the first of which is ϕ_1 with the a's replaced by the p's, the second is ϕ_1 with the b's replaced by the p's, and so on. It follows that if we write

$$\pi_x^m = p_0 x_1^m + m p_1 x_1^{m-1} x_2 + \cdots ,$$

and

$$\phi = (ab)^r (ac)^s \cdots a_x^\rho b_x^\sigma \cdots ,$$

we have for $\delta\phi$ the sum of i symbolical concomitants in the first of which the symbol a is replaced by π, in the second the symbol b by π and so forth.

For illustration if ϕ is the covariant Q of the cubic,

$$Q = (ab)^2 (cb) c_x^2 a_x,$$

then

$$\delta Q = (\pi b)^2 (cb) c_x^2 \pi_x + (a\pi)^2 (c\pi) c_x^2 a_x + (ab)^2 (\pi b) \pi_x^2 a_x.$$

Again the operator δ and the transvectant operator Ω are evidently permutable. Let g, h be two covariants of f and show from this fact that

$$\delta(g, h)^r = (\delta g, h)^r + (g, \delta h)^r.$$

27. Assume

$$f = a_x^3,$$
$$\Delta = (f, f)^2 = (ab)^2 a_x b_x = \Delta_x^2,$$
$$Q = (f, (f, f)^2) = (c\Delta) c_x^2 \Delta_x = (ab)^2 (cb) c_x^2 a_x = Q_x^3,$$
$$R = (\Delta, \Delta)^2 = (ab)^2 (cd)^2 (ac)(bd),$$

and write

$$Q = Q_x^3 = Q_0 x_1^3 + 3 Q_1 x_1^2 x_2 + 3 Q_2 x_1 x_2^2 + Q_3 x_2^3.$$

Then from the results in the last paragraph (26) and those in Table I of Chapter III, prove the following for the Aronhold polar operator $delta = (Q\frac{\partial}{\partial a})$:

$$\delta f = Q,$$
$$\delta \Delta = 2(aQ)^2 a_x Q_x = 2(f, Q)^2 = 0,$$
$$\delta Q = 2(f, (f, Q)^2) + (Q, \Delta) = -\frac{1}{2} R f,$$
$$\delta R = 4(\Delta, (f, Q)^2)^2 = 0.$$

28. Demonstrate by means of Hermite's reciprocity theorem that there is a single invariant or no invariant of degree 3 of a binary quantic of order m according as m is or is not a multiple of 4 (Cayley).

29. If f is a quartic, prove by Gordan's series that the Hessian of the Hessian of the Hessian is reducible as follows:

$$((H,H)^2,(H,H)^2)^2 = -\frac{1}{108}i^2 Jf + \frac{1}{9}H\left(H^2 - \frac{1}{24}i^2\right).$$

Adduce general conclusions concerning the reducibility of the Hessian of the Hessian of a form of order m.

30. Prove by Gordan's series,

$$((f,i)^2,f)^2 = \frac{1}{6}i^2 + \frac{1}{15}(f,i)^4 f,$$

where $i = (f,f)^4$, and f is a sextic. Deduce corresponding facts for other values of the order m.

31. If f is the binary quartic

$$f = a_x^4 = b_x^4 = c_x^4 = \cdots ,$$

show by means of the elementary symbolical identities alone that

$$(ab)^2(ac)^2 b_x^2 c_x^2 = \frac{1}{2}f \cdot (ab)^4.$$

(SUGGESTION. Square the identity

$$2(ab)(ac)b_x c_x = (ab)^2 c_x^2 + (ac)^2 b_x^2 - (bc)^2 a_x^2.)$$

32. Derive the fundamental system of concomitants of the canonical quartic

$$X^4 + Y^4 + 6mX^2Y^2,$$

by particularizing the a coefficients in Table II.

33. Derive the syzygy of the concomitants of a quartic by means of the canonical form and its invariants and covariants.

34. Obtain the typical representation and the associated forms of a binary quartic, and derive by means of these the syzygy for the quartic. The result for the typical representation is

$$f^3 \cdot f(y) = \xi^4 + 3H\xi^2\eta^2 + 4T\xi\eta^3 + (\frac{1}{2}if^2 - \frac{3}{4}H^2)\eta^4.$$

To find the syzygy, employ the invariant J.

35. Demonstrate that the Jacobian of three ternary forms of order m is a combinant.

36. Prove with the aid of exercise 26 above that

$$(f,\phi)^{2r+1} = (a\alpha)^{2r+1} a_x^{n-2r-1} \alpha_x^{n-2r-1}$$

is a combinant of $f = a_x^n$ and $\phi = \alpha_x^n$.

37. Prove that $Q = (ab)(bc)(ca)a_x b_x c_x$, and all covariants of Q are combinants of the three cubics a_x^3, b_x^3, c_x^3 (Gordan).

38. Let f and g be two binary forms of order m. Suppose that ϕ is any invariant of degree i of a quantic of order m. Then the invariant ϕ constructed for the form $v_1 f + v_2 g$ will be a binary form F_i of order i in the variables? v_1, v_2. Prove that any invariant of F_i is a combinant of f, g. (Cf. Salmon, Lessons Introductory to Modern Higher Algebra, Fourth edition, p. 211.)

39. Prove that the Cartesian equation of the rational plane cubic curve

$$x_i = a_{i0}\xi_1^3 + a_{i1}\xi_1^2\xi_2 + \cdots + a_{i3}\xi_2^3 (i = 1, 2, 3),$$

is

$$\phi(x_1, x_2, x_3) = \begin{Vmatrix} |a_0 a_1 x| & |a_0 a_2 x| & |a_0 a_3 x| \\ |a_0 a_2 x| & |a_0 a_3 x| + |a_1 a_2 x| & |a_1 a_3 x| \\ |a_0 a_3 x| & |a_1 a_3 x| & |a_2 a_3 x| \end{Vmatrix} = 0.$$

40. Show that a binary quintic has two and only two linearly independent seminvariants of degree five and weight five.

The result, obtained by the annihilator theory, is

$$\lambda(a_0^4 a_5 - 5a_0^3 a_1 a_4 + 10a_0^2 a_1^2 a_3 - 10a_0 a_1^3 a_2 + 4a_1^5) + \mu(a_0 a_2 - a_1^2)(a_0^2 a_3 - 3a_0 a_1 a_2 + 2a_1^3).$$

41. Demonstrate that the number of linearly independent seminvariants of weight w and degree i of a binary form of order m is equal to

$$(w; i, m) - (w - 1; i, m),$$

where $(w; i, m)$ denotes the number of different partitions of the number w into i or fewer numbers, none exceeding m. (A proof of this theorem is given in Chapter VII of Elliotts' Algebra of Quantics.)

42. If $f = a_x^m = b_x^m = \cdots$ is a ternary form of order m, show that

$$(f, f)^{0,2k} = (abu)^{2k} a_x^{m-2k} b_x^{m-2k}.$$

Prove also

$$((f, f)^{0,2k}, f)^{r,s} = \frac{1}{\binom{2m-4k}{s}} \sum_{i=0}^{s} \binom{m-2k}{i}\binom{m-2k}{s-i}(abc)^r$$

$$\times (abu)^{2k-r}(bcu)^{s-i}(acu)^i a_x^{m-i-2k} b_x^{m-s+i-2k} c_x^{m-r-s}.$$

43. Derive all of the invariant formations of degrees 1, 2, 3, 4 of the ternary cubic, as given in Table VII, by the process of passing by transvection from those of one degree to those of the next higher degree.

44. We have shown that the seminvariant leading coefficient of the binary covariant of $f = a_x^m$,

$$\phi = (ab)^p (ac)^q \cdots a_x^\rho b_x^\sigma \cdots ,$$

is

$$\phi_0 = (ab)^P (ac)^q \cdots a_1^p b_1^\sigma \cdots ,$$

If we replace a_1 by a_x, b_1 by b_z etc. in ϕ_0 and leave $a_2, b_2, \cdots$ unchanged, the factor (ab) becomes

$$(a_1 x_1 + a_2 x_2) b_2 - (b_1 x_1 + b_2 x_2) a_2 = (ab) x_1.$$

At the same time the actual coefficient $a_r = a_1^{m-r} a_2^r$ of f becomes

$$a_x^{m-r} a_2^r = \frac{(m-r)!}{m!} \frac{\partial^r f}{\partial x_2^r}.$$

Hence, except for a multiplier which is a power of x_1 a binary covariant may be derived from its leading coefficient ϕ_0 by replacing in $\phi_0, a_0, a_1, \cdots , a_m$ respectively by

$$f, \frac{1}{m} \frac{\partial f}{\partial x_2}, \frac{1}{m(m-1)} \frac{\partial^2 f}{\partial x_2^2}, \cdots , \frac{(m-r)!}{m!} \frac{\partial^r f}{\partial x_2^r}, \cdots , \frac{1}{m!} \frac{\partial^m f}{\partial x_2^m}.$$

Illustrate this by the covariant Hessian of a quartic.

45. Prove that any ternary concomitant of $f = a_x^m$ can be deduced from its leading coefficient (save for a power of u_x) by replacing, in the coefficient, a_{pqr}, by

$$\frac{p!}{m!} \left(y \frac{\partial}{\partial x} \right)^q \left(z \frac{\partial}{\partial x} \right)^r a_x^m .$$

(Cf. Forsyth, Amer. Journal of Math., 1889.)

46. Derive a syzygy between the simultaneous concomitants of two binary quadratic forms f, g (Chap. VI).

The result is

$$= 2 J_{12}^2 = D_1 g^2 + D_2 f^2 - 2h f g,$$

where J_{12} is the Jacobian of the two forms, h their bilinear invariant, and D_1, D_2 the respective discriminants of f and g.

47. Compute the transvectant

$$(f, f)^{0,2} = (abu)^2 a_x b_x,$$

of the ternary cubic

$$f = a_x^3 = b_x^3 = \sum \frac{3!}{p! q! r!} a_{pqr} x_1^p x_2^q x_3^r,$$

in terms of its coefficients $a_{pqr} (P + q + r = 3)$.

The result for $\frac{1}{2}(f, f)^{0,2}$ is given in the table below. Note that this mixed concomitant may also be obtained by applying Clebsch's translation principle to the Hessian of a binary cubic.

$\alpha_1^2 u_1^2$	$x_1^2 u_1 u_2$	$x_1^2 u_2^2$	$x_1^2 u_1 u_2$	$x_1^2 u_2 u_1$	$x_1^2 u_3^2$
$a_{120}a_{102} - a_{111}^2$	$2a_{111}a_{201} - 2a_{210}a_{102}$	$a_{102}a_{300} - a_{201}^2$	$2a_{210}a_{111} - 2a_{120}a_{201}$	$2a_{201}a_{210} - 2a_{111}a_{300}$	$a_{300}a_{120} - a_{210}^2$

$x_1 x_2 u_1^2$	$x_1 x_2 u_1 u_2$	$x_1 x_2 u_2^2$	$x_1 x_2 u_1 u_3$	$x_1 x_2 u_2 u_3^2$	$x_1 x_2 u_3^2$
$a_{120}a_{012} + a_{102}a_{030}$	$2a_{111}^2 - 2a_{102}a_{120} + 2a_{201}a_{021}$	$a_{102}a_{210} + a_{300}a_{012}$	$2a_{210}a_{021}$	$2a_{201}a_{120}$	$a_{300}a_{030}$

$x_2^2 u_1^2$	$x_2^2 u_1 u_2$	$x_2^2 u_2^2$	$x_2^2 u_1 u_3$	$x_2^2 u_2 u_3$	$x_2^2 u_3^3$
$a_{030}a_{012} - a_{021}^2$	$2a_{021}a_{111} - 2a_{120}a_{012}$	$a_{012}a_{210} - a_{111}^2$	$2a_{120}a_{021} - 2a_{030}a_{111}$	$2a_{111}a_{120} - 2a_{021}a_{210}$	$a_{210}a_{030} - a_{120}^2$

$x_1 x_3 u_1^2$	$x_1 x_2 u_1 u_2$	$x_1 x_3 u_2^2$	$x_1 x_3 u_1 u_3$	$x_1 x_3 u_2 u_3$	$x_1 x_3 u_3^2$
$a_{120}a_{003} - 2a_{111}a_{012} + a_{102}a_{021}$	$2a_{201}a_{012} - 2a_{210}a_{002}$	$a_{300}a_{003} - a_{201}a_{102}$	$2a_{111}^2 - 2a_{201}a_{021} - 2a_{120}a_{201} + a_{210}a_{012}$	$2a_{210}a_{102} - 2a_{300}a_{012}$	$a_{120}a_{021} - 2a_{111}a_{210} + a_{300}a_{021}$

$x_2 x_3 u_1^2$	$x_2 x_3 u_1 u_2$	$x_2 x_3 u_2^2$	$x_2 x_3 u_1 u_3$	$x_2 x_3 u_2 u_3$	$x_2 x_3 u_3^2$
$a_{030}a_{003} - a_{021}a_{012}$	$2a_{021}a_{102} - 2a_{120}a_{003}$	$a_{012}a_{201} - 2a_{111}a_{102} + a_{210}a_{003}$	$2a_{120}a_{012} - 2a_{030}a_{102}$	$2a_{111}^2 - 2a_{021}a_{201} - 2a_{210}a_{012} + 2a_{120}a_{102}$	$a_{210}a_{021} - 2a_{120}a_{111} + a_{030}a_{201}$

$x_x^2 u_1^2$	$x_3^2 u_1 u_2$	$x_3^2 u_3^3$	$x_3^2 u_1 u_3$	$x_3^2 u_2 u_3$	$x_3^2 u_3^2$
$a_{021}a_{003} - a_{012}^2$	$2a_{012}a_{102} - 2a_{111}a_{003}$	$a_{003}a_{201} - a_{102}^2$	$2a_{111}a_{01} - 2a_{021}a_{102}$	$2a_{102}a_{111} - 2a_{012}a_{201}$	$a_{201}a_{021} - a_{111}^2$

48. Prove that a modular binary form of even order, the modulus being $p > 2$, has no covariant of odd order.

(Suggestion. Compare Chap. II, Section 2, II. If λ is chosen as a primitive root, equation (48) becomes a congruence modulo $p - 1$.)

Index